CONSTITUTIONAL RIGHTS IN PRIVATE LAW

This book provides the philosophical foundations for the application of constitutional rights in private law – and more broadly, for social justice-oriented private law reform.

The book connects lessons from political and moral philosophy to legal principles addressing the nature and limits of constitutional and private law. This allows the author to present a framework for bringing constitutional rights to bear on private law's operation and evolution. This is an analytically rigorous yet doctrinally sensitive work, which will be widely welcomed by private lawyers, legal theorists and social justice scholars.

International Studies in the Theory of Private Law: Volume 18

International Studies in the Theory of Private Law

This series of books, edited by a distinguished international team of legal scholars, aims to investigate the normative and theoretical foundations of the law governing relations between citizens. The context for such investigations of private law systems is set by important modern tendencies in systems of governance. The advent of the regulatory state marks the withdrawal of the state from direct control and management of social and economic activity, and the adoption instead of procedural regulation and co-regulatory strategies that promote the use of private law techniques of ordering and self-regulation in social and economic interactions between citizens. The tendency known as globalisation and the corresponding increases in cross-border trade produce the responses of transnational regulation of commerce and private governance regimes, and these new systems of governance challenge the hegemony of traditional national private law systems. Furthermore, these tendencies towards transnational governance regimes compel an interaction between different national legal traditions, with their differences in culture and philosophy as well as their differences based upon variations in market systems, which provokes questions not only about competing policy frameworks but also about nature and adequacy of different kinds of legal reasoning itself.

The series welcomes a diverse range of theoretical approaches in the examination of these issues including approaches using socio-legal methods, economics, critical theory, systems theory, regulation theory, and moral and political theory. With the aim of stimulating an international discussion of these issues, volumes will be published in Germany, France, and the United Kingdom in one of the three languages.

Volumes published with Hart Publishing, Oxford

1. David Campbell, Hugh Collins und John Wightman (eds), *Implicit Dimensions of Contract: Discrete, Relational and Network Contracts* (2003)
2. Christian Joerges, Inger-Johanne Sand and Gunther Teubner (eds), *Transnational Governance and Constitutionalism* (2004)
3. Oren Perez, *Ecological Sensitivity and Global Legal Pluralism: Rethinking the Trade and Environment Debate* (2004)
4. Harm Schepel, *The Constitution of Private Governance* (2004)
5. Nili Cohen and Ewan McKendrick, *Comparative Remedies for Breach of Contract* (2005)
6. Marc Amstutz and Gunther Teubner (eds), *Networks: Legal Issues of Multilateral Co-operation* (2010)

7. Gunther Teubner (edited and with an Introduction by Hugh Collins), *Networks as Connected Contracts* (2010)
8. Christian Joerges and Josef Falke (eds), *Karl Polanyi, Globalisation and the Potential of Law in Transnational Markets* (2011)
9. Poul F Kjaer, Gunther Teubner and Alberto Febbrajo (eds), *The Financial Crisis in Constitutional Perspective: The Dark Side of Functional Differentiation* (2011)
10. Jean Braucher, John Kidwell and William C Whitford (eds), *Revisiting the Contracts Scholarship of Stewart Macaulay: On the Empirical and the Lyrical* (2013)
11. Thomas Dietz, *Global Order Beyond Law: How Information and Communication Technologies Facilitate Relational Contracting in International Trade* (2014)
12. Anna Beckers, *Enforcing Corporate Social Responsibility Codes: On Global Self-Regulation and National Private Law* (2015)
13. Nahel Asfour, *Wrongful Enrichment: A Study in Comparative Law and Culture* (2017)
14. Pablo Marcello Baquero, *Networks of Collaborative Contracts for Innovation* (2020)
15. Christian Joerges, *Conflict and Transformation: Essays on European Law and Policy* (2022)
16. Marcus Moore, *Regulating Boilerplate: Resolving the Issues of Imposition and Unfairness in Standard Form Contracts* (2025)
17. Ernesto Vargas Weil, *Stability and Change in Modern Property Law: A Comparative Approach to the Principle of Numerus Clausus* (2025)
18. Tom Kohavi, *Constitutional Rights in Private Law* (2025)

Volumes published in German by Nomos Verlagsgesellschaft, Baden-Baden

1. Peer Zumbansen, *Ordnungsmuster im modern Wohlfahrtsstaat: Lernerfahrungen zwischen Staat, Geseelschaft und Vertrag* (2000)
2. Dan Wielsch, *Freiheit und Funktion: Zur Struktur- und Theoriegeschichte des Rechts der Wirtschaftsgesellschaft* (2001)
3. Marc Amstutz, *Evolutorisches Wirtschaftsrecht: Vorstudien zum Recht und seiner Methode in den Diskurskollisionen der Marktgesellschaft* (2001)
4. Christian Joerges and Gunther Teubner, Gunther (eds), *Rechtsverfassungsrecht: Recht-Fertigungen zwischen Sozialtheorie und Privatrechtsdogmatik* (2003)
5. Gunther Teubner, *Netzwerk als Vertragsverbund: Virtuelle Unternehmen, Franchising, Just in Time in sozialwissenschaftlicher und juristischer Sicht* (2004)
6. Daniel Dédeyan, *Macht durch Zeichen: Rechtsprobleme der Kennzeichnung und Zertifikation* (2004)
7. Dietrich Claus Becker, *Von Namen und Nummern: Kollisionen unverträglicher Rechtsmassen im Interent* (2005)

8. Vagias Karavas, *Digitale Grundrechte: Elemente einer Verfassung des Informationsflusses im Intenet* (2007)
9. Peter Korth, *Dritthaftung von Ratingagenturen* (2009)
10. Cordula Heldt, *Baukooperation und Franchising als multilaterale Sonderverbindung. Vertragsnetzwerke – Parallelschuldverhältnisse – Personengesellschaften* (2010)
11. Jan Lüsing, *Die Pflichten aus culpa in contrahendo und positiver Vertragsverletzung* (§ 241 II BGB): *Über den hybriden Charakter der Schutzpflichten und zur Selbstbindung ohne Vertrag* (2010)
12. Moritz Renner, *Zwingendes transnationales Recht: Elemente einer Wirtschaftsverfassung jenseits des Staates* (2011)
13. Christoph Lüscher, *Zur Konzeptualisierung von Verbrauchervertragsrecht unter besonderer Berücksichtigung des schweizerischen und europäischen Verbrauchervertragsrechts. Eine Untersuchung im Schnittfeld von Vertragsrecht, Systemtheorie und Ökonomie* (2011)
14. Daniel Klösel, *Compliance-Richtlinien. Zum Funktionswandel des Zivilrechts im Gewährleistungsstaat* (2012)
15. Chunyi Qi, *Rechtstransfer in Chinas Produktionsregime? Zur Kontrolle der Allgemeinen Geschäftsbedingungen im deutschen und chinesischen Recht* (2013)

Constitutional Rights in Private Law

Tom Kohavi

•HART•
OXFORD • LONDON • NEW YORK • NEW DELHI • SYDNEY

HART PUBLISHING

Bloomsbury Publishing Plc

Kemp House, Chawley Park, Cumnor Hill, Oxford, OX2 9PH, UK

1385 Broadway, New York, NY 10018, USA

Bloomsbury Publishing Ireland Limited, 29 Earlsfort Terrace, Dublin 2, D02 AY28, Ireland

HART PUBLISHING, the Hart/Stag logo, BLOOMSBURY and the Diana logo are trademarks of Bloomsbury Publishing Plc

First published in Great Britain 2025

A catalogue record for this book is available from the British Library.

A catalogue record for this book is available from the Library of Congress.

ISBN: HB: 978-1-50997-710-9
ePDF: 978-1-50997-712-3
ePub: 978-1-50997-711-6

Typeset by Compuscript Ltd, Shannon

For product safety related questions contact productsafety@bloomsbury.com

To find out more about our authors and books visit www.hartpublishing.co.uk. Here you will find extracts, author information, details of forthcoming events and the option to sign up for our newsletters.

Contents

1

Introduction

1.1. THE CHALLENGE

CONSTITUTIONAL LAW, AS its name suggests, constitutes the institutions and practices through which political collectives govern themselves, such as elections, legislation and adjudication. Constitutional norms therefore express collective commitments and ideals regarding the creation and preservation of justified social conditions, such as dignity, equality and liberty. Private law, on the other hand, empowers private agents to form relationships or associations (for instance, through contract or marriage) and determines what they owe to each other – both within and outside of such relationships or associations (for instance, as drivers or neighbours). Private law norms therefore focus on what private agents owe to each other – for instance, on questions such as whether a promise was made to an agent or whether they were battered, defamed or negligently harmed.

Constitutional law and private law, seem to address distinct parts of the normative universe. However, in recent decades, as a result of changes both internal and external to these domains, they have not only grown closer but have become set on a collision course. Modern constitutions recognise rights that address not only what the state does to right-holders but also how right-holders are doing in terms of their basic interests: for example, whether they enjoy a sufficient level of public safety, workplace privacy or equal opportunity. Because such rights are also affected by private actions and activities, the constitution encroaches upon private law's normative territory: it addresses not only vertical relationships between the state and its citizens, but also horizontal relationships, associations and practices, from which the state is more remote.

Eviction. After a long period of severe mental problems that resulted in difficulties with regular employment, Fiona's parents took a loan from Capital Home Loans to buy her a home. When they struggled to make payments, the company sought possession of the property. Fiona claimed that her right to respect for home – that the United Kingdom's Human Rights Act 1998 imports from Article 8 of the European Convention on Human Rights – requires subjecting the company's eviction claim to substantive fairness tests, which the prevailing private law regime did not include. Her claim drew support from the jurisprudence of the European Court of Human Rights, which construes Article 8 to cover evictions and holds that states can infringe the right to home indirectly – through the legal regimes regulating evictions. Such regimes must therefore be compatible with the Convention's conditions for justified infringements – most importantly, each infringing regime's social benefits must exceed the harms to the right. The Supreme Court rejected Fiona's claims. It held that the statutory eviction procedure properly and proportionately reconciles considerations such as the parties' interests and the need for clear and stable regulation, which is crucial for the housing market.[1]

We will touch upon many similar cases, in which constitutional rights raise questions about, for example, workplace surveillance, journalistic reporting, discrimination against gay customers, or parental support of children. We will see that constitutional rights obligate political collectives to evaluate and develop private law in light of complex reasons for regulation, which are foreign to private law at a deep structural level: reasons that diverge from private law's focus on what parties owe to each other in their direct relationships – for example, as parties to mortgage agreements – by highlighting vulnerabilities and needs that the parties may not have created or exploited.

To answer questions about how the collective values enshrined in constitutional rights reflect on the regulation of private relationships, associations and practices, legal actors must therefore address structural and allocative factors: for instance, patterns of inequality, invasive data gathering practices, or the role of journalism in modern democracy. This creates strong normative tensions. While it would be unjust and unconstitutional to shield private law from deep and comprehensive constitutional scrutiny, we cannot respond to such normative pressures by simply treating private right-holders as representatives of the political collective and private duty-bearers as cogs in the state's regulatory apparatus. Values enshrined in both private law and modern constitutions (like autonomy, privacy or dignity) resist such a subordination of the interpersonal to the political. This resistance is important not only from private law's perspective: if it is treated as a fully malleable regulatory tool that can be used in any way for policy purposes, our ability to use it to realise constitutional rights (or social justice more generally) effectively and justifiably is significantly diminished. Thus, while the private cannot be isolated from the public, it also cannot be simply subordinated to it.

The collision seems unavoidable. It is both complicated and interesting because it is shaped by and manifests deeper normative conflicts. It raises questions not only about how to understand or apply the law as it is, but also about how it can and should evolve. These are issues that lie at the intersections of moral, political and legal theory. The conflicting parts of the constitution and private law are, in this sense, the tips of two colliding icebergs: two

[1] *McDonald v McDonald* [2016] UKSC 28.

moral paradigms – one more focused on agency and responsibility, the other on vulnerability and beneficence – that frame, guide and constrain reasoning about normative issues, such as the nature and limits of private law's evolution in response to constitutional pressures.

The challenge, familiar to philosophers and legal scholars alike, is how to bridge the apparent chasm between these paradigms. This problem haunts any attempt to bring social justice to bear on private relationships, associations and practices – for example, by adopting complaints procedures or speech codes in universities or workplaces. Because the legal system must resolve this problem in a public, consistent and transparent manner, it has less room than philosophy for abstraction or circumvention. This is why legal responses to the challenge of constitutional horizontality are important and interesting not only for lawyers but more broadly to anyone interested in normative tensions between public and private: responses to this challenge can guide societal normative evolution not only in expressive or symbolic senses, but also in more practical senses, by integrating public values into private normative settings.

This book addresses this challenge and claims that we can do better than a mere *modus vivendi*: rather than rigidly separating constitutional rights and private law or subordinating the latter to the former, we can facilitate an ongoing dialogue between them that also contributes to their effectiveness and justification. Building on central theoretical ideas from both domains, jurisprudence, and contractualist moral theory, this book offers an account of the normative foundations that explain and guide constitutional horizontality. This account strives not only to preserve but to strengthen the basic roles these domains play in modern liberal democracies, and therefore to solidify their moral authority and value. In this sense, it is pluralistic. Yet it is also structured enough to facilitate effective political and legal deliberation about this foundational normative process and its influence in different social spheres.

This chapter introduces the challenge of constitutional horizontality – by locating it in its historical context and presenting the spectrum of possible horizontality models and the moral undercurrents that shape them – and lays out the book's methodology and order. The main theme, developed as we proceed, is that constitutional horizontality introduces into modern legal systems deep moral tensions that they cannot ignore or iron out.

1.2. HISTORICAL BACKGROUND

To understand the challenge of constitutional horizontality, we must locate it in its historical context: as part of the processes through which constitutional law and private law evolve while responding to tensions between moral forces tied to the labels of public and private. Distinctions between public law and private law – grounded in even earlier distinctions between matters of collective interest like citizenship and matters of private interest like the family – were already drawn in Ancient Rome.[2] They faded away during the Middle Ages, when the authority of rulers, occupied with limited public tasks, was vaguely conceptualised in private law terms: internally as an agreement and externally as exchangeable property.[3] They resurfaced as societies entered modernity,[4] and have since been a basic feature of modern legal systems. They underlie two competing idealised visions of law and the state that shape constitutional horizontality.

1.2.1. The Restrained State

The ideal of the restrained state formed as states gradually became the main providers of social goods such as security, education and health – in response to the needs and expectations of an urban middle class, which formed alongside the scientific revolution (that shifted economic activities from agriculture and dispersed manufacturing to centralised industries). These processes of governmental expansion and societal reshuffling created the need for legal regimes capable of coordinating complex activities and interactions, often between strangers, in ways that simpler, convention-based and local legal regimes struggled to. But these processes were also accompanied by a growing fear of the state. The political revolutions in the United States and France introduced the idea that the state should be limited. This principle was complemented by the ideology of the market: the assumption that society benefits from transactions between 'free and equal' agents. These forces shaped the idea that a sphere of human activity should be isolated from state intervention, unless one person harms another.[5]

One outcome of these opposing trends – of empowering and restraining the state – was the consolidation of private law.[6] In continental Europe, it

[2] Eric Descheemaeker, *The Division of Wrongs: A Historical Comparative Study* (Oxford University Press, 2009) 50–57.

[3] JWF Allison, *Continental Distinction in the Common Law: A Historical and Comparative Perspective on English Public Law* (Oxford University Press, 1996) 42–43.

[4] This section draws heavily on RC van Caenegem, *An Historical Introduction to Private Law* (DEL Johnston tr, Cambridge University Press, 1992). See also Nils Jansen, 'Duties and Rights in Negligence' (2004) 24 *Oxford Journal of Legal Studies* 443, 451–58; Charles Donahue Jr, 'Private Law Without the State and During its Formation' (2008) 56 *American Journal of Comparative Law* 541.

[5] Jürgen Habermas, *The Structural Transformation of the Public Sphere: An Inquiry into a Category of Bourgeois Society* (Thomas Burger tr, MIT Press, 1989) 3–12, 74–75; William Lucy, 'What's Private About Private Law?' in Andrew Robertson and Tang Hang Wu (eds), *The Goals of Private Law* (Hart Publishing, 2009) 47, 60–61.

[6] van Caenegem, *An Historical Introduction to Private Law* (n 4) 55–58, 83–85, 116–17, 134–37, 159–65; Habermas, *The Structural Transformation* (n 5) 79–80, 141–42.

manifested in private law codifications (most notably in France and Germany) that remained loyal to their Roman legal foundations. In common law systems (first in England and then in others) this period saw a transition from the formalistic reliance on rigid 'forms of action' to more substantive thinking that utilised concepts like contracts and torts: old rules were connected to deeper ideas, such as consent, duty and harm.[7] In their attempts to legitimise this emerging system, law-creating state agents tended to focus on *laissez-faire* ideas: offering pairs of private agents fair resolutions for 'their' disputes, rather than promoting public goals.[8] Private law's aspirations were modest: mostly, to facilitate market practices and individual choice.[9] Common law judges – pulling most of the weight of creating Anglo-American private law at the time – responded to the changing socio-economic conditions while staying largely loyal to their pragmatic and incremental inclinations, with a strong emphasis on legal stability.[10]

In this picture, public law plays a modest and negative role: limiting the state's actions. Constitutions adopted at the time (like that of the United States) aimed to authorise and restrain but hardly to guide the state; and in some legal systems, like England's, public law was almost non-existent – there was hardly any distinction between public and private or a robust conception of the state, whose actions were often regulated by borrowing private law tools.[11] Private law, on the other hand, took on the basic (and, in many senses, constitutional) role of protecting the citizen's moral status and natural rights – mostly to life, liberty and property.[12] Private law created spheres of autonomy by protecting existing entitlements, facilitating their consensual exchange, and offering recourse for non-consensual harm.[13] This is the foundation of the moral paradigm of the restrained liberal state, the activities of which are regularly limited to passively mediating conflicts of largely negative and robust rights.[14]

[7] Descheemaeker (n 2) 191–95; Steve Hedley, 'Courts as Public Authorities, Private Law as Instrument of Government' in Kit Barker and Darryn Jensen (eds), *Private Law: Key Encounters with Public Law* (Cambridge University Press, 2013) 89, 97–104.

[8] Peter Stein, *Roman Law in European History* (Cambridge University Press, 1999) 120–122; Dan Priel, 'The Political Origins of English Private Law' (2013) 4 *Journal of Law and Society* 481.

[9] Michael Lobban, 'The Politics of English Law in the Nineteenth Century' in Paul Brand and Joshua Getzler (eds), *Judges and Judging in the History of the Common Law and Civil Law: From Antiquity to Modern Times* (Cambridge University Press, 2012) 102, 116–23.

[10] Michael Lobban, 'Common Law Reasoning and the Foundations of Modern Private Law' (2007) 32 *Australian Journal of Legal Philosophy* 39.

[11] I elaborate on this point in the next chapter.

[12] John Henry Merryman, 'The Public Law–Private Law Distinction in European and American Law' (1968) 17 *Journal of Public Law* 3, 11.

[13] Descheemaeker (n 2) 118; Stein (n 8) 104–30; Alice Erh-Soon Tay and Eugene Kamenka, 'Public Law–Private Law' in SI Benn and GF Gaus (eds), *Public and Private in Social Life* (Croom Helm, 1983) 67, 73–81; Hugh Collins, 'Utility and Rights in Common Law Reasoning' (2007) 30 *Dalhousie Law Journal* 1.

[14] Duncan Kennedy, 'The Structure of Blackstone's Commentaries' (1979) 28 *Buffalo Law Review* 209, 366.

1.2.2. The Ambitious State

As the twentieth century progressed, the ideal of the restrained state grew out of tune with the prevailing social conditions and values. It became difficult to justify isolating the injustices suffered by vulnerable individuals in private spheres (such as children, employees or consumers) from state scrutiny and regulation. Two world wars and the emerging global economy induced states to assume extended commitments not only outwards, by joining multinational treaties and organisations,[15] but also inwards, by entering into what were previously thought of as apolitical private spheres. It became clear that the ability to enjoy rights, on both fronts, depends on membership in an effective political unit.[16] Thus, the spread of international human rights treaties spurred and was complemented by the adoption of more ambitious constitutional bills of rights, which burden states with duties to guarantee basic conditions of social justice within their reach. This process mirrors the trust in expertise and political institutions that forms a basic feature of modernity.[17] While regularly under siege, basic aspects of this process resist erosion by the ideal of the restrained state. Extensive regulation in areas such as consumerism, education, public health or housing build on and solidify the responsibilities and authorities of states to solve complex social problems, while assigning coordinated duties to different public and private agents.

This systematic and goal-oriented attitude was reflected in realist, economic, and critical legal theories – which showed that legal institutions are not neutral and could be arranged to better reduce risks of harms,[18] and better spread their costs if they materialise through regulatory schemes, such as workers' compensation.[19] Importantly, it was not only that private law came under pressure to meet such policy goals – it also underwent internal changes that pushed it in these directions:[20] for example, many legal disputes came to involve corporate agents (directly as right-holders or duty-bearers or indirectly as insurers) that can distribute the costs of liability – and they often do not reach a substantive judicial decision but end in out-of-court settlements, according to profit-oriented corporate policies.[21] Such changes, together with the greater

[15] Philip Selznick, *Law, Society, and Industrial Justice* (Russel Sage Foundation, 1969) 245–46.

[16] On the related idea of the 'right to have rights', see Hannah Arendt, 'The Decline of the Nation-State and the End of the Rights of Man' in *The Origins of Totalitarianism* (Schocken Books, 1951).

[17] Anthony Giddens, *The Consequences of Modernity* (Stanford University Press, 1990) 21–39, 114–49.

[18] Roberto Mangaberia Unger, *Law in Modern Society* (The Free Press, 1976) 203.

[19] Jenny Steele, 'Risk Revolutions in Private Law' in Sarah Worthington, Andrew Robertson and Graham Virgo (eds), *Revolution and Evolution in Private Law* (Hart Publishing, 2018) 75.

[20] NE Simmonds, 'The Changing Face of Private Law: Doctrinal Categories and the Regulatory State' (1982) 2 *Legal Studies* 257; Kit Barker, 'Private Law: Key Encounters with Public Law' in *Private Law: Key Encounters with Public Law* (n 7) 3, 5–19.

[21] Linda Mulcahy and Wendy Teeder, 'Are Litigants, Trials and Precedents Vanishing After All?' (2021) 85 *Modern Law Review* 326.

emphasis on policy-promotion, shifted the focus from ex-post dispute resolution to ex-ante regulation. This opened the door for more extensive legislative and administrative influence – quite visible in domains like consumer law and labour law – and encouraged judges to be more comfortable with the law-creating and goal-oriented aspects of their decisions.[22]

It has become quite clear that private law is not only about the protection of entitlements and the facilitation of their consensual exchange; it must also, for example, protect dignity and promote equality. In this regard, to see private law as purely private is to see it, in Owen Fiss's words, as 'rooted in a world that no longer exists. ... a horizontal world, in which people related to one another on individual terms and on terms of approximate equality'.[23] So, the pendulum swings: from private law's dominance, with constitutional law playing a secondary and negative role, to a world where constitutional law and public policy more broadly play foundational roles in shaping the legal system's evolution. It is in the context of this swing, which involves the *de*constitutionalisation of private law – the erosion of the foundational roles that it had during early modernity[24] – that constitutional horizontality enters the picture.

1.3. THE HORIZONTALITY SPECTRUM

In the post-war era, constitutions came to be seen not only as higher law but also as entailing collective obligations – mostly through right-norms – to create social conditions in which people's basic interests are guaranteed in all social spheres.[25] One of the leading legal systems in this regard is Germany, which was rebuilt after the war in an attempt to cement human dignity in its foundation as a response to the horrors of the Nazi regime.

Boycott. In 1950, Veit Harlan, who had previously directed anti-Semitic films, released a new film. Erich Lüth, chairman of the Hamburg press club, called for a boycott. The Federal Constitutional court held that the decisions of local courts, which ordered Lüth to cease his boycott calls, violated his constitutional right to freedom of expression by applying private law without considering this right's horizontal implications.[26]

This conception of constitutional rights as foundational and exerting influence over all areas of law was adopted by European courts as well as by legal systems in other areas of the world, such as Colombia, Israel and South Africa

[22] Collins, 'Utility and Rights' (n 13) 6–14.
[23] Owen M Fiss, 'The Forms of Justice' (1979) 93 *Harvard Law Review* 1, 44.
[24] Merryman (n 12) 17.
[25] It should be noted that while I talk throughout the book about duties to citizens, my claims could apply to other categories of right-holders such as residents or immigrants.
[26] 7 BVerfGE 198 (15 January 1958).

(in which, much like in Germany, constitutional horizontality also responds to past injustices). Even in legal systems where the constitution's horizontal influence is more circumscribed due to the common law's dominance, such as the United States, the United Kingdom and Canada, rights-based horizontal regulation expanded: for example, statutory rights, seen by some theorists as constitutional,[27] extended duties not to discriminate to social spheres like voting, employment, housing and education. Other examples abound of the influence of rights such as privacy, freedom of expression, dignity and autonomy over the regulation of private relationships, associations and practices.

1.3.1. Verticality and Horizontality

Because of the complexity, diversity and depth of these legal developments, any definition of constitutional horizontality must rely on substantive justifications of its aims and limits. Indeed, many definitions exist in constitutional theory and practice.[28] The general starting point is the distinction between the vertical and horizontal dimensions of constitutional rights, which refers to the agents that right-based duties obligate and the actions that they address. Traditional verticality holds that constitutional rights obligate only state agents and address only their actions. This is the accepted reading of the Constitution of the United States, adopted during the *laissez-faire* era of the restrained state: under it, constitutional rights do not obligate state agents to promote basic interests or to protect them from private parties but only to refrain from causing or being intimately involved in harms to basic interests in certain specified ways.

Discrimination. A gay couple wanted to buy a wedding cake from a bakery in Colorado, whose owner declined their request due to his Christian beliefs. The case reached the Supreme Court of the United States after the Colorado Civil Rights Commission and Court of Appeals found that the couple had been discriminated against.[29] The Supreme Court held that the owner's right to religious liberty was violated: not because it was improperly balanced with the couple's rights to equality but because the Commission had shown hostility to religion, both in comments about the baker's beliefs and in his treatment compared to bakers who were allowed not to provide cakes disapproving of gay

[27] Bruce Ackerman, *We the People, Volume 3: The Civil Rights Revolution* (Belknap Press, 2018).

[28] See, eg, Daniel Friedmann and Daphne Barak-Erez (eds), *Human Rights in Private Law* (Hart Publishing, 2001); David Hoffman (ed), *The Impact of the UK Human Rights Act on Private Law* (Cambridge University Press, 2011); Jud Mathews, *Extending Rights' Reach* (Oxford University Press, 2018).

[29] *Masterpiece Cakeshop v Colorado Civil Rights Commission* 584 US 617 (2018).

marriage. Thus, the couple's rights to equality were ignored, and the baker's right to freedom of religion was engaged as addressing the separation of church and state rather than the ability to form or manifest religious beliefs.

We will return to this vertical 'state action' model in the next chapter. The important thing, at this point, is that there are great pressures, when it comes to general and beneficiary-centered rights like equality or freedom of religion, to see them as also addressing social conditions or states of affairs – that is, not only how the state treats individuals but also how they are treated more broadly. Indeed, modern constitutionalism sits quite uneasily with the idea that constitutional rights have nothing to say about how private agents treat each other: for example, if religious belief and equality should be respected by state agents, why not by private agents as well?

This is the basic intuition behind the model on the other end of the spectrum, of direct horizontality, versions of which have been adopted, for example, in South Africa and Ireland. Under this model, constitutional rights impose duties on private agents and can ground remedial liabilities in response to their rights-violating actions. Thus, in cases like *Discrimination*, bakers are obligated to respect the equality rights of gay customers, who must, in turn, respect the religious liberty rights of bakers. This means that beyond exceptional cases of absolute rights (for example, against torture or slavery) some form of reconciliation or balance between constitutional rights is necessary; and therefore private duties will often be weaker than public duties. The important point for us is that the beneficiary-centered and systematic structure of constitutional rights-reasoning is identical whether the potential duty-bearer is a state agent or private agent. In this sense, this model embodies the post-war ideology of the ambitious state and a conception of the constitution as a set of norms that dictate terms of interaction in all social spheres.

The direct horizontality model and its critique will be explored in chapter 3. At this stage, suffice it to say that it faces pressures opposite to the ones faced by the vertical model. Autonomy, responsibility, moral integrity, and the unique normativity of private relationships push back against the imposition of policy-oriented duties through mechanisms that deputise right-holders as private attorneys general and duty-bearers as parts of the state's regulatory apparatus, subjecting them to ongoing constitutional scrutiny. Given the complexity of constitutional rights, the discretion and authority involved in translating them into duties, and the risks posed to relational values by this process and accountability with regard to it, it is not surprising that this model is mostly supported in the context of the human rights-based duties of multinational corporations; and that in the few legal systems in which it was adopted, it usually takes more restrained forms – that draw distinctions between public and private agents in terms of the requirements of constitutional rights.

1.3.2. Indirect Approaches

The pressures on the vertical and direct horizontality models lead us, as I discuss in chapters 4 and 5, to indirect horizontality models, towards which there seems to be a pull in liberal legal systems. This book does not substantiate this empirical claim nor does it rely on it. Rather, it claims that indirect models can both better integrate the political aspects of constitutional rights and the relational aspects of private law and locate different cases on the horizontality spectrum – something the other models struggle to do. In a sense, the very idea of constitutional horizontality, combined with relatively modest liberal commitments, pushes towards nuanced indirect models, at least as a deliberative starting point.

Under indirect models, the agents that constitutional rights obligate and the actions that they address come apart: rights address both public and private actions, but obligate only public agents, including in their law-creating roles. Indirect models take many forms and can overlap with the other models. Crudely, stronger indirect models rely on the idea that state agents have positive duties to ensure that constitutional rights are respected, protected and promoted in all social spheres, whereas weaker indirect models rely on the idea that constitutional rights operate as values that the entire legal system must realise.

In legal systems that adopt indirect models – for example, Germany, Canada and the United Kingdom – we can find traces of both stronger and weaker versions. Their shared basic features are that private agents have no direct constitutional claims against each other – only against the state – and that such claims can address not only state actions but also the state's regulation of private actions and activities. Thus, in a *Discrimination* case, the Supreme Court of the United Kingdom held that bakers and customers can assert their Convention rights – to freedom of religion and expression on one side, and to equality on the other – only against the state; and that a proportional balance between these rights can be struck if the anti-discrimination regime is construed as prohibiting bakers from refusing to provide services to customers just because the latter support gay marriage, while permitting bakers to refuse to provide cakes with messages with which they deeply disagree.[30]

Indirect models aim to expose the private to public influence without subordinating the former to the latter or treating the interpersonal as political. They take seriously the progressive constitutional duties of state agents, who operate on behalf of the political collective; yet they also acknowledge that, to discharge these duties effectively and justifiably, private law's relational structure and

[30] *Lee v Ashers Baking Company Ltd* [2018] UKSC 49, paras 49–57.

underlying values must be taken seriously.[31] Chapters 4 and 5 explore this middle ground, while criticising both stronger and weaker indirect models.

Stronger indirect models will be criticised for structuring state reasoning in an overly consequentialist and goal-oriented manner – mostly by relying too directly on proportionality analysis to shape the horizontal realisation of constitutional rights. While constitutional theory and practice often treat proportionality as a normative framework suitable for all regulatory questions, relying on it without appreciating qualitative distinctions between types of reasons for regulation reintroduces the problems of direct horizontality.

Weaker indirect models will be criticised for structuring state reasoning in ways that deflate the progressive force of constitutional rights: for example, by granting judges too much discretion to decide when and how to realise constitutional rights as open-ended values when developing the common law. While private law theory and practice often highlight the importance of incremental evolution and a focus on isolated disputes – for both institutional and substantive reasons – unbridled discretion is at odds with the point of constitutional horizontality, and exposes indirect models to the problems of traditional verticality.

The criticisms of the models that lie on the constitutional horizontality spectrum lead us to what I take to be the heart of constitutional horizontality: the common law – or a version of it that fits modern regulatory conditions. The common law has been dealing with challenges similar to the challenge of horizontality for centuries. It can therefore not only bridge the academic discourses surrounding this normative phenomenon – political, moral, constitutional, human rights, and private law theories – but also the different models of horizontality. The common law, with its incrementalism and contextualism, allows pushing private law towards better conformity with constitutional rights, while preserving its integrity, coherence and legitimacy as a domain of morally robust rights and duties. While private law faces complex challenges in this regard in modern regulatory conditions, as chapter 6 explains – for example, the involvement of corporations, insurance, or administrative agencies – it still has unique tools to pave horizontal paths for constitutional rights.

1.4. MORAL FOUNDATIONS

While constitutional horizontality forms part of a political and progressive moment of regulatory expansion, it also reflects the resilience of the private

[31] See also Gavin Phillipson and Alexander Williams, 'Horizontal Effect and the Constitutional Constraint' (2011) 74 *Modern Law Review* 878, 879–80.

and the relational. In this sense, it is one of many practices that shape and are shaped by normative tensions between ideal-typical moral visions of law and the state:[32] on the one hand, the restrained state, in which the private is largely isolated from the public – in line with traditional verticality; on the other hand, the ambitious state, in which the private is subordinated to the public, in line with direct horizontality. This phenomenon cannot, therefore, be explained as a natural and neutral feature of the normative universe nor as merely a collision between norms that legal systems currently recognise. It is a process involving ongoing exercises of legal authority and discretion, guided and limited by moral reasons external to law as it currently stands. Explanations or prescriptions that ignore these broader normative forces and tensions between public and private will therefore be partial or reductive – like explanations of mountains that ignore tectonic or erosion processes. It is not only that there are parallels between law and morality here, but that they are continuous in ways that explain constitutional horizontality's nature and limits.

1.4.1. Conflicting Paradigms

Constitutional horizontality brings into legal systems basic moral conflicts between deontology and teleology. It is pulled, from one side, by deontological ideas, which define actions as permitted, required, or forbidden according to their intrinsic features:[33] which focus on whether exercises of agency (*deon* means 'duty' in Greek) wrong people directly – for instance, by subordinating, exploiting, discriminating, or limiting speech. Constitutional horizontality is also pulled, from the other side, by teleological principles (*telos* means 'goal' or 'purpose'), which determine moral status according to the values that the object of evaluation realises: for example, as a form of consequentialism, classical utilitarianism sees agents as obligated to bring about the best states of affairs in terms of social utility.[34] While complex versions of consequentialism can accommodate rights indirectly (say, because regularly upholding systems of norms that recognise rights brings about better results over time),[35] rights

[32] See Kennedy (n 14) 364–68; Martin Loughlin, *Public Law and Political Theory* (Oxford University Press, 1992) 59–61; Jürgen Habermas, 'Paradigms of Law' (1996) 17 *Cardozo Law Review* 771; Hugh Collins, *Employment Law*, 2nd edn (Oxford University Press, 2010) 14–20; Thomas W Merrill, 'Private and Public Law' in Andrew S Gold, John CP Goldberg, Daniel B Kelly, Emily Sherwin and Henry E Smith (eds), *The Oxford Handbook of the New Private Law* (Oxford University Press, 2020) 575.

[33] See generally Larry Alexander and Michael Moore, 'Deontological Ethics' in Edward N Zalta and Uri Nodelman (eds), *The Stanford Encyclopedia of Philosophy* (Winter 2024).

[34] See generally Walter Sinnott-Armstrong, 'Consequentialism' in Edward N Zalta and Uri Nodelman (eds), *The Stanford Encyclopedia of Philosophy* (Winter 2023).

[35] See generally Brad Hooker, 'Rule Consequentialism' in Edward N Zalta and Uri Nodelman (eds), *The Stanford Encyclopedia of Philosophy* (Spring 2023).

violations are seen as bad things that happen in the world.[36] In this sense, consequentialism is beneficiary-centered: our actions as agents are just another factor to be considered when evaluating states of affairs. Deontology (much like private law) resists this form of reasoning. It sees moral norms as obligating each agent separately, while focusing on their responsibilities:[37] thus, we must keep our promise or not punch someone even if by breaking our promise or punching someone we can reduce the number of broken promises or delivered punches in society.

One of the basic themes of the book is that both moral perspectives capture important parts of the normative universe: both a more active and independent side of the moral agent, expressed in our direct interactions and relationships; and a more passive and dependent side, to which state institutions often respond.[38] To be effective and justified, the processes through which constitutional rights are brought to bear on private law rights and duties must accommodate and tend to the conflicts between intuitions and principles from both moral perspectives. Therefore, even if these perspectives often overlap in practice, understanding and guiding constitutional horizontality requires appreciating each perspective's distinct normative features – and seeing their conflicts not as problems to be solved, but as signs of healthy legal systems that engage and try to reconcile foundational aspects of the normative universe.

1.4.2. Horizontality in Context

In this sense – and this is another basic theme of this book – constitutional horizontality is not *sui generis*. It is addressed, even if in slightly different forms, by political and moral theorists exploring how social justice influences interpersonal morality and by private law theorists and practitioners debating how best to accommodate 'policy' reasons, such as the robustness of markets, the free exchange of ideas, innovation, family integrity, and even national security. To a great extent, the main battle lines in private law theory are drawn according to the place of public policy within it: some theorists, with consequentialist tendencies, claim that private law is a malleable tool that can be used to realise any policy goal; while others, who highlight its relational structure, insist

[36] Thomas Scanlon, *What We Owe to Each Other* (Harvard University Press, 1998) 80.

[37] Stephen Darwall, 'Agent-Centered Restrictions from the Inside Out' (1986) 50 *Philosophical Studies* 291.

[38] On this distinction, see Amartya Sen, 'Well-Being, Agency and Freedom' (1985) 82 *Journal of Philosophy* 169; Thomas W Pogge, 'The Problems with Contractarian-Consequentialist Ways of Assessing Social Institutions' (1995) 12 *Social Philosophy and Policy* 241; Martha C Nussbaum, 'Flawed Foundations: The Philosophical Critique of (a Particular type of) Economics' (1997) 64 *University of Chicago Law Review* 1197, 1203–06; David Miller, *National Responsibility and Global Justice* (Oxford University Press, 2007) 5–7; Stephen Darwall, *The Second-Person Standpoint: Morality, Respect, and Accountability* (Harvard University Press, 2006) 126–30.

that doing so not only deviates from its basic principles, but also creates deep moral problems. These debates shed additional light on the normative picture: we must understand not only what constitutional rights ask of private law, but also how private law can respond – and as should be quite clear, these questions are intertwined.

It will be claimed that while there are good reasons for private law's resistance to open-ended policy reasoning, well-structured forms of reasoning can integrate public goals within the normative structure of private rights-and-duties relationships. Private law autonomy cannot be achieved by ignoring its regulatory context – it requires its careful integration in this context. Constitutional rights, properly understood, leave room for this integration by normally working behind the scenes – focusing on the social conditions and states of affairs created by the basic structure of society. In fact, their horizontal dimensions are more effective and justified when shaped by relational private law principles. In this sense, constitutional horizontality expresses the fact that constitutional rights and private law need and depend on each other.

These moral undercurrents push us towards flexibility and context-sensitivity, as a response to the predicament of moral pluralism:[39] towards seeing constitutional horizontality as exhibiting more or less 'publicness' or 'privateness' in different ways and moments.[40] This presents a unique challenge. A theory of constitutional horizontality must explain how it can justifiably and effectively move along this normative spectrum: how it can operate as a transmission mechanism between constitutional rights and private law. This mechanism must not deflate the horizontal dimensions and progressive potential of constitutional rights: after all, the point of constitutional horizontality is to subject private law to effective scrutiny touching how the political collective realises constitutional rights in all social spheres. On the other hand, this mechanism must meet basic rule of law requirements, such as transparency, stability and practicability; and it must leave room for distinctions between public and private and for the relational normativity and underlying values of private relationships, associations and practices. This requires constitutional horizontality to rest on solid and deep moral foundations.

1.5. RIGHTS AND JUSTIFICATIONS

The constitutional horizontality challenge is multifaceted and complex, yet two of its features stand out: first, as noted in the previous section, it manifests

[39] Stanley I Benn and Gerald F Gaus, 'The Liberal Conception of the Public and the Private' in *Public and Private in Social Life* (n 13) 31; William Lucy and Alexander Williams, 'Public and Private: Neither Deep not Meaningful?' in *Private Law: Key Encounters with Public Law* (n 7) 45.

[40] Tay and Kamenka (n 13) 83; Lucy, 'What's Private About Private Law?' (n 5); Barker, 'Private Law: Key Encounters' (n 20) 20–21.

tensions between two moral paradigms; second, and this is the focus of this section, it is about rights. On the constitutional side, many norms or principles can justify the constitutionalisation of other areas of the legal system, including private law:[41] for example, rule of law principles.[42] Yet the main challenge of horizontality is rights-based, for two reasons. First, in terms of force: rights-based claims about horizontality are not about, for example, goodness, efficiency, charity or community – they are part of relational arguments about what people are owed by the political collective, in terms of the realisation of their basic interests. Failures wrong people as right-holders. Second, the rights-based challenge is more complex, because individual interests are sensitive to private law's ability to respond effectively and justifiably to constitutional pressures – and in this sense, rights-based constitutional horizontality is not a pure top-down process.

Interestingly, it is not only that constitutional rights apply forceful and complex pressures on private law to evolve, but that on private law's side rights push strongly against such external pressures. While reasons of judicial competence or authority and legal stability and coherence push back as well, we will see that their force is limited – especially when it comes to legislative activities. Reasons touching the dependence of private law's value as a form of regulation on its rights-based structure – and therefore on the partial isolation of its forms of empowerment and guidance from constitutional or other large-scale reasons – are more comprehensive. Rights are therefore on both sides of constitutional horizontality. They push us to bring constitutional reasons to bear on private law but without politicising or instrumentalising it or eroding the unique normativity of private rights-and-duties relationships.

Resolving this challenge is not merely a matter of achieving conceptual precision and clarity: for example, by dissecting rights into the claims, liberties, powers and immunities that comprise them, in the spirit of Wesley Hohfeld's famous analysis.[43] In both constitutional law and private law we treat clusters of such normative parts as complex wholes, and pay greater attention to what ties them together and gives them force in normative conflicts.[44]

This challenge is also not about the existence conditions that such clusters must meet to be labelled as rights. In the fierce debate about the nature of rights, 'will' theories focus on the ability to control their correlated duties and the freedom from such duties,[45] while 'interest' theories focus on how rights justify

[41] See Martin Loughlin, 'What is Constitutionalisation?' in Petra Dobner and Martin Loughlin (eds), *The Twilight of Constitutionalism?* (Oxford University Press, 2010) 47.

[42] See Lisa M Austin and Dennis Klimchuk (eds), *Private Law and the Rule of Law* (Oxford University Press, 2014).

[43] See Heidi M Hurd and Michael S Moore, 'The Hohfeldian Analysis of Rights' (2018) 63 *American Journal of Jurisprudence* 295.

[44] See Alon Harel, 'Theories of Rights' in Martin P Golding and William A Edmundson (eds), *The Blackwell Guide to the Philosophy of Law and Legal Theory* (Blackwell Publishing, 2005) 191.

[45] HLA Hart, 'Legal Rights' in *Essays on Bentham* (Oxford University Press, 1982) 162, 183.

the imposition of different duties on different agents in different circumstances by relying on foundational values.[46] Both theories offer us valuable insights. The will theory's emphasis on enforcement and relationships reflects some of private law's basic features. However, as HLA Hart, one of its prominent expositors, conceded, while it is helpful in explaining rights in 'ordinary' law, it struggles with general constitutional rights.[47] Here, the interest theory, with its beneficiary-centered and systematic structure, often does a better job. If the will theory sees 'the right-holder as the manager of a network of normative relations connecting her to others', the interest theory sees the 'right-holder as the passive beneficiary of a network of protected and supportive duties shared by others'.[48] However, while the instrumentalism of the interest theory is a benefit in the public domain, it must be refined and limited in the constitutional horizontality context. Thus, we see here that because the recognition of rights responds to the deepest features of the person and society,[49] it also reflects the tensions between the two moral paradigms presented above. This is where theories of the nature of rights run out of resources: to understand the nature and limits of constitutional horizontality we must rely on more substantive ideas that address the normative structure and underlying values of constitutional and private law rights.

1.5.1. Contractualism

This book turns for this purpose to contractualist moral theories. They have been prominent in the past decades, thanks to philosophers such as John Rawls and TM Scanlon. The core idea is that mutual recognition and respect shape the reasonableness of the moral justifications that we can offer to others, and therefore constrain the content of moral principles. Three features of this justificatory structure are important for us: first, it responds both to the intrinsic features of actions and to their consequences, thereby locating middle grounds between deontology and teleology; second, it locates these middle grounds in different normative contexts, like the basic structure of society, allocative practices, and rights-and-duties relationships; and third, it grounds moral reasoning in these contexts in unified structural and substantive foundations.

Contractualism is important for us because rights draw much of their force from their recognition as valid claims in normative practices like constitutional

[46] Joseph Raz, 'The Nature of Rights' in *The Morality of Freedom* (Oxford University Press, 1986) 165, 166; Jeremy Waldron, 'Rights in Conflict' (1989) 99 *Ethics* 503, 509–12.

[47] Hart, 'Legal Rights' (n 45) 193. On pluralism and the nature of rights, see also Horacio Spector, 'Value Pluralism and the Two Concepts of Rights' (2009) 46 *San Diego Law Review* 819; Siegfried Van Duffel, 'The Nature of Rights Debate Rests on a Mistake' (2012) 93 *Pacific Philosophical Quarterly* 104.

[48] LW Sumner, *The Moral Foundation of Rights* (Clarendon Press, 1997) 47.

[49] Thomas Nagel, *Equality and Partiality* (Oxford University Press, 1991) 140.

law and private law.[50] As claims, they operate within relational normative structures that contractualism explains. Rights grant their holders (or their representatives) the standing and authority to call the duty-bearer to account, on the right-holder's own behalf and at their own discretion.[51] They do not constrain duty-bearers merely because they are well-placed to benefit others (as public rules do). Rather, they express the fact that duty-bearers are accountable and responsible to the right-holder in certain regards; that they wrong the right-holder in particular if they fail to discharge their duties; and that reactive attitudes like blame by the right-holder and remedial obligations are justified in response to such wrongs.[52] The duty-bearer's failure does not consist of merely acting wrongly in ways that happen to affect the right-holder,[53] as is the case, say, with not recycling or not voting: we do not wrong anyone by discounting the (good) reasons to do these things. Rights highlight the fact that when our conduct affects other people's basic interests, we must justify ourselves directly to them rather than portraying ourselves as 'benevolent bureaucrats' who distribute benefits and burdens in society.[54]

Contractualism highlights the fact that rights and the relational normative structures in which they operate form parts of, and can be shaped by, social institutions and practices, which can alter the ways in which the values that underlie rights are translated into duties – for example, by creating right-holder vulnerabilities or assigning duty-bearers responsibilities.[55] A basic premise of this book is that while some vulnerabilities are unique to public activities and practices (such as elections or trials), many of the interests that underlie constitutional rights are sensitive to both public and private activities and practices. Because these interests are general, complex and tentacular, much work must be done on the agent-centered side of the ledger: specifically, we will have to explore how different notions of agency and responsibility lead us from such interests to different duties and duty-bearers.

Constitutional rights express an expansive and prescriptive notion of collective responsibility, which responds to the fact that state agents have no autonomy interests in their official capacities and to their authority and ability

[50] Joel Feinberg, 'The Nature and Value of Rights' (1970) 4 *Journal of Value Inquiry* 243, 252–53.

[51] Alan Gewirth, 'Why Rights are Indispensable' (1986) 95 *Mind* 329, 335–37; Stephen Darwall, 'Bipolar Obligation' in *Morality, Authority, and Law: Essays in Second-Personal Ethics I* (Oxford University Press, 2013) 20, 26–31; Rowan Cruft, *Human Rights, Ownership, and the Individual* (Oxford University Press, 2019) 46–61, 80–83.

[52] Darwall, *The Second-Person Standpoint* (n 38) 6–7. See also Cruft, *Human Rights, Ownership, and the Individual* (n 51) 39–43; R Jay Wallace, *The Moral Nexus* (Princeton University Press, 2019) 49–51, 57–59.

[53] Michael Thompson, 'What it is to Wrong Someone? A Puzzle about Justice' in R Jay Wallace, Philip Pettit, Samuel Scheffler and Michael Smith (eds), *Reason and Value: Themes from the Moral Philosophy of Joseph Raz* (Oxford University Press, 2006) 333, 352, 372.

[54] Thomas Nagel, 'War and Massacre' (1972) 1 *Philosophy & Public Affairs* 123, 136–38.

[55] On these justificatory paths, see Matthew H Kramer, 'Rights Without Trimmings' in *A Debate Over Rights: Philosophical Enquiries* (Oxford University Press, 2000) 7, 35–39. See also Jeremy Waldron, *The Right to Private Property* (Oxford University Press, 1988) 70–71.

to solve social problems as part of the state's institutional apparatus. These rights therefore entail duties not only to avoid treating right-holders in certain ways but also to make sure that right-holders are treated in certain ways. Private law rights, on the other hand, express a restrictive and choice-sensitive notion of personal responsibility, which ensures that there is a tight fit between our duties to others and our responsibilities to them. Negative and concrete duties not to harm can be justified universally in this context, but positive or complex duties (say, to protect from third parties) are imposed mostly when duty-bearers assume extended responsibilities towards others. Therefore, it is difficult to justify general private law duties – say, to promote equality or protect privacy; but such general rights are regularly recognised by constitutional law, and for good reasons: concretising and specifying rights against the state will often slow our progress towards social justice.

The beneficiary-centeredness and loose relationality of constitutional rights and the agent-centeredness and strict relationality of private law rights are not existence conditions: they touch the force and value of rights as part of the social normative fabric. Contractualism enters the picture at this point, to explain why constitutional law rights operate closer to the paradigm of the ambitious state, with its teleological overtones, while private law rights operate closer to the paradigm of the restricted state, with its deontological overtones. While these distinctions are not clear-cut, we must understand them and the foundational normative forces underlying them to grasp the nature and limits of constitutional horizontality. The problem of constitutional horizontality is, in many ways, that the progressive orientation of constitutional rights expands them into private spheres, where it erodes their force and value as private rights.

1.5.2. Normative Layers

By building on contractualism – and tying it to basic ideas in constitutional theory, private law theory, and jurisprudence – we can achieve more than a *modus vivendi* between constitutional rights and private law: we can adopt forms of reasoning that at least partly integrate their basic principles by giving them priority in their natural normative habitats, while carefully reconciling their political and relational aspects in a contextual and incremental manner.

The first important activity in this regard is the delineation of the horizontal dimensions of constitutional rights. I rely on John Rawls's theory to explain how constitutional rights bring social justice principles to guide and constrain private law's evolution as regulatory ideals. They are shaped by relational and deontological reasons, but only to the extent that they address the political collective's ability to pursue social justice through the institutions that comprise the basic structure of society. On the other hand, these abstract ideals do not obligate private agents directly, in most cases, thereby leaving room for more relational and less political moral principles in choices of regulatory regimes.

With regard to the realisation of constitutional rights – their translation into private law norms, while resolving their conflicts with competing reasons for regulation – I will claim that we must be careful with the consequentialist tendencies of open-ended proportionality analysis. I rely on TM Scanlon's theory to distinguish between decisions to adopt regulatory regimes – say, public insurance or tort law – and decisions about the structure or content of these regimes. I claim that in both cases we must compare individual claims on a contextual basis, while taking into account reasons that address the kind of relationships that the regimes create or allow, and second-order reasons about when and how to engage in systematic regulatory reasoning. Relational reasons operate in choices of regulatory regimes only to the extent that they shed light on their allocative implications for all affected parties; however, if a rights-and-duties private law regime is adopted, policy reasons must be diluted and adequately combined with relational reasons to gain weight in decisions about the structure or content of these relationships.

Having said that, against weak accounts of horizontal realisation that treat constitutional rights as mere values that the common law's development should gradually accommodate, it will be claimed that there is ample room for constitutional rights to shape the details of private law rights-and-duties relationships. Mutual recognition and respect can invite such external influence and allow its integration within relational normative structures of standing, responsibility, accountability, reactive attitudes, and remedies. This structure operates as an effective filtering mechanism that complements proportionality analysis in constitutional horizontality cases, on the ground. It sheds light on the creative and authoritative dimensions of this process: social practices, such as a constitutionally-oriented private law, not only respond to but also shape our expectations from and responsibilities towards each other and therefore our standing to claim and blame and the adequacy of remedial responses.

The general contours of the challenge of constitutional horizontality should be visible at this point. Private law realises many values: some internal to private relationships (like intimacy or trust) and others external to them (like social equality or market stability). Its ability to realise values depends on the normative robustness of its right-norms: if they become mere placeholders – if private law is treated as a malleable form of top-down regulation – private law's ability to create and sustain relationships of mutual recognition and respect, and to bring communal values to bear on such relationships, is diminished.

Private relationships are delicate ecosystems. But change is necessary. Injustice is common: from racism and inequality, through breaches of privacy, to workplace abuse and harassment. We must therefore find ways to effectively realise constitutional rights through private law while preserving its ability to tap into the unique normative tapestry of private relationships and activities.

Sometimes, we may want private agents to, for example, ensure equal access to education or protect online privacy – even if they did not cause the social conditions in which the rights to equality or privacy are threatened. This goes beyond private law's traditional purview – which is why it needs the constitution to give it a forceful push. But for this push to be effective and justified, it must respond to private law's unique normative features. This is the normative challenge of constitutional horizontality. Responses to this challenge can take the form of traditional verticality (say, when it comes to the rights against the establishment of religion or to a fair trial), of direct horizontality (say, when it comes to the rights against torture or slavery), of strong indirect horizontality (say, when it comes to choices of regulatory regimes), or of weak indirect horizontality (say, when it comes to the incremental common law development of private law regimes). This book relies on the contractualist framework to explain the nature and limits of these responses – gradually working towards a pluralistic account of constitutional horizontality as a normative practice that requires all state branches to collaborate while transitioning between incremental evolution and comprehensive reform.

1.6. METHODOLOGICAL REMARKS

The book has two complementary goals: to explain what constitutional horizontality is and the place of private law in a legal system in which the constitution expands horizontally. In a sense, the book addresses constitutional aspects of the political theory of private law: its roles and justifications as an exercise of state authority and power. As a form of political theory, it locates legal institutions in the broader normative universe by using philosophical tools and drawing qualitative distinctions. However, because it deals with legal institutions, it must take seriously their past and present as reliable repositories of moral principles and considered judgments.[56] As Bernard Williams claimed, because the legal system must settle normative disputes, we have good reasons to take legal principles into account when addressing philosophical questions: not only the particular answers that the law gives but also its ways of framing and resolving moral conflicts, given the forces that operate on it as a political institution.[57]

This book therefore addresses many pieces of legislation and judicial cases from common law jurisdictions, but from a philosophical and political

[56] See Sandy Steel, 'Justifying Civil Recourse for Wrongs' (2023) 27 *Jerusalem Review of Legal Studies* 1, 8; Hanoch Dagan and Avihay Dorfman, *Relational Justice* (Oxford University Press, 2024) 8–9.

[57] Bernard Williams, 'Afterword: What Has Philosophy to Learn from Tort Law?' in David G Owen (ed), *Philosophical Foundations of Tort Law* (Clarendon Press, 1995) 487, 492.

perspective. This back and forth – between central features of legal practices and more theoretical insights – aims to elucidate the nature and limits of constitutional horizontality as a complex legal activity. Because it does not aim to merely describe legal practices but to present constitutional horizontality as a morally legitimate process, it also touches on legal choices that are morally wrong, if their wrongness can enrich the process of reaching effective equilibrium about constitutional horizontality questions.[58] This process, I note in this section, must be internally structured and externally comparative and diligent.

1.6.1. The Central Case

This book engages constitutional horizontality by focusing on an idealised scenario, in which loosely relational and beneficiary-centered constitutional rights apply pressure on strictly relational and agent-centered private law rights, in liberal and reasonably effective and justified common law legal systems.[59] I focus on this scenario not necessarily because it is common or prevalent (though it is) or because it expresses the timeless essence or nature of these right-types (though there are pressures on rights in these domains to take these forms). Rather, I focus on this scenario for explanatory reasons: it serves as the deliberative starting point that best contributes to our understanding of how constitutional horizontality can and should form part of the law's evolution towards better coherence, integrity and justification.[60]

Focusing on this scenario is important because constitutional horizontality, similarly to new constitutions, still operates within thin normative frameworks, is not fully internalised by agents and institutions, and the collaborative efforts of developing it – thereby moving it to the background of legal practices – are still ongoing.[61] To place constitutional horizontality on solid foundations, we should start with the scenario that poses the most complex (and thus interesting) problems. If constitutional rights are strictly relational and state-centered or if private law rights are loosely relational and policy-oriented, there are still moral challenges, but less friction between the constitution and private law. It is when constitutional rights expand horizontally and private law rights resist external influence that the deep conflict between moral paradigms appears.

[58] See generally Carl Knight, 'Reflective Equilibrium' in Edward N Zalta and Uri Nodelman (eds), *The Stanford Encyclopedia of Philosophy* (Spring 2025).

[59] On the methodology of using central cases, see John Finnis, *Natural Law and Natural Rights*, 2nd edn (Paul Craig ed, Oxford University Press, 2011) 9–11.

[60] On this kind of explanation and constitutional horizontality, see Hugh Collins, 'Private Law, Fundamental Rights, and the Rule of Law' (2008) 121 *West Virginia Law Review* 1, 23–25.

[61] On constitution-building, see James Fowkes, *Building the Constitution: The Practice of Constitutional Interpretation in Post-Apartheid South Africa* (Cambridge University Press, 2016) 131–42.

My definitions of constitutional law, private law, and their rights-norms are therefore aimed at exposing and explaining this conflict. While narrower definitions can alleviate the conflict, they are better seen as downstream conclusions that are substantively justified by reliance on considerations that the complex scenario reveals. This methodology mirrors thinking about democracy or secularism as ideal-types, even if there are no, or even if there can be no, perfectly democratic or secular societies.

The proposed account of constitutional horizontality is therefore normative and philosophical,[62] and reconstructs the materials it engages.[63] A basic theme running through it is that the structures and basic principles of constitutional rights and private law are co-dependent: constitutional rights need private law's relational structure and ties to interpersonal morality to be realised effectively and justifiably in private settings; and private law needs constitutional rights that highlight collective commitments to meet basic interests and needs to secure its legitimacy. In a sense, each area of law allows the other to focus on its unique regulatory roles.

Having said that, the proposed account is not prescriptive: it does not advocate the recognition of specific loosely relational constitutional rights or strictly relational private law rights by applying comprehensive moral principles to the circumstances of particular legal systems. Rather, it assumes, upstream, that such forms of recognition are sufficiently common and justified – and it will be claimed that we have good (yet not necessarily conclusive) reasons to recognise these right-types – to illuminate constitutional horizontality. It also makes no prescriptive claims about the horizontal realisation of constitutional rights in specific regulatory contexts: it only aims to inform and provide theoretical foundations for such downstream claims by specialists in areas like tort law, labour law or family law.

1.6.2. Neighbouring Approaches

Much attention must be given, when constructing a normative explanation of such legal phenomena, to competing theoretical accounts. I should say a few words about how this book is positioned relative to them. First, it should already be clear that this book does not merely offer a taxonomy of different models, which focuses on their technical differences, nor advocate a specific model. While this book builds on and responds to such accounts, it aims to go deeper

[62] Isaiah Berlin, 'Does Political Theory Still Exist?' in *Concepts and Categories*, 2nd edn (Henry Hardy ed, Princeton University Press, 2014) 187.

[63] Ronald Dworkin, 'Integrity in Law' in *Law's Empire* (Harvard University Press, 1986) 225. See also Stephen A Smith, *Contract Theory* (Oxford University Press, 2004) 4–13.

by exploring the nature and limits of constitutional horizontality as a practice (within which the models can be distinguished and compared).

Second, some theories pull towards direct horizontality at this deeper level because they engage the challenge from a public perspective: for instance, by tying it to equal citizenship,[64] or to sovereignty and the relations between minorities and majorities.[65] From this perspective, as Johan van der Walt claimed, constitutional horizontality seems disappointing: it 'has largely remained a conceptual or jurisprudential revolution',[66] and 'will probably never effect progressive social revolutions or reforms',[67] which requires subordinating 'all private relations to fundamentally public norms and concerns'.[68] I will explain my concerns about such claims, but it should already be noted that I engage constitutional horizontality from a more pluralistic perspective, one that takes seriously the normative uniqueness of private relationships.

Another type of account that tends to pull towards direct horizontality does so because it focuses on the duties of multinational corporations, often in less effective legal systems.[69] Given the enforcement difficulties that arise in that context, such accounts are suspicious of state-oriented indirect models. I will go back to this scenario, which is both common and concerning. However, as noted above, by starting with cases in which there is more resistance to the imposition of constitutionally-grounded duties on private agents, we can better understand when each form of horizontality is justified – and avoid, for example, the mistake of engaging all private agents as if they have the capabilities and goals of profit-oriented companies.

The aforementioned accounts of constitutional horizontality expose the political dimensions of private relationships, associations and practices, and the limits of the state's ability to guide private agents towards the realisation of public goals. The private cannot be hermetically isolated from the public. However, they must be integrated within a broader normative framework that pays close attention to the normative structure and underlying values of private law as well. I will claim, in this regard, that states have important roles to play in the efforts to realise constitutional rights in private social spheres. This role can be disputed. A notable challenge in this regard

[64] Eleni Frantziou, *The Horizontal Effect of Fundamental Rights in the European Union: A Constitutional Analysis* (Oxford University Press, 2019).

[65] Johan van der Walt, *The Horizontal Effect Revolution and the Question of Sovereignty* (De Gruyter, 2014).

[66] ibid 7.

[67] ibid 9.

[68] ibid 10.

[69] See, eg, Florian Wettstein, *Multinational Corporations and Global Justice: Human Rights Obligations of a Quasi-Governmental Institution* (Stanford University Press, 2009); David Jason Karp, *Responsibility for Human Rights: Transnational Corporations in Imperfect States* (Cambridge University Press, 2014); David Bilchitz, *Fundamental Rights and the Legal Obligations of Business* (Cambridge University Press, 2021).

is Jean Thomas's constitutional horizontality theory: in fact, a moral argument, grounded in a reconstruction of constitutional and human rights that divorces them from their state-centered origins, for the recognition of new private law rights.[70] Against 'the waning of the modern state',[71] Thomas sees state-centered approaches as less effective because they can be worked around by, say, big corporations.[72] Thomas claims that private agents must be able to figure out which duties they are under, even ahead of judicial decisions – a normative process on which the state should not encroach.[73] Thomas's theory is important because it takes us from questions of the horizontal scope of constitutional rights, with which vertical and direct horizontality models are occupied, to questions of horizontal realisation; and from a relatively doctrinal occupation with law as it is to a more philosophical occupation with is evolution. I also agree that moral arguments must properly constrain constitutional horizontality reasoning without collapsing into an open-ended and ad hoc form of policy analysis. However, against Thomas, I will claim that modern legal systems contain the normative resources to construct well-structured reasoning mechanisms, and that states have important roles to play in the processes through which such mechanisms are relied upon to translate constitutional rights into private law rights.

Because my account explains constitutional horizontality as an evolutionary normative process, it also sidelines some factors that might influence its outcomes: for example, political cultures or the relations between federal governments and states or provinces in federal systems or between constitutional courts and other courts or the legislature.[74] Such factors are obviously important, but can be addressed after we get a better understanding of the substantive aspects of constitutional horizontality. This order is important, because once we strip constitutional horizontality of some of its institutional garments, we can see that similar questions were dealt with in political and moral philosophy: for instance, in debates about the relations between collective and personal responsibilities or between distributive and corrective justice. I build on some of the main themes in such philosophical debates to shed light on latent yet basic features of constitutional horizontality. Interestingly, it is not only that philosophical insights can help us understand constitutional horizontality as a legal phenomenon, but also the other way around: as noted above, justice, morality, and law are intertwined in this context, and we can therefore see legal

[70] Jean Thomas, *Public Rights, Private Relations* (Oxford University Press, 2015) 25–28, 40–49, 109–13.

[71] ibid 5.

[72] ibid 14.

[73] ibid 145–48.

[74] See Mathews, *Extending Rights' Reach* (n 28); Mark Tushnent, 'The Issue of State Action/Horizontal Effect in Comparative Constitutional Law' (2003) 1 *International Journal of Constitutional Law* 79.

attempts to tackle problems of constitutional horizontality as part-moral arguments. One of the most important roles of this book is to expose and explain the connections between these normative discourses, thereby grounding constitutional horizontality in solid normative foundations that can explain, guide, and limit our collective progress towards social justice.

A final cluster of theories with which this book engages are theories of constitutional law and private law: that, for instance, criticise the open-ended nature of proportionality or the rigid separation of private law from social justice. Constitutional and human rights lawyers tend to think about constitutionally-grounded reform of private law without considering private law's nature and limits; meanwhile private lawyers, on their part, tend to either accept private law's subordination to external reasons (often labelled as policy reasons) or assume that it is immune to their influence. The book aims to better integrate their claims about their respective fields, while allowing each group to benefit from the unique perspective of the group standing on the other side of the fence.

1.7. THE ROAD AHEAD

The book is structured around criticisms of different models of constitutional horizontality.[75] It starts, in the next chapter, by criticising traditional verticality, while exposing and explaining the moral forces that push constitutional rights to expand horizontally – centrally, the beneficiary-centeredness and demandingness of the interests that underlie them and their role as collective commitments – and their resulting normative structure, which allows them to guide and constrain the regulation of private relationships, associations and practices, as general ideals.

Chapter 3 criticises direct horizontality, while exposing and explaining the moral forces that push back against attempts to take horizontal expansion to its logical conclusions – imposing constitutional duties on private agents: centrally, personal responsibility and the inherent relationality of rights-and-duties relationships. It explains why the normative structure of rights that private agents exercise with and claim against private agents, whether legal or constitutional, are pushed to be concrete and exclude or marginalise non-relational reasons.

Chapters 2 and 3 therefore present constitutional and private law rights as pulling constitutional horizontality in opposing directions, while relying on central ideas in constitutional and human rights theory and in private law theory

[75] Condensed versions of these criticisms are presented in Tom Kohavi, 'Moral Pluralism and Constitutional Horizontality' (2024) 37 *Canadian Journal of Law and Jurisprudence* 475.

that express foundational moral principles about the nature of agency, responsibility, well-being, and rights. These opposing forces take us, as noted above, to indirect horizontality models. These models locate the action not in the delineation of constitutional rights – whether they obligate only state agents with regard to state actions or also private agents with regard to private actions – but in their realisation: a result of the fact that they obligate only state agents, but also pertain to private actions and activities.

Chapter 4 criticises strong indirect models for eroding, ignoring, or distorting the unique relational normativity of private rights-and-duties relationships by subordinating state reasoning about constitutional rights realisation to consequentialist forms of proportionality analysis; while chapter 5 criticises weak indirect models for isolating private rights-and-duties relationships too strongly from structural and allocative reasons for regulation. While strong models envision realisation reasoning as top-down regulatory reasoning, weak models depict it as bottom-up common law reasoning. I will explain why both perspectives are necessary for state agents to realise constitutional rights effectively and justifiably in private social spheres.

These pressures highlight the fact that constitutional horizontality is a collaborative practice, in which all state branches participate, while transitioning between more contextual and incremental moments that focus on relational considerations, and more general and systematic moments that bring structural and allocative considerations into the mix. Second-order reasons – about how to see the choice situation – are crucial to preserve the balance between stability and reform, and between the protection of private relationships, associations and practices from harm by external scrutiny and their development towards better constitutional conformity.

Chapter 6 piles up additional pressure by complicating the picture of private law, highlighting the many public inroads into it: for instance, corporations, liability insurance, regulatory third parties, general standards, and norms that respond to vulnerability and need in areas like family law, employment law, consumer law, or discrimination law. The emerging picture seems to be too messy for any structured and principled account of constitutional horizontality to explain or guide. Private law itself seems to be disintegrating into policy-oriented clusters of norms – on which constitutional rights simply pile on additional pressure. I will claim that this messy picture actually shows not only that constitutional horizontality is already part of private law and that private law has the tools to respond to it, but also that this process can contribute to private law's integrity, coherence and legitimacy. By locating and solidifying normative bridges from collective responsibilities to personal responsibilities within private rights-and-duties relationships, constitutional horizontality highlights private law's unique regulatory and moral roles. Private law need not collapse under these pressures. It can thrive under them. It need not be overhauled but merely recalibrate its normative lens to be able to identify when it must respond to constitutional rights-based reasons for reform. Importantly, when responding to them it must keep doing what it has been doing for centuries: integrating reasons for regulation into private rights-and-duties relationships. This is what its basic institutional, procedural, substantive and conceptual apparatus is suited to – even if it must be given a constitutional push, which this book explains and justifies.

2

Horizontal Expansion

2.1. INTRODUCTION

THIS CHAPTER AND the next one deal with the scope of constitutional rights. This chapter explains how constitutional horizontality emerges with the constitution's expansion from the strictly relational and state-centered domain it occupied during the *laissez-faire* era, while the next one explains why this expansion often stops before recognising private constitutional duties. The starting point is the constitution's horizontal expansion.

Before getting started, I must note that I adopt a rather inclusive definition of 'constitutional'. While the archetypal case of a constitutional right includes formal entrenchment and the ability to strike down legislation, my claims apply, with minor modifications, to legislative bills of rights,[1] civil rights,[2] nationally recognised international law rights,[3] and even common law rights.[4] When thinking about constitutional horizontality, the important features of constitutional rights are that they guide and constrain legal activities as collective commitments cemented at the foundations of the legal system.

Often inspired by international documents such as the Universal Declaration of Human Rights (1948), modern constitutional rights address diverse issues: basic goods like water, food, education, shelter or health services; activities like voting, working, marrying or manifesting one's religious beliefs; and interests that entail complex prescriptions about goods, activities, and forms of treatment like security, liberty (including freedoms of movement, assembly, expression, conscience, and so on), equality, dignity, property and privacy. This chapter explains why such rights are under pressure to take beneficiary-centered, abstract, and loosely relational forms – to address not only the state's actions or activities but every action or activity that can impact the interests underlying them. The goal-oriented layers around the deontological cores of these rights shift the focus from what states do to right-holders, to how right-holders are

[1] eg New Zealand Bill of Rights Act 1990.
[2] eg United States' Civil Rights Act 1964.
[3] eg United Kingdom's Human Rights Act 1998.
[4] See, eg, Mark Elliot and Kirsty Hughes (eds), *Common Law Constitutional Rights* (Hart Publishing, 2020).

doing – to social conditions or states of affairs. I claim, against concerns about expansive accounts of rights in philosophy and law, that merely loosely relational constitutional rights are not only conceptually possible but also morally attractive: if treated as obligating the political collective (at the very least, state agents acting on its behalf) they can not only effectively empower right-holders and constrain duty-bearers but also guide the legal system's ongoing evolution towards social justice by shaping the allocation of rights and duties grounded in constitutional rights to different agents in different circumstances.

This does not mean that there is no place for state-centered and strictly relational rights in modern constitutions. On the contrary: they still capture important aspects of liberal political morality, which is rightly concerned about the abuse of state authority. I do not offer an account of the nature or essence of constitutional rights but, as noted in the previous chapter, an account of the rights whose basic normative features elucidate the challenge of constitutional horizontality. Having said that, loosely relational rights – whose general, beneficiary-centered, and teleological normative structure constantly pushes them to expand horizontally – are actually central in modern practices of constitutional rights-claiming, realising and adjudicating. This adds to the importance of understanding their nature and normative implications.

2.2. TRADITIONAL VERTICALITY

In the classical liberal story, one of the constitution's basic goals is to protect private social spheres from state intervention: liberty is dependent on a limited government, majority rule is legitimate only within boundaries, and constitutional rights aim to keep the state in check and prevent excessive state action, thereby leaving citizens free to interact, unless they harm others, in civil society and various markets. This story stands behind what was referred to as a 'culture of authority', which sees constitutional rights as focusing on 'delimiting the borders of public action'.[5] Rights operate as judicially-policed boundaries that cannot be crossed, and, in this sense, do not guide policy-oriented legislative or administrative activities but limit them.[6]

This story can lead to non-relational state-centeredness. For example, it can be claimed that in some social domains – say, religion or the arts – state

[5] Moshe Cohen-Eliya and Iddo Porat, *Proportionality and Constitutional Culture* (Oxford University Press, 2010) 112–14, 118.

[6] On this conception of constitutional rights, see Julian Rivers, 'Proportionality and Variable Intensity of Review' (2006) 65 *Cambridge Law Journal* 174; Pavlos Eleftheriadis, 'Human Rights as Legal Rights' (2010) 1 *Transnational Legal Theory* 371, 385–86; Luc B Tremblay, 'An Egalitarian Defense of Proportionality-Based Balancing' (2014) 12 *International Journal of Constitutional Law* 864, 866–68; Malcolm Thorburn, 'Proportionality' in David Dyzenhaus and Malcolm Thorburn (eds), *Philosophical Foundations of Constitutional Law* (Oxford University Press, 2016) 305, 309–10.

intervention should be prohibited.[7] It can also be claimed that when courts face legitimacy deficits, they should focus on the official processes through which rights are infringed rather than on the substantive justifications of the infringement.[8] In this spirit, constitutional jurisprudence in the United States often addresses questions about what amounts to the establishment of religion or content-based limitations of speech: the state does not violate rights if it infringes them incidentally while trying to promote legitimate goals, regardless of how severe the impact is on the right-holder's interests.[9] This reflects the fact that the focus is not on these interests but on how the state conducts itself:[10] we are more concerned, for example, about the state's neutrality in religious matters than about the ability of people to actually pursue, revise or practise religious beliefs.

Such categorical state-centeredness can also be strictly relational – grounded in the sensitivity of certain interests to harm by state action.[11] The obvious cases relate to activities like elections, adjudication, or incarceration. But there are also general interests that can entail strictly relational state duties. For example, while states tolerate foreseeable loss of life (e.g., car accidents),[12] they can be prohibited from deliberately sacrificing lives, even to save lives.[13] Similar claims could be made about the rights against torture, to equality or to freedoms of speech or religion.[14] While these rights are not all absolute, they can have categorical aspects that focus on interactions between the state and right-holders taken in isolation. If the justification of the right-holder's standing in the case of non-relational state-centered rights is instrumental (as a supervisor of sorts), in the case of strictly relational rights, this standing is morally tied to their ability to stand up for themselves and protect their interests.

[7] Alan Gewirth, 'Are All Rights Positive?' (2002) 30 *Philosophy & Public Affairs* 321.

[8] Robert Spano, 'The Future of the European Court of Human Rights – Subsidiarity, Process-Based Review and the Rule of Law' (2018) 18 *Human Rights Law Review* 473.

[9] Michael C Dorf, 'Incidental Burdens on Fundamental Rights' (1996) 109 *Harvard Law Review* 1175.

[10] Richard H Jr Fallon, 'Individual Rights and the Powers of Government' (1993) 27 *Georgia Law Review* 343, 358–59, 364–65; Matthew D Adler, 'Rights against Rules: The Moral Structure of American Constitutional Law' (1998) 97 *Michigan Law Review* 1, 13–14; Ashutosh Bhagwat, *The Myth of Rights* (Oxford University Press, 2010) 4, 64.

[11] See generally Mattias Kumm and Alec D Walen, 'Human Dignity and Proportionality: Deontic Pluralism in Balancing' in Grant Huscroft, Bradley W Miller and Grégoire Webber (eds), *Proportionality and the Rule of Law: Rights, Justification, Reasoning* (Cambridge University Press, 2014) 67.

[12] See Steven Lukes, 'Comparing the Incomparable: Tradeoffs and Sacrifices', in Ruth Chang (ed), *Incommensurability, Incomparability and Practical Reason* (Harvard University Press, 1997) 184, 191–92.

[13] See Alon Harel, 'Necessity Knows No Law' in *Why Law Matters* (Oxford University Press, 2014) 108.

[14] Richard H Fallon Jr, *The Nature of Constitutional Rights: The Invention and Logic of Strict Judicial Scrutiny* (Cambridge University Press, 2019) 72.

A prominent example of state-centeredness in the theory of constitutional rights is Ronald Dworkin's theory of rights as trumps.[15] According to it, the main point of rights against the state is not to protect interests but to exclude suspicious justifications for state action.[16] Constitutional rights therefore apply solely against the state,[17] entail duties that are discharged by the state 'person by person',[18] in separate state–citizen relationships, and tolerate balancing or tradeoffs only in 'catastrophic' cases.[19] Whether as a result of Dworkin's concerns about utilitarian reasoning or the tyranny of the majority (or both), he portrayed constitutional rights as strong and even rigid protections against the promotion of political or collective goals.

State-centered rights are important parts of the liberal menu of rights against the state. These rights obligate the state to treat or avoid treating particular right-holders in certain ways and to operate in areas of social activity that are sensitive to political influence in an even-handed and formally neutral manner. These rights are by no means easy to discharge and can have wide-scale implications. However, their horizontal implications are quite limited.

2.2.1. The State Action Model

The state action or strongly vertical model holds not only that constitutional rights entail only state duties, but also that these duties address only state actions that harm right-holders or that tie the state to such harms, to the extent that it is intimately involved in them. This is the case both when rights are grounded in interests particularly sensitive to state action and when they are grounded in interests that are also sensitive to private actions. Normally, what the state owes to one right-holder is unaffected by what it owes to another: the state is obligated to protect or promote rights, which might involve imposing duties on private agents, only when it assumes extended responsibilities to particular right-holders (say, by imprisoning inmates together).

Domestic Violence. When Joshua was a baby, a divorce court gave custody of him to his father. Despite several police and hospital reports about potential abuse and concerns by a social worker who visited their home, the department of social services did not remove Joshua from the father's custody. After one of these visits, the father beat young Joshua so badly that he fell into a coma.

[15] For similar accounts, see also George Letsas, *A Theory of Interpretation of the European Convention on Human Rights* (Oxford University Press, 2007) 23–24, 105, 117–18; Moshe Cohen-Eliya and Iddo Porat, 'Proportionality and Justification' (2014) 64 *University of Toronto Law Journal* 458, 469–76.

[16] Paul Yowell, 'A Critical Examination of Dworkin's Theory of Rights' (2007) 52 *American Journal of Jurisprudence* 93, 130.

[17] Jeremy Waldron, 'Pildes on Dworkin's Theory of Rights' (2000) 29 *Journal of Legal Studies* 301, 304.

[18] Ronald Dworkin, *Justice for Hedgehogs* (Harvard University Press, 2013) 330.

[19] ibid 473.

The damage left him disabled and confined to a medical institution for the rest of his life. Joshua's mother sued the state on his behalf: she claimed that the failure to protect him by not removing him from his father's custody amounted to a violation of his constitutional rights. The Supreme Court of the United States rejected the claim.[20] It was held that the constitutional right to due process prevents the state from depriving individuals of life, liberty and property in certain ways, but does not create duties to protect these rights. Such positive duties are imposed when the state's involvement creates a 'special relationship' with the right-holder, but it was held that this was not the case with Joshua.

Under the traditional vertical model, the constitution extends horizontally only when state actions amount to assumptions of responsibilities to prevent or respond to harms to protected constitutional interests by private parties.[21] This model sees public law as an extension of private law, and therefore applies to the state an interpersonal conception of responsibility:[22] a conception that reflects a default position of mutual freedom and grounds duties in their bearer's actions towards the right-holder.

This gives an odd shape to constitutional rights: the right to equality, for example, might not only permit the state to ignore private discrimination, but also prohibit affirmative action initiatives, as their justification exceeds isolated relationships.[23] This constitutional focus on how the state treats each right-holder in isolation fits with the political theory behind this veteran of constitutional horizontality models, which focuses on state abuses of power and sees private law as protecting people's basic rights (a role that can receive constitutional protection by recognising rights against state intervention in forms of private ordering).[24]

2.2.2. Moral Concerns

Criticising the state action model seems almost futile, given the barrage of criticism already directed at it.[25] However, two criticisms are important for our

[20] *DeShaney v Winnebago County* 489 US 189 (1989).

[21] See generally Erwin Chemerinsky, 'Rethinking State Action' (1986) 80 *Northwestern University Law Review* 503.

[22] On this general theme, see Susan Bandes, 'The Negative Constitution: A Critique' (1990) 88 *Michigan Law Review* 2271, 2313–26; Martin Loughlin, 'The State, The Crown and the Law' in Maurice Sunkin and Sebastian Payne (eds), *The Nature of the Crown: A Legal and Political Analysis* (Oxford University Press, 1999) 33; Janet McLean, *Searching for the State in British Legal Thought: Competing Conceptions of the Public Sphere* (Cambridge University Press, 2012) 289; Olivier Beaud, 'Conceptions of the State' in Michael Rosenfeld and András Sajó (eds), *The Oxford Handbook of Comparative Constitutional Law* (Oxford University Press, 2012) 269, 281.

[23] Ian Haney-López, 'Intentional Blindness' (2012) 87 *New York University Law Review* 1779.

[24] The seminal case in this regard is *Lochner v New York* 198 US 45 (1905).

[25] See Lillian BeVier and John Harrison, 'The State Action Principle and Its Critics' (2010) 96 *Virginia Law Review* 1767. See also Stephen Gardbaum, 'The "Horizontal Effect" of Constitutional Rights' (2003) 102 *Michigan Law Review* 387, 415–22; Frank I Michelman, 'The Bill of Rights, the

purposes. For the sake of brevity, I assume that even if state action jurisprudence in the United States is a 'conceptual disaster area',[26] it does offer a workable reasoning structure. The problems I focus on are deeper and substantive: they address its libertarian moral myopia. They are about how its reliance on interpersonal moral ideas when reasoning about the political collective's constitutional obligations leads it to ignore or distort important reasons for regulation.

Anthropomorphisation. As noted above, this model of horizontality relies on a common-sense, choice-sensitive, and restrictive conception of responsibility.[27] According to it, we owe to strangers mostly negative duties not to harm them in relatively concrete ways – shaped by distinctions between, for example, acts and omissions, doing and allowing, or intending and foreseeing. Complex or affirmative duties are limited to special relationships, in which agents assume extended responsibilities towards particular others.[28] This conception reflects the priority that liberal interpersonal morality gives to our ability to control our duties to others over our interest in receiving protection or aid.[29]

While there are justifications for some degree of similar state control over its duties to citizens, the state action model gives it nearly absolute discretion without fully justifying it in ways that reflect the fact that the state has no autonomy interests. The problem is that if constitutional scrutiny follows only harmful state actions, intimate state involvement in harmful private actions, or state assumptions of extended responsibilities, there are no constraints on state decisions not to act – for example, on how the state deals with the risks posed by abusive fathers, as long as it does not assume extended responsibilities, which, as we saw in *Domestic Violence*, even police reports and concerns by social workers might not amount to.

Thomas Nagel claimed in his famous critique of Robert Nozick's libertarian theory that it assumes that 'it is possible to determine what governments may and should do by first asking what individuals, taken a few at a time in isolation from large-scale society, may do'.[30] Social justice, for Nozick, is not about patterns or end-states: it is procedural and backwards-looking, in the sense that states of affairs are justified if no relational wrongs were committed in bringing them about.[31] Beyond the prevention of such wrongs, regulation rests

Common Law, and the Freedom-Friendly State' (2003) 58 *University of Miami Law Review* 401, 401–06; Johan van der Walt, *The Horizontal Effect Revolution and the Question of Sovereignty* (De Gruyter, 2014) ch 3; Jud Mathews, *Extending Rights' Reach* (Oxford University Press, 2018) ch 5.

[26] Charles L Black, Jr, 'The Supreme Court, 1966 Term – Foreword: "State Action", Equal Protection, and California's Proposition 14' (1967) 81 *Harvard Law Review* 69, 95.

[27] See Samuel Scheffler, 'Individual Responsibility in a Global Age' in *Boundaries and Allegiances: Problems of Justice and Responsibility in Liberal Thought* (Oxford University Press, 2002) 32, 36–38.

[28] Hart famously distinguished in this regard between 'general' and 'special' rights – *see* HLA Hart, 'Are There Any Natural Rights?' (1955) 64 *Philosophical Review* 175, 183–88.

[29] Dworkin, *Justice for Hedgehogs* (n 18) 285–89, 300–03.

[30] Thomas Nagel, 'Libertarianism Without Foundations' (1975) 85 *Yale Law Journal* 136, 139–40.

[31] Robert Nozick, *Anarchy, State and Utopia* (Blackwell, 1974) 26–35, 149–74.

on foundations of consent. To an extent, as in the feudal era, the libertarian state is a 'private law state';[32] its powers and duties are conceptualised by relying on private law tools, such as trust or contract;[33] and moral rights are realised through political activities, when doing so wins sufficient social support.

The state action model similarly applies small-scale normative principles to large-scale political questions of constitutional justice. There are technical ways to expand the horizontal scopes of constitutional rights in this regard:[34] for example, to see corporations as state agents when they have strong market power over basic goods like electricity or water; to see the state's involvement in private activities – say, subsidising university fees or allowing the customers of a restaurant to park in a public parking lot – as tying the state more intimately to harms caused by these activities; or by construing more state actions – say, the home visits of social workers – as assumptions of extended responsibilities. Judges often use such techniques, which reduce the harmful consequences of the problem of anthropomorphisation and the reliance on the restrictive conception of responsibility. But they expose another big problem.

Fetishisation. Even when state actions open the door for constitutional scrutiny, the state action model asks the wrong questions: not about the extent of harms or deprivations suffered by individuals but about the trail that might lead from such harms or deprivations to the state.[35] For example, in *Domestic Violence* we do not ask what the state can do to protect children from abusive parents, but whether the state's actions in different factual patterns amount to assumptions of duties to protect children. To take another pair of examples, it was held that one private university's sports association is private for constitutional purposes because it does not receive but only indirectly benefits from public funds,[36] while a similar association is public because the state became 'pervasively entwined' in its operation by approving some of its rules and covering its employees' pensions.[37] Even if such distinctions can provide definitive answers about which duties should be imposed on state agents,[38] the problem remains that they are often grounded in inadequate reasons.

Discrimination. An African-American family bought a house in Missouri in 1945, but a restrictive covenant prohibited 'people of the Negro or Mongolian race' from occupying it. Kraemer, a local resident, claimed that the covenant prevented the family from taking possession of the house.

[32] Peter Vallentyne, 'Libertarianism and the State' (2007) 24 *Social Philosophy and Policy* 187, 194–96.

[33] See Seth Davis, 'The Private Law State' (2018) 63 *McGill Law Journal* 727.

[34] David Bilchitz, *Fundamental Rights and the Legal Obligations of Business* (Cambridge University Press, 2021) 135–74.

[35] Gautam Bhatia, *Horizontal Rights: An Institutional Approach* (Hart Publishing, 2023) 33–34.

[36] *National Collegiate Athletic Association v Smith* 525 US 459 (1999).

[37] *Brentwood Academy v Tennessee Secondary School Athletic Association* 535 US 971 (2002).

[38] For criticisms of the state action model in this regard, see Bilchitz, *Fundamental Rights and the Legal Obligations of Business* (n 34) 143–46.

The Supreme Court of the United States held that while racially restrictive covenants, being private agreements, cannot be unconstitutional, their enforcement amounts to state action that violates the constitutional right to equal protection of the law.[39]

While this decision reaches a substantively justified result, it does so in the wrong way. It does not reflect a constitutional concern for reducing discrimination in the housing market, but only tries to keep the state at a safe distance from such private wrongs. The problem is that when injustices are deep and pervasive, merely keeping the state away from them does little to alleviate them.[40] If we care about the values that underlie constitutional rights, what we *fundamentally* care about is not the nature of state involvement but how individuals fare in terms of their basic interests. We cannot be alarmed when a police officer misreads a search warrant but indifferent to the threat to privacy by big tech corporations.

By construing the scope of constitutional rights according to how the state treats us or what it does to us – as opposed to how we are treated or how we do – the state action model makes questions of constitutional horizontality incoherent. The actions and activities of parents, employers, landlords, journalists, doctors, and other private agents are addressed primarily by private law, with its focus on personal responsibility and choice (more on that below). Any intervention in private law is seen as a political policy choice. Private law is seen as a domain of principle and rights that can be coherently and systematically explained and justified, while external interventions in it are seen as morally opaque and unprincipled rather than expressions of collective moral commitments that aim to realise social justice.

But political collectives, as I claim below, have constitutional duties to monitor and regulate private actions and activities when they affect the values that underlie constitutional rights. Blind trust in the political process in this regard is not only practically questionable but also a conceptual, constitutional and moral failure to respond to the requirements of constitutional rights: to adopt the teleological and systematic approach that is necessary to respect, protect and promote their underlying values to a justified extent.

The state action model's 'Hansel and Gretel' type of constitutional scrutiny both undermines private law's legitimacy and weakens the pursuit of social justice. Constitutional rights lose much of their progressive and goal-oriented normativity and their ability to push the regulation of private relationships, associations and practices towards better conformity with constitutional and social justice. This might not worry those that trust the democratic process and the market to push society in these directions – even if over time. But in recent decades this trust has been unfounded in most liberal democracies.

[39] *Shelley v Kraemer* 334 US 1 (1948).

[40] For an illuminating illustration through equality in voting, see Mathews (n 25) 129–32.

This raises additional moral concerns about traditional verticality. The next sections move from these concerns to more positive claims about the kind of agency and responsibility that underlies modern constitutional rights – and, as a result, about their normative structure and horizontal expansion.

2.3. POLITICAL FOUNDATIONS

Modern constitutional rights often express a notion of responsibility that is not restrictive and individualistic but prescriptive and collective – tied to the beneficiary-centered nature of the values that underlie these rights: liberty, equality, dignity or privacy, for instance, imply intricate demands regarding social conditions and states of affairs. Because constitutional rights draw their force and value from how they respond to these demands, delineating their scopes based solely on the nature or extent of state action makes little sense.

The starting point, in this regard, is that, as Samuel Scheffler claims, the foundations of the restrictive conception of responsibility – a vision of social relations as consisting primarily in direct and clearly demarcated interactions and a phenomenology of agency that distinguishes between acts and omissions, near and remote effects, and individual and group involvements – are destabilised in modern societies.[41] Indeed, when thinking about problems like poverty, discrimination, online privacy, or pandemics, the restrictive conception is rigid and limited – they require more systematic and complex conceptions of responsibility, which do not 'apply essentially interpersonal concepts outside the domain in which they have a genuine application'.[42]

The problem with traditional verticality in this regard is that, as feminist, socialist and other progressive theorists and practitioners claim, many injustices materialise in social spheres in which the state is not directly or intimately involved: for example, in the family or in various markets.[43] In fact, in modern and legally-saturated societies, the privateness of relationships, associations and practices – facilitated and shaped by state regulation – depends on state choices: regulatory abstention, in this sense, is not natural or neutral, especially when legal regulation can reduce power disparities or prevent harms.[44]

[41] Scheffler, 'Individual Responsibility in a Global Age' (n 27) 38–46.

[42] Samuel Scheffler, 'Morality and Reasonable Partiality' in *Equality and Tradition: Questions of Value in Moral and Political Theory* (Oxford University Press, 2012) 41, 69–72. See also Jeremy Waldron, 'Nozick and Locke: Filling the Space of Rights' (2005) 22 *Social Philosophy and Policy* 81, 108–09.

[43] GA Cohen, 'Where the Action is: On the Site of Distributive Justice' (1997) 26 *Philosophy & Public Affairs* 3; Susan Moller-Okin, 'Justice and Gender: An Unfinished Debate' (2004) 72 *Fordham Law Review* 1537. *See also* Alon Harel, 'Public and Private Law' in Markus D Dubber and Tatjana Hornle (eds), *The Oxford Handbook of Criminal Law* (Oxford University Press, 2014) 1040.

[44] Van der Walt (n 25) 151–54; Marco Jimenez, 'Distributive Justice and Contract Law: A Hohfeldian Analysis' (2016) 43 *Florida State University Law Review* 1265, 1299–1306.

To think about social justice, we therefore must 'cut off the head of the king', to borrow Michel Foucault's words.[45] Social injustices are not only about what the state does but can also be brought about by complex and diffuse social processes and structures, formed through the often-benign activities of numerous agents, which become unjust only in accumulation – also in nuanced ways, through beliefs, stereotypes or predispositions.[46] The injustices caused, for example, by lending practices, housing conditions, online data gathering or workplace subordination are often dynamic, complex and interdependent. It is naïve to expect markets, civil society or the political process to rise above and dismantle them on their own. And it is difficult to respond to them by relying solely on strictly relational constitutional rights that focus on direct state involvement. Therefore, for constitutional rights to effectively realise their underlying values, they must build on a more comprehensive notion of collective responsibility that transcends rigid public–private divides.

2.3.1. The Basic Structure of Society

One of the most prominent expressions of these ideas is John Rawls's theory of social justice. As part of the liberal social contract tradition, it unpacks values inherent in the political relationship between free and equal citizens, who justify to each other their collective use of coercive power.[47] Reciprocity and respect require the principles of social justice (for Rawls, of basic liberties, equal opportunities, and equality of basic goods unless inequalities serve the worse-off) to be justified in terms that reasonable citizens can accept: by placing idealised deliberating citizens behind a 'veil of ignorance', Rawls aimed to ensure that moral reasoning reflects social solidarity and is not distorted by historical contingencies.[48]

One of the basic features of Rawls's theory, to which we will return in later chapters, is that it does not focus on limited allocations of goods and burdens to individuals, but on the basic structure of society as a whole: the main political, social, legal and economic institutions, as a unified and

[45] Michel Foucault, *The History of Sexuality – Volume 1: An Introduction* (Robert Hurley tr, Pantheon Books, 1978) 88–89. See also Victor Tadros, 'Between Governance and Discipline: The Law and Michel Foucault' (1998) 18 *Oxford Journal of Legal Studies* 75.

[46] On such injustices, see Iris Marion Young, *Responsibility for Justice* (Oxford University Press, 2011); Robert Goodin, *Perpetuating Advantage: Mechanisms of Structural Injustice* (Oxford University Press, 2023).

[47] John Rawls, *Justice as Fairness: A Restatement* (Erin Kelly ed, Harvard University Press, 2001) 40, 182.

[48] ibid 5–6, 15–16.

dynamic system.[49] One of the main purposes of this focus is to avoid the libertarian reduction of the political to the interpersonal. The profound and pervasive impact of the basic structure justifies the political collective's obligations to respond through it to complex behavioural patterns that involve roles, relationships, attitudes, habits, and so on.[50] It is highly unlikely that uncoordinated private activities could attain or sustain social justice: the accumulated results of isolated fair actions can be unfair from a broader perspective, which private agents lack the capacity and authority to respond to. We need a dynamically-adjusted institutional framework to correct these unjust trends: for example, by ensuring access to higher education, imposing progressive taxes, or adopting anti-discrimination rules. Rawls emphasised in this vein and in response to criticisms from the left that 'if the so-called private sphere is a space alleged to be exempt from justice, then there is no such thing'.[51]

This collective obligation to attain and sustain 'background justice' is translated to constitutional norms when they can contribute to this political project. In Rawls's scheme, after we agree on principles of social justice (and for our purposes here, we need not agree on their content) delegates to a hypothetical 'constitutional convention' must 'adopt, from among the constitutions that are both just and workable the one that seems most likely to lead to just and effective legislation'.[52] The problem, in our context, is that the state action model (that is, state-centered delineations of constitutional rights) is much less likely to lead to just and effective legislation, because it ignores decisions about both *how* and *whether* to regulate private relationships, which lie at the heart of the collective endeavour of securing background justice – that, as the next chapters show, is supported in many ways by public practices of constitutionally-guided regulation.

Modern constitutional rights resist the Hayekian thought that 'nobody has the responsibility or the power to assure that these separate actions of many will produce a particular result for a certain person'.[53] The political collective has this responsibility, even if it involves responses to complex social structures.[54] This moral principle is reflected in the nature and structure of constitutional rights – and, importantly for us, in their horizontal dimensions.

[49] ibid 10–12, 181–82.

[50] ibid 55–57; John Rawls, *Political Liberalism*, 2nd edn (Columbia University Press, 2005) 266, 269–71, 282. See also Thomas Nagel, *Equality and Partiality* (Oxford University Press, 1991) 83–84.

[51] Rawls, *Justice as Fairness* (n 47) 164, 166. We will discuss this aspect of Rawls's theory at greater length in chapter 4.

[52] Rawls, *Political Liberalism* (n 50) 336.

[53] FA Hayek, *Law, Legislation, and Liberty: Volume 2 – The Mirage of Social Justice* (Routledge, 1982) 33.

[54] Owen M Fiss, 'The Forms of Justice' (1979) 93 *Harvard Law Review* 1, 22.

2.3.2. Collective Responsibility

Before getting to constitutional rights, though, two basic features of this expansive conception of responsibility must be clarified. First, this responsibility is collective, in the sense that it rests with political communities.[55] By adopting constitutions, collectives entrust agglomerations of institutions to act on their behalf as states – and may thereby burden these institutions with responsibilities that exceed those of individual citizens.[56] While there are many complexities in debates about collective agency,[57] it is generally agreed that the state is a collective agent that can form attitudes, make choices, and take actions. One of the most foundational collective responsibilities is to evaluate and respond to the normative status quo, to ensure that it meets the demands of social justice.[58] This responsibility falls on the shoulders of 'we the people' rather than on those of individuals or even 'aggregates of *I's*',[59] in the sense that all members of the political collective, combined, are responsible to create justified social conditions.[60] This collective responsibility lies with the political community, acting through the state.

Second, this collective responsibility is forward-looking. Because the state is an institutional apparatus that acts on the collective's behalf, autonomy and moral integrity justify weaker constraints on the scope of its responsibilities: its greater capabilities (say, in terms of information analysis) and authorities (say, in terms of law-creation) justify focusing not only on what it has done – for instance, whether it was directly involved in harms or assumed extended responsibilities to prevent them – but also on what it can do. When thinking about the state's responsibility to sustain social justice, we also think prescriptively. The notion of a 'social contract' is metaphorical and abstract: while we must also pay attention to the meaning of the political collective's past choices, the idea of a 'living constitution' implies that even if our interpretation of such choices remains stable, changes in social conditions and moral principles can change the constitution's content.[61] This invites, when delineating constitutional rights, forward-looking reasons about the political collective's responsibility to

[55] See Marion Smiley, 'Future-Looking Collective Responsibility: A Preliminary Analysis' (2014) 38 *Midwest Studies in Philosophy* 1.

[56] Alan Gewirth, *The Community of Rights* (The University of Chicago Press, 1996) 54–62; Toni Erskine, 'Assigning Responsibilities to Institutional Moral Agents' (2001) 15 *Ethics and International Affairs* 67, 69–74; David Miller, *National Responsibility and Global Justice* (Oxford University Press, 2007) 97–104.

[57] See generally Marion Smiley, 'Collective Responsibility' in Edward N Zalta and Uri Nodelman (eds), *The Stanford Encyclopedia of Philosophy* (Fall 2023).

[58] Young, *Responsibility for Justice* (n 46) 107–12.

[59] Christopher Kutz, *Complicity: Ethics and Law for a Collective Age* (Cambridge University Press, 2000) 7.

[60] On the connections between agent-neutral values and collective obligations, see Derek Parfit, *Reasons and Persons* (Oxford University Press, 1984) 27.

[61] See David A Strauss, *The Living Constitution* (Oxford University Press, 2010).

secure social justice. Pressures to address such reasons accompany better access to knowledge about injustices and means of alleviating them.[62]

Bringing these ideas together, it could be said that unlike private agents, the state can disrespect us as citizens by ignoring our interests and not only by mistreating us directly. While in private relationships respect for dignity normally requires that we treat others as 'inviolable' rather than as 'unignorable', in relationships with the state these two aspects of dignity are prominent and their conflicts are therefore more visible.[63] The state's greater ability to predict and respond to complex harms makes systematic risk-management and social coordination unavoidable aspects of its activities.[64] Thus, 'within the appropriate limits, public decisions will be justifiably more consequentialist than private ones. They will also have larger consequences to take into account.'[65] Given the public dimensions of the practice of constitutional horizontality, systematic reasoning can therefore show greater respect for the equal moral status of persons and their separateness than rigid libertarian reasoning.[66] Because we will get to the reduced ability and authority of private agents only in the next chapter, we can hold at this point that *at least* when it comes to the state, there is no reason to narrow the scope of collective responsibilities to realise social justice to isolated actions or activities: there is at least one agent, acting on behalf of the collective, that can effectively discharge responsibilities to, for example, promote equality or protect privacy in private social spheres.

Moral, political, legal and constitutional theories often ignore these points: they think 'in hopelessly individualistic terms';[67] focus on individual obligations;[68] rely on legalistic and personified conceptions of responsibility;[69] and ignore the state's uniqueness as an agent.[70] Dworkin, for example, saw his account of rights as trumps as 'the political equivalent of the most familiar sense in which the idea is used in personal morality',[71] while assuming that these normative domains are continuous. However, if we pay careful attention

[62] Carol Rovane, 'Forward-looking Collective Responsibility: A Metaphysical Reframing of the Issue' (2014) 38 *Midwest Studies in Philosophy* 12, 23–24.

[63] Kasper Lippert-Rasmussen, 'Moral Status and the Impermissibility of Minimizing Violations' (1996) 25 *Philosophy and Public Affairs* 333.

[64] Barbara H Fried, 'What Does Matter? The Case for Killing the Trolley Problem (or Letting it Die)' (2012) 62 *Philosophical Quarterly* 505, 509–17.

[65] Thomas Nagel, 'Ruthlessness in Public Life' in Stuart Hampshire (ed), *Public and Private Morality* (Cambridge University Press, 1978) 75, 82–84. See also R Jay Wallace, *The Moral Nexus* (Princeton University Press, 2019) 227–29.

[66] See Will Kymlicka, 'Rawls on Teleology and Deontology' (1988) 17 *Philosophy & Public Affairs* 173; Iwao Hirose, 'Aggregation and the Separateness of Persons' (2013) 25 *Utilitas* 182, 193–97.

[67] Henry Shue, 'Mediating Duties' (1988) 98 *Ethics* 687, 695–96.

[68] See Christopher Kutz, 'The Collective Work of Citizenship' (2002) 8 *Legal Theory* 471, 472.

[69] See Young, *Responsibility for Justice* (n 58) 97–100.

[70] See Robert E Goodin, *Utilitarianism as a Public Philosophy* (Cambridge University Press, 1995) 60–62; David Enoch, 'Intending, Foreseeing, and the State' (2007) 13 *Legal Theory* 69, 91.

[71] Dworkin, *Justice for Hedgehogs* (n 18) 327–29.

to our conceptions of the state and the political, we notice important qualitative differences.[72] This section described them in terms of agency and responsibility. The next section further unpacks them by focusing on the normative structure that these moral forces push constitutional rights to take.

2.4. GENERAL RIGHTS

If the political collective, acting through the state, is the agent primarily or at least preliminarily constrained by constitutional rights,[73] its expansive responsibility allows the normative structure of constitutional rights to take a more general form, as abstract ideals that guide regulatory activities and public deliberations as part of the basic structure of society. This role is reflected in the expansion of constitutional (and human) rights practices in the post-war period:[74] moving beyond the traditional, negative and state-centered model, legal systems began recognising rights that entail positive duties to protect or aid – rights that fulfil foundational roles in guiding the political collective towards social justice, including in private social spheres.

One of the basic features of this now common constitutional model is a two-stage reasoning structure: the first stage delineates the scope of constitutional rights to see if they were adversely affected by a duty-bearer's actions; if the answer is positive, the second stage evaluates these actions to determine if they amount to a justified infringement or an unjustified violation. This distinction allows rights to be delineated broadly, because while more actions come under constitutional scrutiny, they can regularly be deemed justified infringements.[75]

The common model has drawn much criticism. While much of it addresses the realisation stage (specifically, its reliance on proportionality and balancing), some of it addresses the delineation stage. The expansion of the scopes of constitutional rights, critics have argued, erodes their status, force, and distinction from mere values, goals or ideals.[76] This criticism builds on and echoes a

[72] Quentin Skinner, 'A Genealogy of the Modern State' (2009) 162 *Proceedings of the British Academy* 325, 361–64; Martin Loughlin, *Foundations of Public Law* (Oxford University Press, 2010) 183, 205–08.

[73] *See generally* Onora O'Neill, 'Agents of Justice' in Andrew Kuper (ed), *Global Responsibilities: Who Must Deliver on Human Rights?* (Routledge, 2005) 37, 38–42.

[74] Grégoire Webber, *The Negotiable Constitution: On the Limitation of Rights* (Cambridge University Press, 2009) 55–86; Kai Möller, *The Global Model of Constitutional Rights* (Oxford University Press, 2012); Alec Stone Sweet and Jud Mathews, *Proportionality Balancing and Constitutional Governance: A Comparative and Global Approach* (Oxford University Press, 2019).

[75] Gerhard van der Schyff, 'Interpreting the Protection Guaranteed by Two-Stage Rights in the European Convention on Human Rights: The Case for Wide Interpretation' in Eva Brems and Janneke Gerards (eds), *Shaping Rights in the ECHR* (Cambridge University Press, 2013) 65; Kai Möller, 'Proportionality and Rights Inflation', in *Proportionality and the Rule of Law* (n 11) 155.

[76] Onora O'Neill, 'The Dark Side of Human Rights' (2005) 81 *International Affairs* 427; Grégoire Webber, 'On the Loss of Rights' in *Proportionality and the Rule of Law* (n 11) 123.

philosophical debate about the nature of rights. Say that I broke into a secluded cabin and used its contents to survive an unexpected storm. Both the 'specificationist' and the 'generalist' hold that if my actions were unjustified, I violated the owner's property rights; but their positions diverge if my actions were justified: while the specificationist holds that this means the owner has no property rights here, the generalist holds that it is possible and often more accurate to say that the owner has such rights, which were justifiably infringed.[77]

With the specificationist, critics of the common constitutional model claim that the scopes of constitutional rights should extend only to cases in which they defeat all competing considerations.[78] For example, if libel law justifiably limits a form of expression to protect privacy, it is excluded from the scope of the right to freedom of expression. General rights – say, to freedom of expression, period – are merely presumptive or *prima facie* rights, in the sense that some parts of them are not 'real' rights. Advocates of specificationism in the constitutional domain claim that it creates a less antagonistic relationship between rights and state action – if rights are general, they are regularly infringed; makes rights-based reasoning more coherent by reducing the conflicts between rights and competing reasons;[79] and increases the force and therefore the value of rights by treating them as conclusive and peremptory norms, that – unlike general rights – are fully action-guiding and determine who actually owes what to whom.[80]

2.4.1. Conceptual Foundations

What worries specificationist critics of the common model is that it seems to deviate from the normative structure of a right: of a claim about the right-holder's interests that constrains the duty-bearer's agency.[81] Under-specification might be an insurmountable hurdle in this regard. For example, if there are no pre-legal principles that determine which duties rights to complex goods

[77] John Oberdiek, 'Lost in Moral Space: On the Infringing/Violating Distinction and Its Place in the Theory of Rights' (2004) 23 *Law and Philosophy* 325; John Oberdiek, 'Specifying Rights Out of Necessity' (2008) 28 *Oxford Journal of Legal Studies* 127. This famous example is taken from Joel Feinberg, 'Voluntary Euthanasia and the Inalienable Right to Life' (1978) 7 *Philosophy & Public Affairs* 93.

[78] Webber, *The Negotiable Constitution* (n 74) 116–46; Francisco J Urbina, *A Critique of Proportionality and Balancing* (Cambridge University Press, 2017) 244–51.

[79] John Oberdiek, 'Specifying Constitutional Rights' (2010) 27 *Constitutional Commentary* 321.

[80] Grégoire Webber, 'Human Goods and Human Rights Law' in Tom Angier, Iain T Benson, and Mark D Retter (eds), *The Cambridge Handbook of Natural Law and Human Rights* (Cambridge University Press, 2022) 324, 332–35. See also Cristián Rettig, 'The Claimability Condition: Rights as Action-Guiding Standards' (2020) 51 *Journal of Social Philosophy* 322, 330–33.

[81] See generally John Tasioulas, 'Taking Rights out of Human Rights' in Roger Crisp (ed), *Griffin on Human Rights* (Oxford University Press, 2014) 9, 18–21. See also Urbina (n 78) 98–110, 232–33; Eric R Boot, *Human Duties and the Limits of Human Rights Discourse* (Springer, 2017) 65–67.

like health or education entail for each agent (as opposed to rights to simpler goods like bodily integrity or negative liberty) and effective duty-allocating legal institutions do not exist, how can rights have any practical import in terms of empowerment and guidance?[82]

This is a valid concern; but it is weaker in the context on which we focus: the constitutional practices of reasonably justified and effective legal systems – as opposed to, for example, purely moral rights or constitutional rights in 'rogue' or 'weak' states.[83] We focus on cases in which the state, operating on behalf of the political collective, can be seen as an organised fallback duty-bearer against which constitutional rights can always be claimed and can always constrain.[84] Because social coordination is one of the state's basic functions, and because state agents operate in a heavily regulated institutional environment, constitutional rights against the state (and thus the political collective) can create robust relational normative ties, even if they do not entail concrete duties – not only for private agents, but also for state agents – and even if it is unclear whether their full realisation is actually feasible.

Thus, as noted in the previous chapter, Hart, one of the advocates of the will theory of rights, conceded that its rival – the interest theory – is better equipped to explain general constitutional rights. According to the interest theory, rights are not final outputs of normative reasoning that are perfectly paired with duties: rather, they are inputs – or 'intermediate conclusions' – which build on values to justify the imposition of duties.[85] Rights do so dynamically: they can entail different duties for different agents in different circumstances;[86] and agents might have to figure out which duties rights entail for them.[87] This form of discretion does not mean that agents are under no constraints: it means that rights can provide a more complex and ongoing type of guidance that obligates duty-bearers to resolve normative conflicts in response to the right's changing requirements. Duty-bearers can therefore be responsible and obligated to right-holders both to acknowledge their concrete duties under specific factual and normative conditions and, at times, to establish the conditions necessary for such duties to arise.[88]

[82] See generally Pablo Gilabert, 'The Feasibility of Basic Socioeconomic Human Rights: A Conceptual Exploration' (2009) 59 *Philosophical Quarterly* 659.

[83] See O'Neill, 'Agents of Justice' (n 73) 41–50.

[84] See Adam Etinson, 'Human Rights, Claimability, and the Uses of Abstraction' (2013) 25 *Utilitas* 463, 479.

[85] Joseph Raz, *The Morality of Freedom* (Oxford University Press, 1986) 165; Joseph Raz, *Practical Reason and Norms*, 2nd edn (Oxford University Press, 1999) 187.

[86] Jeremy Waldron, 'Rights in Conflict' (1989) 99 *Ethics* 503, 509–12.

[87] Amartya Sen, 'Elements of a Theory of Human Rights' (2004) 32 *Philosophy & Public Affairs* 315, 338–42.

[88] Etinson (n 84) 481–82; Hugh Breakey, 'Positive Duties and Human Rights: Challenges, Opportunities and Necessities' (2015) 63 *Political Studies* 1198, 1210–11.

We need not, for example, hold that a right to basic healthcare does not cover a certain treatment because it is very expensive, or that the right to freedom of expression does not cover defamation: we can define 'healthcare', 'expression', or other values enshrined in general constitutional rights while focusing on the right-holder's interests and 'human capacities, available resources, and general features of social life',[89] thereby relegating reasons about the burdens on or nature of involvement of agents to the second reasoning stage.

While all rights must be realised through a system of consistent action-guiding norms,[90] they can start their normative life as more abstract ideals that are largely agnostic about how to realise them in practice.[91] They do not possess 'peremptory force', in the sense of providing categorical and conclusive reasons that 'cut off deliberation, debate, or argument'.[92] As Joseph Raz explained when laying out his interest theory of rights, rights have a 'special' force, 'expressed by the fact that they are grounds of duties, which are peremptory reasons'.[93] That is, rights can provide non-peremptory reasons, as long as their entailed duties, as opposed to duties entailed by other types of norms or mere responsibilities, are peremptory and relational, and failures to abide by them wrong right-holders.[94] It is only at the end of their normative life that rights must be fully specified. This means that their full specification at the preliminary stage of their recognition and delineation is not an existence condition but an option, justified in specific contexts.[95] The pressing question is therefore whether constitutional rights that have the mere capacity to entail duties are not only conceptually permissible but also justified and non-redundant.[96]

[89] John Tasioulas, 'The Moral Reality of Human Rights' in Thomas Pogge (ed), *Freedom from Poverty as a Human Right: Who Owes What to the Very Poor?* (Oxford University Press, 2007) 75, 88–95. See also James Griffin, *On Human Rights* (Oxford University Press, 2008) 44, 127–28; Laurens Lavrysen, 'The Scope of Rights and the Scope of Obligations' in *Shaping Rights in the ECHR* (n 75) 162; Dimitrios Krytisis, *Where Our Protection Lies* (Oxford University Press, 2017) 182–89.

[90] Elizabeth Ashford, 'The Inadequacy of our Traditional Conception of the Duties Imposed by Human Rights' (2006) 19 *Canadian Journal of Law and Jurisprudence* 217.

[91] See David Bilchitz, *Poverty and Fundamental Rights* (Oxford University Press, 2007) 89–92; Jacob Weinrib, *Dimensions of Dignity: The Theory and Practice of Modern Constitutional Law* (Cambridge University Press, 2016) 219–20; Rowan Cruft, *Human Rights, Ownership, and the Individual* (Oxford University Press, 2019) 143–49.

[92] HLA Hart, 'Commands and Authoritative Legal Reasons' in *Essays on Bentham* (Oxford University Press, 1982) 243, 253. See also Webber, 'On the Loss of Rights' (n 76) 146; NE Simmonds, 'Constitutional Rights, Civility, and Artifice' (2019) 89 *Cambridge Law Journal* 175, 181–85.

[93] Raz, *The Morality of Freedom* (n 85) 249. See also ibid 183, 192.

[94] See Corinna Mieth, 'On Human Rights and the Strength of Corresponding Duties' in Gerhard Ernst and Jan-Christoph Heilinger (eds), *The Philosophy of Human Rights* (De Gruyter, 2012) 159, 181–82; Simon Hope, 'Kantian Imperfect Duties and Modern Debates Over Human Rights' (2014) 22 *Journal of Political Philosophy* 396.

[95] See Etinson (n 84) 479.

[96] See also Griffin (n 89) 97, 107–10.

2.4.2. Moral Foundations

The justification of generalism in constitutional rights law must show that there is value in seeing their entire scopes as imbued with the relational normativity of rights. Some defenders of the common model justify the expansionist trend by portraying it as part of a transition from a 'culture of authority' to a 'culture of justification',[97] at the centre of which lies a moral right to have the state substantively justify to us actions that harm our interests:[98] the broader constitutional rights are, the broader the state's duties to justify such actions are.

While accountability to the right-holder is part of the deontological core of rights, it is important not to put the cart before the horse in this regard. Delineation reasoning is more basic, in the sense that it asks what should duty-bearers be accountable to right-holders for. Holding that duty-bearers should be constitutionally accountable for every adverse impact on the well-being of citizens raises the aforementioned concerns about the erosion of the force and value of rights. But the deeper problem is that, even if we have an interest in having the state justify to us all harmful actions, we also have other interests, not only in what the state says but also in what it does: providing goods, creating social conditions, preventing harms, and so on.[99]

Delineations of constitutional rights must prime the legal system to regulate in ways that adequately realise their underlying values; and in this regard, accountability is also of derivative importance, as it can elucidate the regulatory requirements of rights. This is why the scopes of constitutional rights are not fixed or rigid,[100] nor do they cover all actions that fall within their 'semantic reach'.[101] Mistaken expansion is often preferable to mistaken contraction, because the former only moves us to a second reasoning stage in which mistakes can be corrected.[102] But this is not always the case, as sometimes the values underlying constitutional rights are better served by contracting their scopes: for instance, to protect their symbolic value or avoid destabilising other rights. At a deeper level, even if broad scopes are justified, these rights must rely on solid moral foundations to properly empower and guide. They must be stable

[97] Cohen-Eliya and Porat, *Proportionality and Constitutional Culture* (n 5) 111–22.

[98] Kai Möller, 'Justifying the Culture of Justification' (2019) 17 *ICON* 1078.

[99] See Jeff King, *Judging Social Rights* (Cambridge University Press, 2012) 309. On a related distinction between the justificatory and regulatory dimensions of constitutional rights, see Frank I Michelman, *Constitutional Essentials: On the Constitutional Theory of Political Liberalism* (Oxford University Press, 2022) 3–6.

[100] Webber, *The Negotiable Constitution* (n 74) 120, 130; Oberdiek, 'Specifying Rights' (n 77) 127–28.

[101] Urbina (n 78) 230–31, 246–48. See also Cruft, *Human Rights* (n 91) 149–56.

[102] Mark Tushnet, 'Rights Inflation in Canada and the United States' in Richard Albert and David R Cameron (eds), *Canada in the World: Comparative Perspectives on the Canadian Constitution* (Cambridge University Press, 2017) 209.

and focused enough to operate as intermediate conclusions that facilitate and guide both legal and political deliberation.[103] Seeing these rights as fully specified conversation-stoppers will reduce their ability to fulfil their normative roles when it comes to complex regulatory decisions, about issues such as building a road, approving a drug for sale, or revising workplace safety rules. If they are fully specified, the kind of actions that they permit, require or forbid with regard to complex and changing social conditions will often deviate from their underlying values.[104]

Constitutional rights must be general to properly empower and guide because the values underlying them are complex and tentacular. For example, the core of privacy is sensitive to workplace data gathering practices, the core of equality is sensitive to gentrification processes, and the core of freedom of expression is sensitive to the policies of online social media platforms. Because we cannot determine in advance which regulatory schemes realise such values justifiably and effectively, we must not only see the rights grounded in them as primarily obligating collective agents, but also see these rights as obligating such agents to respond to complex social patterns through coordinated regulatory efforts.[105] Constitutional rights grounded in such complex values must provide ongoing guidance about the progress towards social justice, rather than merely establish minimal and rigid thresholds:[106] they must make dynamic and systematic prescriptions as part of the basic structure of society.[107] This systematicity is expressed not only in their primary objects – terms like equality, privacy, dignity or expression – but also in the fact that each right serves many interests, including interests covered by other rights.[108]

In this spirit, the level of generality in which rights are often recognised in declarations, proclamations and conventions lies between mere value-affirmations and concrete rules: an intermediate position that keeps them at enough distance from existing or proposed legal norms to serve as critical standards, but not so distant as to lose practical value.[109] Such constitutional rights

[103] Alon Harel, 'Why Rights Matter: The Interdependence of Rights and Values' in *Why Law Matters* (Oxford University Press, 2014) 13.

[104] See Griffin (n 89) 71–75.

[105] Elizabeth Ashford, 'The Nature of Violations of the Human Right to Subsistence' in Adam Etinson (ed), *Human Rights: Moral or Political?* (Oxford University Press, 2018) 337, 353–54.

[106] Griffin (n 89) 37–38; Samantha Besson, 'The Allocation of Anti-Poverty Rights Duties: Our Rights, but Whose Duties?' in Krista Nadakavukaren Schefer (ed), *Poverty and the International Economic Legal System: Duties to the World's Poor* (Cambridge University Press 2013) 408, 413–15.

[107] This point, it should be noted, goes beyond (and perhaps conflicts with) Rawls's claims in this regard.

[108] John Tasioulas and Effy Vayena, 'Just Global Health: Integrating Human Rights and Common Goods' in Thom Brooks (ed), *The Oxford Handbook of Global Justice* (Oxford University Press, 2020) 139, 144–46. On this feature of the interest theory, see Cruft, *Human Rights* (n 91) 143–51; Alon Harel, 'Revisionist Theories of Rights' (1997) 11 *Canadian Journal of Law and Jurisprudence* 227.

[109] Tom Campbell, 'Human Rights Morality and Human Rights Practice' in Tom Campbell and Kylie Bourne (eds), *Political and Legal Approaches to Human Rights* (Routledge, 2017) 3, 11–12.

are treated as normative inputs, in the spirit of the interest theory.[110] This means that right-based reasons – as opposed to right-based duties – can conflict without being adjusted at the constitutional level. The exclusion or outweighing of such reasons is contextual and sub-constitutional: these reasons keep operating at the constitutional level as ideals, and can therefore justify a different regulatory solution if social conditions or moral principles evolve.[111]

Importantly, the entire scope of general constitutional rights must be imbued with the special normative force of rights: even those parts of them that lack immediate deontic implications can be important for understanding the constitution as a whole, guiding regulatory decisions, or framing public deliberations.[112] While duty-bearers are not formally obligated to reflect on their entire scopes but only to adequately realise them, the system of constitutional rights is so complex that regular reflection is necessary in practice; and duty-bearers must therefore adopt certain dispositions and mechanisms to ensure that rights are properly engaged, and that their partial realisation is properly justified to their holders.[113]

In this sense, constitutional rights operate as complex relational goals.[114] For example, denying a person access to a hospital wrongs them by failing to respect their right to access basic medical care; but so does a failure to adopt the goal of ensuring that there are enough hospitals or to regulate hospital policies.[115] Rights can entail reasons not only about which options to choose now but also about altering our set of options.[116] They can therefore operate as aspirational, comprehensive, and at present (but not in principle) unrealisable ideals[117] that give duty-bearers some leeway about how to realise them, while still constraining them.[118] In this spirit, for example, the Constitutional Court of South Africa held that the right to access to adequate housing gives the state leeway to realise it progressively, but obligates it to 'devise a comprehensive and workable plan', which must 'clearly allocate responsibilities and tasks', 'ensure that the appropriate financial and human resources are available', and pay close

[110] Joseph Raz, 'Legal Rights' (1984) 4 *Oxford Journal of Legal Studies* 1, 11.

[111] Aharon Barak, *Proportionality: Constitutional Rights and Their Limitations* (Cambridge University Press, 2012) 86. See also ibid 38–42, 83–98.

[112] Lawrence Sager, 'Material Rights, Underenforcement, and the Adjudication Thesis' (2010) 90 *Boston University Law Review* 579, 584–85.

[113] See Mattias Kumm, 'Is the Structure of Human Rights Practice Defensible? Three Puzzles and Their Resolution' in Vicky C Jackson and Mark Tushnet (eds), *Proportionality: New Frontiers, New Challenges* (Cambridge University Press, 2017) 51, 57.

[114] See James W Nickel, 'Goals and Rights: Working Together?' in Malcolm Langford, Andy Sumner and Alicia Ely Yamin (eds), *The Millennium Development Goals and Human Rights: Past, Present and Future* (Cambridge University Press, 2015) 37, 42–45.

[115] Pablo Gilabert, *Human Dignity and Human Rights* (Oxford University Press, 2018) 75–76.

[116] ibid 71, 79–80. See also Ashford, 'The Nature of Violations' (n 105) 354.

[117] Kimberley Brownlee, 'Dwelling in Possibility: Ideals, Aspirations, and Human Rights' in *Human Rights: Moral or Political?* (n 105) 313.

[118] Boot (n 81) 45–47.

attention to 'those whose needs are the most urgent'.[119] In this sense, constitutional rights are not only about 'here and now'.[120] This idea applies not only to socio-economic rights. For example, there can be stringent duties to protect people from concrete threats of violence but also more dynamic and open-ended duties to reduce the homicide rate in society.[121]

From this perspective, partial rights realisation is a moral tragedy, but one that can have moral value.[122] By helping political collectives recognise the tragic reality of moral pluralism, this perspective can also facilitate moral progress:[123] for instance, by focusing our collective attention on social and psychological barriers to rights-realisation.[124] For example, it can be justified to recognise reasonable access to housing or health services as constitutional rights not despite but because of the fact that it is difficult to secure these goods in capitalistic societies. In such cases, the recognition of general rights can both cement collective commitments and focus political and legal debates on the basic interests of right-holders. To borrow Jeremy Waldron's words, these rights are not 'moral absolutes, standing tragically unemployed, on the sidelines of a world riven by distasteful conflict and hard choices. On the contrary, they are supposed to be our best, most honest, and most respectful response to such a world.'[125] While this does not mean that specification is never justified, it does mean that it should operate as a rich normative ideal – more strongly tied to the interests that underlie modern constitutional rights – rather than a rigid conceptual requirement that all rights must meet.

2.5. LOOSE RELATIONALITY

The grounding of constitutional rights in expansive aspects of collective responsibility allows them not only to operate as general progressive ideals but also to take a loosely relational form. Even if these rights primarily obligate the state, they can therefore still address actions and activities external to state–citizen relations if they affect the interests underlying these rights. However, it

[119] *Government of the Republic of South Africa v Grootboom* [2000] ZACC 19, paras 37–44.

[120] David Bilchitz, 'Fundamental Rights as Bridging Concepts: Straddling the Boundary Between Ideal Justice and an Imperfect Reality' (2018) 40 *Human Rights Quarterly* 119, 136. See also Katharine G Young, 'Waiting for Rights: Progressive Realization and Lost Time' in Katharine G Young (ed), *The Future of Economic and Social Rights* (Cambridge University Press, 2019) 654.

[121] Stijn Smet, 'The "Absolute" Prohibition of Torture and Inhuman or Degrading Treatment in Article 3 ECHR: Truly a Question of Scope Only?' in *Shaping Rights in the ECHR* (n 75) 273.

[122] Ashford, 'The Nature of Violations' (n 105) 352. On moral tragedies, see Martha Nussbaum, 'The Costs of Moral Tragedy: Some Moral Limits of Cost-Benefit Analysis' (2000) 29 *Journal of Legal Studies* 1005.

[123] See Jeremy Waldron, 'Rights' in Robert E Goodin, Philip Pettit and Thomas Pogge (eds), *A Companion to Contemporary Political Philosophy*, 2nd edn (Blackwell, 2007) 745, 748.

[124] Gilabert, *Human Dignity and Human Rights* (n 115) 69.

[125] Waldron, 'Nozick and Locke' (n 42) 109.

is important to stress that these rights are not non-relational. Their two-term structure as 'rights to x' (liberty, equality, privacy, and so on) can be seen as ignoring the duty-bearer.[126] But it is more accurate and better reflects the inherent relationality of rights to say that general two-term rights implicitly assume the existence of a duty-bearer: the political collective. We can move the duty-bearer to the background but not entirely out of the picture.

Even merely moving the duty-bearer to the background pushes the agent-neutral and beneficiary-centered values that underlie these rights closer to their surface. When reasoning about individual duties (say, in criminal law or private law), our liberal instinct is to keep a tight fit between people's choices, actions, responsibilities and duties. This instinct, as noted above, is reflected in the traditional state action model. But when responsibility is collective and prescriptive, we can pay more attention to interests and needs: we might, for instance, recognise rights to liberty rather than against false imprisonment, to equality rather than against discrimination, or to dignity rather than against defamation. In this sense, general constitutional rights wear their moral hearts on their sleeves: the constitution obligates the political collective to create the social conditions in which the values underlying such rights can be realised. The forms of involvement of public or private agents in the social processes through which these rights are realised are only of secondary and derivative importance.

Because there is still relationality here, general constitutional rights are not redundant: mere summaries of their underlying values.[127] The point here is not just that these rights need not cover the entire scope of their underlying values. It is also that their adoption as goals that form part of the basic structure of society has relational implications: the very existence of these rights, prior to their realisation through sub-constitutional norms, already frames and guides the normative reasoning of countless agents within countless institutions and practices. Agents must adopt certain predispositions or mechanisms to ensure that they meet the ongoing requirements of constitutional rights. This also means that their broad delineation can be owed to right-holders, even if delineation decisions are inherently systematic and also consider the interests of others. Once we expose the structural regulatory implications of right-delineation decisions, their relational connections to individual claims become evident: connections that are, in turn, strongly tied to their large-scale teleological dimensions, given the nature of their underlying values. This is especially important in our context: because constitutional horizontality is still at the building stage, the results-oriented aspects of delineation decisions are more visible.[128] It can

[126] See John Finnis, *Natural Law and Natural Rights*, 2nd edn (Paul Craig ed, Oxford University Press, 2011) 201, 218–19; Paul Yowell, *Constitutional Rights and Constitutional Design: Moral and Empirical Reasoning in Judicial Review* (Hart Publishing, 2018) 26.

[127] On this claim about general rights, see Oberdiek, 'Specifying Rights' (n 77) 133–34.

[128] See generally James Fowkes, *Building the Constitution: The Practice of Constitutional Interpretation in Post-Apartheid South Africa* (Cambridge University Press, 2016) 137–39.

therefore be said that the horizontal expansion of constitutional rights is owed to right-holders even prior to their realisation, because of the normative ripple effects of this expansion. Because state agents must, at the very least, ensure that constitutional rights, whose underlying values are beneficiary-centered and complex, are realised to a justified extent, these rights justify regular scrutiny of the consequences of private activities and actions.

2.5.1. Constitutional Disputes

I noted in the previous chapter that during the Middle Ages political rule was conceived in private terms: as a contract between the ruler and the ruled and as exchangeable property. Constitutional practices still contain traces of this strict relationality – reflected, for example, in the habit of using private law tools to regulate constitutional activities while treating the state as a private agent.[129] This strict relationality can be reflected not only in substantive principles, like the state action doctrine, but also in the procedural structure through which rights are claimed and adjudicated. Traditionally, constitutional adjudication was limited to an injury suffered by a particular claimant, much like in private law. This model of adjudication was described as a 'private rights model'[130] and a 'private-law model of public law';[131] and the Supreme Court of the United States was criticised, in a similar vein, for operating as a 'private law court in a public law system' – for following a dispute resolution model that focuses on isolated interactions, treats rights as negative protections, and disregards third-party and collective interests.[132]

A 'public law litigation model' emerged in the post-war period.[133] As apex courts adjudicating constitutional disputes became central actors in the development of political and legal systems, there was a transition to a 'public action paradigm',[134] or a 'public interest conception of public law'.[135] Constitutional disputes became the political collective's business, reflecting the teleological

[129] Jason NE Varuhas, *Damages and Human Rights* (Hart Publishing, 2016) 171–72, 181–84. See also Skinner (n 72) 354–60.

[130] Henry P Monaghan, 'Third Party Standing' (1984) 84 *Columbia Law Review* 277, 279–80.

[131] Cass R Sunstein, 'Standing and the Privatization of Public Law' (1988) 88 *Columbia Law Review* 1432.

[132] Jamal Greene, 'A Private Law Court in a Public Law System' (2018) 12 *Law & Ethics of Human Rights* 37.

[133] Abram Chayes, 'The Role of The Judge in Public Law Litigation' (1976) 89 *Harvard Law Review* 1281.

[134] Monaghan (n 130) 279–80.

[135] Jason NE Varuhas, 'The Public Interest Conception of Public Law: Its Procedural Origins and Substantive Implications' in John Bell, Mark Elliott, Jason NE Varuhas and Philip Murray (eds), *Public Law Adjudication in Common Law Systems: Process and Substance* (Hart Publishing, 2016) 45.

and loosely relational normative structure of modern constitutional rights. Under this model, judges have more authority and control over the proceedings; standing rules are relaxed, so that administrative agents, civic organisations, and even concerned citizens can raise constitutional claims; remedies are more flexible and forward-looking; and therefore the focus is no longer only on the vindication of a particular claimant's right.[136] This procedural framework is heavily shaped by instrumental considerations, and right-holders are often seen as private attorneys general.[137] As Cass Sunstein noted, the problem with the old model of public law adjudication is that sometimes 'the right–duty relationship between the government and any particular legal complainant is not crisp and bilateral'.[138] Right-holders do not just claim that the state wronged them, but also that the constitutional system is flawed: they call duty-bearers to account not just in their capacity as an aggrieved party to an isolated relationship but also as representatives of the political collective.[139] To say that the interest claimed by constitutional right-holders is just not having their rights limited in improper ways[140] gets things backwards – and reflects an individualistic and overly adversarial account of constitutional rights. The state is not a private service provider we all happen to have separate legal relationships with, but a qualitatively different agent, who also represents us and operates on our behalf.

This more loosely relational procedural structure has substantive implications. Constitutional rights-based disputes and deliberations need not have a zero-sum nature or exclude external considerations. Loosely relational constitutional rights can therefore be limited not only to respect, protect or promote the rights of others, but also to promote various collective goals.[141] This means that legal agents, including judges, cannot treat constitutional disputes or wrongs as isolated incidents:[142] the question is not, as it often is in private law, who between the litigating parties should bear a concrete burden. Rather, it is how the respective legal rights and duties of the parties fit in a justified and properly adjusted scheme of constitutional rights.

[136] See Chayes (n 133) 1302; Varuhas, 'The Public Interest Conception' (n 135) 57–60.

[137] Richard H Fallon, 'As-Applied and Facial Challenges and Third-Party Standing' (2000) 113 *Harvard Law Review* 1321, 1363–68; Louis J Jaffe, 'The Citizen as Litigant in Public Actions: The Non-Hohfeldian or Ideological Plaintiff' (1968) 116 *University of Pennsylvania Law Review* 1033.

[138] Sunstein (n 131) 1446.

[139] It was claimed that these are two distinct domains of public law: see Jason NE Varuhas, 'Taxonomy and Public Law' in Mark Elliott, Jason NE Varuhas and Shona Wilson Stark (eds), *The Unity of Public Law? Doctrinal, Theoretical and Comparative Perspectives* (Hart Publishing, 2018) 39, 63–71.

[140] Monaghan (n 130) 285–86, 312–13. See also Fallon, 'As-Applied and Facial Challenges and Third-Party Standing' (n 137) 1360–62.

[141] Barak, *Proportionality* (n 111) 80–82, 262–77. See also King, *Judging Social Rights* (n 99) 193–98.

[142] Fiss, 'The Forms of Justice' (n 54) 46–50.

2.5.2. Horizontality

The argument made so far – about the political foundations of modern constitutional rights in collective responsibility, their generality as regulatory and justificatory ideals, and their merely loose relationality, which is reflected in constitutional disputes – deepens the criticisms of traditional verticality and therefore explains the horizontal expansion of constitutional rights. It underlies the idea that the political collective can violate its constitutional duties not only by causing or being intimately involved in harms or deprivations but also by failing to prevent or respond to them: there can be not only constitutional wrongness but also *wrongdoing* even if no individual agent wronged another directly, as a wrong was committed by a collective political agent.

Modern constitutional rights law takes a bird's eye view of society, while rejecting the notion that there can be social domains immune to constitutional scrutiny.[143] Every rights-affecting action or inaction must meet the constitution's substantive requirements. The constitution no longer views society as a collection of discrete interactions between individuals and the state. Instead, it recognises society as an interconnected web of relationships, associations and practices, where private actions can be as impactful on constitutional rights as state actions. From this perspective, it becomes clear that limiting constitutional scrutiny to state actions alone is insufficient. Constitutional rights grounded in values like equality, privacy and dignity inevitably require protection against private actors, compelling their horizontal expansion.

This blurs traditional boundaries between public and private domains, revealing the inadequacies of constitutional distinctions that once confined rights to state actions alone. Even if it is morally worse for the state to harm us intentionally or directly rather than as an indirect result of pursuing permissible goals or just doing nothing,[144] the latter cases are also constitutionally important. Moreover, when constitutional rights are general and grounded in values like equality, privacy or dignity, they cannot but address private action-types like discrimination, surveillance or defamation. Even before getting to questions about who actually owes what to whom – how constitutional rights should be realised in practice – it is clear that they can no longer be limited to the vertical relationship between the state and the citizen. Thus, the horizontal expansion of constitutional rights is not just an extension but a necessary evolution of their normative structure, reflecting the political collective's broader moral and constitutional responsibilities.

[143] Aharon Barak, *The Judge in a Democracy* (Princeton University Press, 2006) 194. See also TRS Allan, *The Sovereignty of Law* (Oxford University Press, 2013) 9, 12.

[144] Adam Omar Husein, 'Doing, Allowing, and the State' (2014) 33 *Law and Philosophy* 235.

2.6. PUBLIC LEGITIMACY

Before concluding this chapter, it must be noted that the substantive and procedural features of general constitutional rights – that underlie and shape their horizontal expansion – are both culturally dependent and shape our political and legal cultures. To understand the nature and limits of constitutional horizontality, we must therefore see that constitutional rights express, develop and concretise moral conceptions of the person, society, agency and well-being.[145] This function of rights has implications, as we will see, both for allocative institutions and for rights-and-duties relationships. In this chapter, we focus on the basic structure of society. In this regard, constitutional rights highlight ideals that this structure should strive to attain as standards of social justice: touching, for instance, property accumulation, marriage, public speech, access to medical services, or privacy on social media platforms.

By addressing such questions as part of social normative practices, constitutional rights help political collectives achieve clarity about their moral values while drawing force from those values. As James Madison wrote over two centuries ago, rights must 'become incorporated with the national sentiment' to 'counteract the impulses of interest and passion'.[146] They are not just reflections of political and legal cultures, nor measures agreed on in moments of collective moral transcendence: they refine values and imbue them with special force, derived from the relational normativity of rights, without grinding them into rigid rules. From this perspective, their weak 'organic connection with the existing legal rules' is not a cause for concern,[147] but part of the promise they hold as evaluative standards.

An infamous example in this regard is the holding of the Supreme Court of the United States that desegregation must occur 'with all deliberate speed'.[148] It was followed by slightly stronger measures when the pace was too slow,[149] but only with partial success.[150] This is a failure to properly recalibrate the system of rights: for example, by extending concrete holdings to more comprehensive principles and categories,[151] with different balancing tests, burdens of proof or argumentation, or stringent cores. A better example is the changes to policing that resulted from the recognition of procedural rights: courts were more

[145] Harel, 'Why Rights Matter' (n 103).

[146] Letter to Thomas Jefferson (17 October 1788). See also Rex Martin, *A System of Rights* (Oxford University Press, 1993) 60–64, 69.

[147] Simmonds, 'Constitutional Rights' (n 92) 191–92.

[148] *Brown v Board of Education* 349 US 294, 301 (1955).

[149] Mark Tushnet, *Weak Courts, Strong Rights: Judicial Review and Social Welfare Rights in Comparative Constitutional Law* (Princeton University Press, 2007) 248, 254–58.

[150] Erwin Chemerinsky, 'The Segregation and Resegregation of American Public Education: The Court's Role' (2003) 81 *North Carolina Law Review* 1597.

[151] King, *Judging Social Rights* (n 99) 289–325.

diligent and effective in pushing regulatory practices in desirable directions,[152] thereby integrating respect for rights not just in regulatory practices but also in the broader political culture.

The form of blame involved in failures in this regard is not only collective, but also less 'juridical' than lawyers are often accustomed to:[153] it is not about commands to make specific choices, take specific actions, or follow specific norms whose violations merit sanction; rather, it is about the pursuit of ideals through ongoing efforts and activities – and responses to failures are therefore also forward-looking, in the sense of aiming to facilitate moral improvement by better orienting us towards our goals. General constitutional rights sit at the heart of such processes, especially when it comes to complex structural injustices. They guide the allocation of more concrete responsibilities and duties to particular agents and their integration in social practices.

In this sense, the use of the concept of rights to refer to loosely relational constitutional rights is not just a 'linguistic and procedural accident'.[154] Their normative robustness means that we cannot tolerate 'banal … recourse to rights language'.[155] They must underlie constant scrutiny and reform of social practices. Think, for example, about reducing discrimination in different markets, ensuring fairer criminal trials, or making family structures more flexible. Rights (for example, to equality or liberty) have been utilised by activists and reformers to overhaul antiquated legal rules, principles and doctrines; they induced political collectives to evaluate the most distant corners of their legal systems in light of social justice principles. Such processes are facilitated by the simultaneous expansion of the scopes of constitutional rights (construed broadly as general ideals) and by their ability to retain their relational normativity, from which they draw much of their force and value. That is, such processes simultaneously rely on and develop the teleological and merely loosely relational structure of modern constitutional rights.

These political aspects of constitutional rights are especially important for private law. As Katharina Pistor claims, private law is part of the 'code of capital' that protects and facilitates forms of property accumulation and exchange that contribute to inequality in modern societies (especially given the ease with which the rich evade their – often lenient – tax duties).[156] In such senses and

[152] David Luban, 'The Warren Court and the Concept of a Right' (1999) 34 *Harvard Civil Rights–Civil Liberties Law Review* 7, 17.

[153] On such notions of blame, see Robin Zheng, 'Moral Criticism and Structural Injustice' (2021) 30 *Mind* 503.

[154] Eoin Daly, 'Freedom as Non-Domination in the Jurisprudence of Constitutional Rights' (2015) 28 *Canadian Journal of Law and Jurisprudence* 289, 309.

[155] Martti Koskenniemi, 'The Effect of Rights on Political Culture' in *The Politics of International Law* (Hart Publishing, 2011) 133, 134, 151.

[156] Katharina Pistor, *The Code of Capital: How the Law Creates Wealth and Inequality* (Princeton University Press, 2019).

others – say, creating the basic building-blocks of the family, social media, or sports – private law is in dire need of political guidance and legitimation. Therefore, constitutional horizontality can potentially contribute to private law's effectiveness and justification – and the ways in which it can and should do so will occupy us in the rest of the book.

2.7. CONCLUSION

If constitutional rights were inherently strictly relational,[157] there would be much less rights-based horizontality to talk about. However, just as there is no single conception of rights, there is no single conception of constitutional rights. Conflicts about the nature of rights are not pathological but result from the nature of human life and modern society. Claims that rights in general or constitutional rights in particular are inherently strictly relational exhibit what Charles Taylor called a 'Maginot Line mentality': defining a concept over-narrowly to defeat a theoretical adversary, but at the cost of making the concept itself less useful.[158] An example is Dworkin's transition from his early conception of rights as general principles that can be limited, even to promote important public goals,[159] to his mature conception of rights as strictly relational trumps – which has been criticised for being individualistic, suspicious of the state, blind to structural injustices, rigidly distinguishing public and private, and portraying non-judicial state agents as constant threats.[160]

This chapter has claimed that there is conceptual and moral room for political collectives to express and solidify their commitments to realise social justice in terms of loosely relational constitutional rights – to the extent that using the language of rights can help them engage and discharge these commitments. As will become clearer as we proceed, at least from the constitutional horizontality perspective, this is often the case: seeing all constitutional rights as strictly relational not only fails to take into account many contexts in which these rights actually do matter – it also tends to bring about less justified outcomes in terms of the realisation of rights in private social spheres in which the state is less intimately involved.

[157] See, eg, Avihay Dorfman, 'Private Law Exceptionalism? Part I: A Basic Difficulty with the Structural Arguments from Bipolarity and Civil Recourse' (2016) 35 *Law and Philosophy* 165, 187–89.

[158] Charles Taylor, 'What's Wrong with Negative Liberty?' in *Philosophy and the Human Sciences* (Cambridge University Press, 1985) 211, 215.

[159] Ronald Dworkin, 'Taking Rights Seriously' in *Taking Rights Seriously* (Harvard University Press, 1977) 184, 194, 199–200.

[160] Robin West, 'Rights, Harms, and Duties: A Response to Justice for Hedgehogs' (2010) 90 *Boston University Law Review* 819; Robin L West, 'Tragic Rights: The Rights Critique in the Age of Obama' (2011) 53 *William and Mary Law Review* 713; Jamal Greene, 'The Supreme Court 2017 Term – Foreword: Rights as Trumps?' (2018) 132 *Harvard Law Review* 37, 38–56, 67–74.

This chapter ends with the conclusion that we can and often should see modern constitutional rights as merely loosely relational and therefore as applying horizontally. This conclusion, however, invites another expansion: if constitutional rights are about private actions and activities, should they not obligate both public and private agents? This takes us to the next chapter, in which we see that this further step, while it seems almost natural, raises moral concerns tied to private law's relational normative structure.

3

Relational Resistance

3.1. INTRODUCTION

THIS CHAPTER IS, in many ways, the mirror image of the previous chapter. There, criticisms of the state action model led us to expansive notions of collective responsibility, which ground constitutional rights in the basic structure of society and push them to take a general and loosely relational form. Here, criticisms of direct horizontality will lead us to restrictive notions of personal responsibility, which locate rights that private agents exercise with and claim against other private agents in their relationships, and push them to take a specified and strictly relational form – that, importantly, resists external (including constitutional) influence. The previous chapter claimed that constitutional rights can and should include private actions and activities in their scopes. This chapter adds that while they can sometimes obligate private agents, the more general and complex they are, the stronger the resistance is to their direct entailment of private duties.

This issue could be addressed in a top-down manner, by asking whether constitutional rights law has the normative resources to reach justified conclusions about rights and duties in private relationships. The direct horizontality model can be seen as assuming that it does (perhaps with slight modifications) and therefore that constitutional rights can generally obligate private agents directly. This chapter contests the direct horizontality model's substantive conclusion, arguing that constitutional rights should not, at least as a general starting point, obligate private agents. While doing so, it also contests its top-down direction of reasoning: if the previous chapter criticised the libertarian tendency to resolve large-scale normative questions with interpersonal moral principles, this chapter criticises the opposite utilitarian tendency to resolve interpersonal normative questions with large-scale moral principles.

This chapter explains why the direct horizontality model is morally problematic by relying on principles implicit in the current rights-based regulation of private relationships, often referred to as private law. The goal is not to offer an account of the essence or nature of private law. After all, the basic point of constitutional horizontality is to push private law towards better conformity with the constitution. Rather, the goal is to understand how far private law can be pushed in this regard. This is important because, as will be shown, there are morally important similarities between constitutional rights that apply horizontally and private law rights: their similar relational structures bring with them moral concerns that private law has a long tradition of dealing with – for instance, by relying on concepts like choice or consent when recognising forms of private ordering and foreseeability or reasonableness when imposing mandatory tort duties. It will be claimed that implicit in such 'core' or 'traditional' areas of private law are moral principles that also shape the evolution of more novel and policy-oriented domains, and are therefore relevant for the recognition of constitutionally-grounded horizontal rights and duties.[1]

The limits of constitutional horizontality that private law highlights are not grounded in specific substantive values like liberty, privacy or autonomy: after all, constitutions can also recognise these values.[2] Rather, the limits derive from the normative structure of private rights-and-duties relationships. A central theme in private law theory is that its normative structure is relational, bipolar, bilateral or correlative. This not only distinguishes it from public forms of regulation, but also imposes constraints on how its norms are applied and developed.[3] These constraints apply whenever the legal system recognises rights that private agents exercise with and enforce against other private agents – even if they are labelled 'constitutional'. Such rights must be justifiably and effectively integrated within morally robust relational systems of claims, standing, responsibility, accountability, reactive attitudes, and remedies. This is one of private law's main normative functions – and there is no way around it for constitutional horizontality. To a great extent, this is the main challenge that constitutional horizontality faces.

Private law's resistance to crude instrumental uses of its norms to realise public goals, which exceed private relationships, can be explained and justified in many ways. Private law theory often relies, in this regard, on the limits of adjudication or litigation. However, because much of modern private law is shaped by legislative and administrative agents, explanations of constitutional horizontality that address only judicial decisions are limited. At their best, I will claim, its explanations must address regulation as a cooperative practice in which private agents and public agents from all state branches participate. This is why I focus, when explaining the nature and limits of constitutional horizontality, on the fact that at the end of the legal production line are private agents, ready to exercise and claim rights in private relationships.

This means that while constitutional rights and concerns about problems like racism or poverty must influence private law, for this influence to be effective and

[1] On this core–margins distinction, see Thomas W Merrill and Henry E Smith, 'The Morality of Property' (2007) 48 *William and Mary Law Review* 1849.

[2] See Dawn Oliver, *Common Values and the Public–Private Divide* (Butterworths, 1999).

[3] See Ernest J Weinrib, *The Idea of Private Law*, 2nd edn (Oxford University Press, 2012); Arthur Ripstein, *Private Wrongs* (Harvard University Press, 2016); John Gardner, *From Personal Life to Private Law* (Oxford University Press, 2018); Peter Benson, *Justice in Transactions: A Theory of Contract Law* (Harvard University Press, 2019); John CP Goldberg and Benjamin C Zipursky, *Recognizing Wrongs* (Harvard University Press, 2020).

justified, it must respond to private law's nature and limits as a regulatory tool. The important point in this regard is that its ability to realise justice or do good depends on its ability to integrate reasons for regulation within relational rights-and-duties structures. This distinguishes it from public forms of regulation (like criminal law or tax law). Treating private law as 'public law in disguise',[4] its use of morally-grounded concepts as technical or detached,[5] or its duties as mere 'price tags' that we can violate if we pay,[6] can therefore not only lead to moral wrongs or wrongdoings but also fail to make the most effective use of private law as a regulatory tool.

We must therefore take seriously the constitutive aspects of private rights-and-duties relationships and engage with them on their own terms, as expressions of mutual accountability, recognition and respect. In this sense, constitutional horizontality, like private law, must be continuous with (but not necessarily mirror) 'ordinary',[7] 'moderate',[8] or as I will refer to it, 'relational', morality – that guides and constrains our reasoning within private rights-and-duties relationships. This continuity creates a reasoning structure that determines the place and weight of constitutional reasons for or against the legal recognition of private rights – touching the congruence between the duty-bearer's personal responsibility to the right-holder and the right-holder's legitimate expectations from and claims against the duty-bearer – that later chapters develop.

3.2. DIRECT HORIZONTALITY

The previous chapters touched on the progressive post-war momentum in constitutional and human rights practices. To a great extent, direct horizontality expresses this momentum – as reflected in Johan Van der Walt's claim that to live up to its progressive promise, constitutional horizontality must bring about a 'subordination of all private relations to fundamentally public norms and concerns', such as the eradication of forms of social domination.[9]

According to the direct horizontality model, constitutional rights obligate both public and private agents to make adequate efforts to realise them in society. Of course, some rights cannot apply horizontally, such as the rights to a fair trial or against the establishment of religion. But whenever the interests underlying a right are sensitive to private actions or activities, private agents will

[4] Leon Green, 'Tort Law Public Law in Disguise' (1959) 38 *Texas Law Review* 1.

[5] Luis Duarte D'Almeida, 'Legal Statements and Normative Language' (2011) 30 *Law and Philosophy* 167.

[6] Stephen A Smith, 'The Normativity of Private Law' (2011) 31 *Oxford Journal of Legal Studies* 215.

[7] Shelly Kagan, *The Limits of Morality* (Oxford University Press, 1989) 2–4.

[8] Samuel Scheffler, *Human Morality* (Oxford University Press, 1992) 100.

[9] Johan van der Walt, *The Horizontal Effect Revolution and the Question of Sovereignty* (De Gruyter, 2014) 10.

be obligated to realise them to the extent required by the constitution. Because private agents also have constitutional rights, their constitutional duties will often be less cumbersome than the duties of public agents regarding those same rights. However, each failure to realise constitutional rights by an agent capable of doing so must be justified by appealing to similar systematic constitutional considerations on a social scale.

This model has some resonance in the horizontality jurisprudence of Ireland and South Africa.[10] Irish constitutional law allows private lawsuits for violations of constitutional rights. While judges have been cautious in applying constitutional rights when private law addresses an issue, the constitution has been applied when it does not.[11] For example, the Irish Supreme Court held that an employer that required employees to sign contracts obligating them to join a specific trade union violated their right to freedom of association.[12] The South African Interim Constitution of 1993 adopted a weak model of horizontality, which sees rights as mere values.[13] The Constitution of 1996 adopted a stronger model, holding that 'the Bill of Rights applies to all law, and binds the legislature, the executive, the judiciary and all organs of state' and all 'natural or juristic persons', taking into account the nature of the right.[14]

Defamation. A newspaper article stated that a South African politician was under police investigation for his involvement with bank robbers. The tort law rule was that the burden to prove the truthfulness and public benefit or reasonableness of defamatory media statements rested with the publishers. The publishers claimed that this rule violated their constitutional right to freedom of speech. The Constitutional Court held that this right 'is of direct horizontal application in this case', but that the burden on the publishers was constitutional: the rule struck a justified balance by encouraging 'editors and journalists to act with due care and respect for the individual interest in human dignity prior to publishing defamatory material'.[15]

The justifications for this direct horizontal application are often beneficiary-centered. If constitutional rights are about realising justified social conditions, why should we not enlist all agents who can contribute to this collective effort?[16] For example, why should we absolve publishers of duties to respect human

[10] Aoife Nolan, 'Holding Non-State Actors to Account for Constitutional Economic and Social Rights Violations: Experiences and Lessons from South Africa and Ireland' (2014) 12 *International Journal of Constitutional Law* 61.

[11] Colm O'Cinneide, 'Irish Constitutional Law and Direct Effect – A Successful Experiment?' in Dawn Oliver and Jörg Fedtke (eds), *Human Rights and the Private Sphere: A Comparative Study* (Routledge, 2007) 213.

[12] *Meskell v CIE* [1973] IR 121.

[13] *Du Plessis v De Klerk* [1996] 3 SA 850.

[14] Articles 8(1), (2).

[15] *Khumalo v Holomisa* [2002] 5 SA 401, paras 33, 41–43.

[16] David Bilchitz, *Fundamental Rights and the Legal Obligations of Business* (Cambridge University Press, 2021) 175–82. For a similar claim about social justice, see Liam Murphy, 'Institutions and the Demands of Justice' (1998) 27 *Philosophy & Public Affairs* 251.

dignity – and those threatening to stifle journalistic efforts of duties to guarantee freedom of speech? But there can also be agent-centered justifications. For example, from a republican perspective, it can be claimed that private agents should be incorporated in the collective constitutional project and made accountable to others in this regard to reinforce their normative ties to the polity and to its members.[17]

3.2.1. The Public Sides of Private Rights

Because the direct horizontality model steps into private law's traditional domain of privately exercised and enforced rights, it is helpful to explain this model against the background of non-constitutional attempts to use private law to promote complex policy goals. While this chapter explains the resistance to such attempts, it is important to appreciate – and I will later develop this claim – that private law regularly addresses reasons that exceed isolated private relations: say, about the effectiveness of markets or the facilitation of forms of private ordering.[18] As the twentieth century progressed, following the influence of progressive thinkers like Marx and Bentham who called for the demystification and scrutiny of social institutions,[19] these public sides of private law were exposed – for example, by legal realists.[20] Gradually, legal theorists and actors grew more comfortable with seeing private law as part of the state's regulatory apparatus, which can and should be shaped to best serve society's needs and goals.

These ideas are often associated with economic theories of private law,[21] which see, for instance, tortious negligence as a failure to prevent harms whose social costs outweigh their social benefits,[22] and contractual parties as having no duties to perform contracts if social costs are reduced by breaching and paying compensation.[23] However, the complementary features of instrumentalism and consequentialism – seeing private law as a malleable regulatory tool that should be used to bring about desirable states of affairs – can also be exhibited by approaches that are more sensitive to distributive and non-economic goals.[24] Private right-holders, under such accounts, call private duty-bearers to

[17] Christina Bambrick, 'Horizontal Rights: A Republican Vein in Liberal Constitutionalism' (2020) 52 *Polity* 401.

[18] Stephen Waddams, *Dimensions of Private Law* (Cambridge University Press, 2003) 191–221.

[19] HLA Hart, 'The Demystification of Law' in *Essays on Bentham* (Oxford University Press, 1982) 21.

[20] See generally Hanoch Dagan, *Reconstructing American Legal Realism & Rethinking Private Law Theory* (Oxford University Press, 2013).

[21] Guido Calabresi, *The Future of Law and Economics* (Yale University Press, 2016) 7.

[22] Richard A Posner, 'A Theory of Negligence' (1972) 1 *Journal of Legal Studies* 29.

[23] Richard A Posner, 'Let Us Never Blame a Contract Breaker' in Omri Ben-Shahar and Ariel Porat (eds), *Fault in American Contract Law* (Cambridge University Press, 2010) 3.

[24] See William Lucy, *Philosophy of Private Law* (Oxford University Press, 2007) 328, 335–37.

account as co-promoters of public goals:[25] the private enforcement of rights is seen as a regulatory extension of the state, and right-holders as 'private attorneys general' who call duty-bearers to account on the public's behalf.[26] This allows private law to operate as a bottom-up and decentralised form of regulation – which gains moral importance, for instance, when industries like tobacco, guns, pharma, oil or tech endanger public interests while evading top-down forms of regulation. In this sense, private law performs public or even constitutional roles,[27] which the direct horizontality model can solidify.

This approach to private law underlies reforms, such as the replacement of negligence regimes for harms caused in workplaces, on roads, or by defective products with no-fault (strict liability) regimes – often coupled with some form of public or private insurance; the consolidation of norms that address special vulnerabilities in contracts between sellers and buyers or employers and employees or against private forms of discrimination in various social spheres; and more egalitarian norms for the creation and dissolution of different family structures. We will address these examples in later chapters, but it is already important to keep in mind the ways in which private law forms of regulation are often used to realise public policy goals, whose justifications extend beyond isolated interactions between pairs of private agents.[28]

3.2.2. Moral Concerns

Like public approaches to private law, direct horizontality models evaluate actions within private relationships, associations or practices as part of broader social states of affairs. The actions of public and private agents alike are therefore never evaluated in isolation – which means that obligating private agents, for example, to promote equality, alleviate poverty or protect privacy, can be justified not because of what they did but because of what they can do.

Two broad types of criticism are directed against such consequentialist principles. The beneficiary-centered type is that they allow too much: for example, allow others to sacrifice our life to save more lives. This criticism is less important in our context, in which rights form part of the good to be realised: we can hold that life should be sacrificed, for example, only in highly unusual and catastrophic circumstances. The more pressing criticisms in our context are

[25] Bernard Williams famously referred to this type of responsibility as 'negative' in 'A Critique of Utilitarianism', in *Utilitarianism: For and Against* (Cambridge University Press, 1973) 77, 93–96.

[26] Jules L Coleman, *The Practice of Principle* (Oxford University Press, 2001) 19; Jules L Coleman, 'Doing Away with Tort Law' (2008) 41 *Loyola of Los Angeles Law Review* 1149. See also William B Rubenstein, 'On What a "Private Attorney General" is – And Why it Matters' (2004) 57 *Vanderbilt Law Review* 2129.

[27] Michael L Rustad, 'Torts as Public Wrongs' (2011) 38 *Pepperdine Law Review* 433, 470.

[28] Guido Calabresi, 'A Broader View of the Cathedral' (2014) 77 *Law and Contemporary Problems* 1.

therefore agent-centered ones – that consequentialist principles demand too much: for example, that we sacrifice our life to save more lives, even of distant strangers. The problems in our context do not arise at the level of the primary duties that we end up with: our constitutional rights (say, to life or to autonomy) can prevent the imposition of disproportionate duties. Rather, the problems arise at the deeper levels of figuring out what our primary duties are and of being potentially called to account in this regard by every agent in every social setting. First-order balancing cannot fully resolve these problems.

Complexity. 'Human rights due diligence' is the process in which business corporations identify their direct and indirect adverse impacts on rights, take prevention or mitigation steps, track their effectiveness, remedy failures, and justify themselves to affected parties. To a great extent, direct horizontality expects individuals to engage in similar processes (even if, usually, on a smaller scale).[29] Thus, David Bilchitz, who advocates a direct model, claims that duty-bearers must be 'required to understand the relevant factors applicable to the context in which they operate and take responsibility for – and be able to justify – the decisions that they make'; and criticises reliance on more concrete rules for leading to 'mechanical box-ticking'.[30] The problem is that most individuals and even corporations lack the abilities or resources to effectively reason about the duties entailed by complex, general, and interconnected rights (including whether the social benefits of particular rights-realising acts outweigh their social costs). As Rawls noted with regard to his focus on the basic structure of society, it is often difficult for private agents to 'comprehend the ramifications of their particular actions viewed collectively'.[31] The problem is not only the abstraction of constitutional rights: private law also guides with abstract standards,[32] and we will see that often for good reasons. But these standards usually do not obligate private agents to evaluate normative and factual factors on a social scale; and even when they do, this burden correlates with the duty-bearer's responsibility to the right-holder, which means that in practice such duties are limited to defined relationships, activities or roles.

Intrusion. Even if private agents could handle such demanding forms of evaluation and reasoning, burdening them with duties to do so because of their potential contribution to collective efforts to realise shared goals – because of their abilities or resources rather than their choices, projects or relationships – undermines their autonomy and sense of authorship of their lives: it can erode the delicate and already flimsy notion that our lives are lived 'from within'.[33]

[29] Bilchitz (n 16) 195–96.

[30] ibid 227.

[31] John Rawls, *Political Liberalism*, 2nd edn (Columbia University Press, 2005) 268.

[32] Jeremy Waldron, 'Clarity, Thoughtfulness, and the Rule of Law' in Geert Keil and Ralf Poscher (eds), *Vagueness and Law: Philosophical and Legal Perspectives* (Oxford University Press, 2016) 317.

[33] Bernard Williams, 'Consequentialism and Integrity' in Samuel Scheffler (ed), *Consequentialism and its Critics* (Oxford University Press, 1988) 20, 35. See also Gardner, *From Personal Life to Private Law* (n 3) 172–75; Joseph Raz, 'Being in the World' (2010) 23 *Ratio Juris* 433, 451.

The problem is that such complex duties 'never sleep', to borrow Dworkin's words;[34] and their tentacular prescriptions reach many corners of our private lives: they are not limited to concrete actions that harm others or to cases in which we assume extended responsibilities to others. Private agents carry an ongoing burden to figure out where they stand, constitutionally.

Crowding out. Direct models also blur the already vague boundaries between our lives, which private law, with its focus on agency, helps solidify;[35] and they erode our ability to recognise and respect people with whom we interact directly in private relationships.[36] Painting private relationships in political colours by prioritising the pursuit of shared public goals can crowd out the dispositions, attitudes, emotions or evaluations that facilitate the forms of communication and attachment that constitute private relationships.[37] Take, for example, proportionality as a justification for rights infringements.[38] In its constitutional form, it operates on a social scale and addresses all affected parties. To justify ourselves to others like that – say, to violate a tenancy contract because doing so promotes equality – is to step back from our direct relationships and to treat others as members of a group of beneficiaries of our actions. Such detachment would often reduce the value of private relationships and can even amount to moral wrongdoing (there are exceptions, but figuring out if they apply raises the previous problems).

Scrutiny. Giving private agents the standing and authority to call other private agents to account for failures to properly respond to general moral reasons can be justified.[39] But calling others to account as constitutional wrongdoers, in the name of the political collective, can give practices of private right-claiming features of denunciation practices, under which public order is enforced from the bottom-up through interpersonal scrutiny and accountability.[40] The problem is not that we are answerable to too many private agents but that we are answerable to the political collective: failures to act in certain ways towards neighbours, co-workers or students would wrong not just them but also 'us'. Such heavy normative machinery is traditionally operated by public agents, who are under strict public law constraints: this is one reason why criminal prosecutions are normally brought by state agents in the name of the political collective while

[34] Ronald Dworkin, *Law's Empire* (Belknap Press of Harvard University Press, 1986) 294.

[35] Gardner, *From Personal Life to Private Law* (n 3) 58–87.

[36] Tony Honoré, *Responsibility and Fault* (Hart, 1999) 10, 93.

[37] Emad H Atiq, 'Why Motives Matter: Reframing the Crowding Out Effect of Legal Incentives' (2014) 123 *Yale Law Journal* 1070.

[38] See also Bilchitz (n 16) 273–79.

[39] See Seana Valentine Shiffrin, 'Inducing Moral Deliberation: On the Occasional Virtues of Fog' (2010) 123 *Harvard Law Review* 1214, 1227.

[40] See generally Sheila Fitzpatrick and Robert Gellately, 'Introduction to Practices of Denunciation in Modern European History' (1996) 68 *Journal of Modern History* 747.

tort claims are brought by private right-holders on their own behalf.[41] But the more constraints we extend to private agents in this regard, the more we integrate them into the state's apparatus, thereby only deepening the infiltration of the public into the private.

Authority. Burdening private agents with duties to discharge collective responsibilities involves recognising their discretion, because we cannot specify in advance what they must do to adequately realise complex general rights.[42] If this responsibility delegation – a soft form of privatisation – is not accompanied by strict administrative oversight, it raises concerns, especially given power disparities in litigation and its increasing rarity.[43] Think, for example, about how the difficulty of calling social media platforms to account leaves them with *de facto* authority to shape the market of ideas. One problem in this regard is that the normative environments in which private agents operate – say, profit-oriented corporations – are less likely to induce them to realise the values underlying rights. But even if the results in terms of rights-realisation are good, a problem remains: constitutional decisions about rights-realisation should be made by agents accountable to the political collective not only through litigation but through more ongoing and entrenched institutional mechanisms.[44] These mechanisms not only ensure responsibility to the public and better norm-conformity, but also allow for better coordination of regulatory decisions, which must respond to each other in complex normative arenas.

The problems of complexity, intrusion, crowding out, scrutiny and authority figure in many normative debates: for example, about discrimination or privatisation. They often justify distinctions between public and private, which are generally accepted, in non-binary and nuanced forms, in political, moral and legal philosophy – and are reflected in the architecture, principles and norms of liberal legal systems. Rawls's theory of social justice goes in that direction as well. Its focus on the basic structure is meant not only to prevent the libertarian reduction of the political to the interpersonal by expanding our moral expectations from the political collective, with its resources and authority, beyond our expectations from private agents. It also aims to prevent the utilitarian subordination of the interpersonal to the political: holding individuals to less exacting

[41] RA Duff and SE Marshall, 'Public and Private Wrongs' in James Chalmers, Fiona Leverick and Lindsay Farmer (eds), *Essays in Criminal Law in Honour of Sir Gerald Gordon* (Edinburgh University Press, 2010) 70; Jesse Wall, 'Public Wrongs and Private Wrongs' (2018) 31 *Canadian Journal of Law & Jurisprudence* 177.

[42] David Bilchitz and Laura Ausserladscheider Jonas, 'Proportionality, Fundamental Rights, and the Duties of Directors' (2016) 36 *Oxford Journal of Legal Studies* 828, 844–45, 849.

[43] See Carlo Vittorio Giabardo, 'Private Law in the Age of the "Vanishing Trial"' in Kit Barker, Karen Fairweather and Ross Grantham (eds), *Private Law in the 21st Century* (Hart Publishing, 2017) 547.

[44] See generally Avihay Dorfman and Alon Harel, 'Against Privatisation as Such' (2016) 36 *Oxford Journal of Legal Studies* 400. For a Rawlsian perspective, see Chiara Cordelli, 'The Institutional Division of Labor and the Egalitarian Obligations of Nonprofits' (2012) 20 *Journal of Political Philosophy* 131.

and complex norms and standards allows social justice to leave room for autonomy, privacy and the moral values endemic to private relationships, associations and practices.[45]

If the state action model treats all agents as private while ignoring collective notions of responsibility, the direct horizontality model treats all agents as public while ignoring personal notions of responsibility: it ignores the ways in which the force and value of rights that private agents exercise and claim in private relationships depend on their integration within these relationships. While the constraints imposed on the content of rights by their form are often loose in relationships with the state (state action models go wrong here), they are stricter in private relationships. This leaves room for some constitutional rights and duties: for example, against torture or slavery. However, the recognition of loosely relational private duties to promote equality or protect privacy, for example, has worrying moral implications; and it is therefore no coincidence that such duties form parts of constitutional law but take (as we will see) more limited forms in private law. The direct horizontality model fails to accommodate this distinction because the status of the duty-bearer is irrelevant: only the ability to realise constitutional rights matters.

It is therefore not surprising that the direct model was also rejected by most legal systems, and even its adoption in Ireland and South Africa met difficulties.[46] It can be justified in special circumstances of severe social injustice, or when it comes to the operation of big business corporations in weak legal systems, whose authority is undermined.[47] However, in modern, liberal, and only moderately unjust legal systems, this model is difficult to justify as a general account of the scope of constitutional rights. Importantly, like the state action model, the direct model – because of its focus on social states of affairs and the little attention it pays to relational moral considerations – struggles to determine when it should apply and when it should not.

3.3. RELATIONAL FOUNDATIONS

If the moral ideas that underlie the criticisms of traditional verticality touch expansive notions of collective responsibility, the moral ideas that underlie the criticisms of direct horizontality touch restrictive notions of personal

[45] Rawls, *Political Liberalism* (n 31) 267–69; Samuel Scheffler, 'The Division of Moral Labour: Egalitarian Liberalism as Moral Pluralism' (2005) 79 *Proceedings of the Aristotelian Society* 229, 231–37; Samuel Freeman, 'The Basic Structure of Society as the Primary Subject of Justice' in Jon Mandle and David A Reidy (eds), *A Companion to Rawls* (John Wiley & Sons, 2014) 88, 101–05.

[46] See Sibo Banda, 'Taking Indirect Horizontality Seriously in Ireland: A Time to Magnify the Nuance' (2009) 31 *Dublin University Law Journal* 263; Nick Friedman, 'The South African Common Law and the Constitution: Revisiting Horizontality' (2014) 30 *South African Journal of Human Rights* 63; Michael Dafel, 'The Directly Enforceable Constitution: Political Parties and the Horizontal Application of the Bill of Rights' (2015) 31 *South African Journal on Human Rights* 56.

[47] This seems to be the central case in Bilchitz (n 16) 74–75; Jean Thomas, *Public Rights, Private Relations* (Oxford University Press, 2015) 13.

responsibility. Despite the growing awareness that private interactions always form parts of broader social institutions or practices, personal responsibility remains deeply rooted in private law's foundations:[48] because duties are justified by grounding them in their bearer's responsibility to specific right-holders,[49] doctrines and principles utilise responsibility or related concepts like foreseeability and consent.[50] Therefore, while welfare schemes, for example, can respond to setbacks to well-being that were not caused by anyone, private law must tie such setbacks to the actions of particular agents. On the other hand, private law is not only about agency: victimless wrongs or public wrongs against the political collective, for example, normally fall outside private law. In private law, agency and well-being must both be present, and connected in normatively salient ways.[51] While private law must answer some non-relational questions (for example, what constitutes harm or who qualifies as a competent agent), much of its focus is on relational ones. To understand this relational focus, we must first locate private law in its normative neighbourhood: morally robust relationships of mutual accountability, recognition and respect.

3.3.1. Moral Relationships

The moral landscape is vast and diverse. It shapes and is shaped by private law in many ways. But the broadest, most robust, bridges stretch from private law to the moral domain of rights, duties and wrongs. In this domain, to borrow Stephen Darwall's terms, moral obligations are not grounded in third-personal and impartial reasons (say, about the beauty of art) or in first-personal and self-referential reasons (say, about the virtue of discipline), but in second-personal and other-regarding reasons: the force and value of moral obligations are derived from claims that other people can press against us (say, that we must not punch them).[52] Moral obligations therefore operate within relational normative structures, comprised of inherently relational and interdependent concepts – standing, authority, responsibility, accountability, wrongs, reactive

[48] Weinrib, *The Idea of Private Law* (n 3) 1.

[49] Coleman, 'Doing away' (n 26) 1161; John CP Goldberg and Benjamin C Zipursky, 'Rights and Responsibility in the Law of Torts' in Donal Nolan and Andrew Robertson (eds), *Rights and Private Law* (Hart Publishing, 2012) 251, 258.

[50] Lucy, *Philosophy of Private Law* (n 24) 25, 35.

[51] See Weinrib, *The Idea of Private Law* (n 3) 124–25; Stephen R Perry, 'The Mixed Conception of Corrective Justice' (1992) 15 *Harvard Journal of Law & Public Policy* 917, 924–32; Arthur Ripstein, 'Private Law and Private Narratives' in Peter Cane and John Gardner (eds), *Relating to Responsibility* (Hart Publishing, 2001) 37, 57–58; Peter Benson, 'Misfeasance as an Organizing Normative Idea in Private Law' (2010) 60 *University of Toronto Law Journal* 731, 748–49, 768.

[52] Stephen Darwall, *The Second-Person Standpoint: Morality, Respect, and Accountability* (Harvard University Press, 2006) 35–38, 300–04, 320. See also RJ Wallace, *The Moral Nexus* (Princeton University Press, 2019) 49–61.

attitudes (like blame) and remedies – which 'comprise an interdefinable circle' that claims about obligations must tap into to gain moral traction.[53]

Such relational moral structures take looser forms when duties are not owed to any individual in particular, and agents are responsible not to do wrong and are accountable to the community at large – the paradigmatic legal case in this regard being criminal law. But these structures take stricter forms when duties are owed to individuals and tied to their standing and authority to call the duty-bearer to account on their own behalf for wronging them – the paradigmatic legal case in this regard being private law.[54] This strictness expresses the fact that, as R Jay Wallace explains, when we are obligated to people whose interests are central in the justification of the obligation and stand to be wronged by how we discharge it, disregard for the obligation is disregard for these people as sources of valid claims.[55] This principle echoes Nagel's distinction between 'administrative' justifications – as 'benevolent bureaucrats' that distribute benefits and burdens in society, 'to countless other beings, with whom one may have various relations or none' – and 'interpersonal' justifications to a person, which address the ways in which our actions affect them in particular.[56] Consequentialism is loosely relational, at best, because it sees our obligations as being about others rather than as owed to others: failures to discharge obligations, if they are wrong, wrong the moral community. In this sense, offering a purely consequentialist justification to a person affected by our actions disrespects them.

When we stand in relationships of mutual accountability, recognition and respect with others, their interests have not only impartial value that everyone has reasons to realise: they also have agent-relative value, grounded in the nature of our relationship, that justifies our obligations to them.[57] This means that interests cannot be automatically translated into obligations. The translation is easier in constitutional law, where, as we saw in the previous chapter, there are strong justifications to add on top of the restrictive notion of responsibility more expansive and collective notions. However, as argued in the first chapter, it is still too early to declare the triumph of collectivist notions of responsibility, more remote from the daily lives of individuals, when it comes to what we owe to each other as private agents.[58] It is therefore crucial, to understand the moral foundations of the resistance to policy-oriented impositions of duties in

[53] Darwall, *The Second-Person Standpoint* (n 52) 6–13. It should be noted that I slightly modify some features of Darwall's theory – yet, as I see it, while remaining loyal to its basic principles.

[54] Stephen Darwall, 'Bipolar Obligation' in *Morality, Authority, & Law: Essays in Second-Personal Ethics I* (Oxford University Press, 2013) 20.

[55] Wallace (n 52) 82–86, 157–63, 176–77.

[56] Thomas Nagel, 'War and Massacre' (1972) 1 *Philosophical & Public Affairs* 123, 136–38.

[57] See Samuel Scheffler, 'Relationships and Responsibilities' (1997) 26 *Philosophy & Public Affairs* 189.

[58] Samuel Scheffler, 'Individual Responsibility in a Global Age' in *Boundaries and Allegiances: Problems of Justice and Responsibility in Liberal Thought* (Oxford University Press, 2002) 32, 41–44.

private law, to expose the gatekeeping function that personal responsibility still performs in many normative practices, including legal ones.

3.3.2. Restrictive Responsibility

While the conditions of being responsible (or response-able) in general can focus on the agent in isolation (say, on their cognitive capacities), the conditions of being responsible *to* someone about something are more contextual and relational.[59] Responsibility in the latter sense is important because while not located at the ground level of normative reasoning, it is more basic than duties: the duty-bearer's responsibility must pre-exist and justify the duty – and if the duty correlates with a right, also the right-holder's standing to call the duty-bearer to account.[60]

This foundational type of responsibility is backwards-looking, but in a more nuanced sense than this term is often used. It is not the ascription of responsibility for an existing state of affairs (for example, I am responsible to clean up the mess that I made in the kitchen), which Hart referred to as 'liability-responsibility':[61] a narrow and remedial notion of responsibility.[62] The kind of responsibility that underlies primary rights and duties is dynamic, in the sense that it consists of norms that determine how we become accountable and obligated to others with regard to certain things. Future actions or states of affairs have moral weight here (for example, Seller is responsible to disclose information to Buyer to avoid misleading them).[63]

What we find in relational morality, in this regard, is a choice-sensitive and restrictive notion of responsibility, mentioned in the previous chapter: that limits our world as agents by distinguishing between what we do and what we fail to prevent and between people with whom we have special relationships and strangers.[64] This conception is reflected in Hart's distinction between 'general' duties that we cannot unburden ourselves of and therefore take more concrete forms (say, not to batter others) and 'special' duties that can be more demanding because they are assumed towards particular others (say, by entering a contractual agreement).[65] This conception of responsibility gives priority to our ability

[59] On this distinction, see Angela M Smith, 'Responsibility as Answerability' (2015) 58 *Inquiry* 99, 111–13.

[60] John Martin Fischer and Neal A Tognazzini, 'The Physiognomy of Responsibility' (2011) 82 *Philosophy and Phenomenological Research* 381, 394.

[61] See generally Lucy, *Philosophy of Private Law* (n 24) ch 2.

[62] See John Gardner, 'Hart and Feinberg on Responsibility' in Matthew H Kramer, Claire Grant, Ben Colburn and Antony Hatzistavrou (eds), *The Legacy of H.L.A. Hart: Legal, Political, and Moral Philosophy* (Oxford University Press, 2008) 121, 132–33.

[63] See Peter Cane, *Responsibility in Law and Morality* (Hart Publishing, 2002) 30–35.

[64] Scheffler, 'Individual Responsibility in a Global Age' (n 58) 36–38.

[65] HLA Hart, 'Are There any Natural Rights?' (1955) 64 *Philosophical Review* 175, 183–88. See also Robert E Goodin, *Protecting the Vulnerable* (The University of Chicago Press, 1985) 16–22, 29–32.

to control our normative situation as agents and our duties to others over our ability to have our well-being served by other people's actions.[66]

This conception of responsibility does not require our complete control of situations,[67] nor does it require that responsibilities be assumed voluntarily:[68] it requires a reasonable level of awareness of the normative implications of our actions and the ability to avoid them. The important thing for us is that the fact that we can benefit others is not enough to establish that we are responsible to them to do so: ascriptions of responsibilities must be grounded in an exercise of our agency in our relationship with them. This notion of responsibility does not merely put its thumb on the agent's side of the normative scales when balancing it against well-being – which would mean that extreme vulnerabilities or needs can directly justify conscripting us to aid others. Rather, this notion of responsibility engages obligations from a qualitatively different perspective, which utilises relational forms of evaluation and reasoning. This, I contend, is the key to understanding the resistance to direct horizontality.

3.4. PRIVATE RIGHTS

In this section, we move from the moral to the legal: to the ways in which relational morality, with restrictive responsibility at its centre, underlies and shapes private law's procedural structure; and in which through this structure, it exerts substantive influence over private law's evolution – and thus also over the recognition of constitutionally-grounded private rights and duties. The starting point is that the relational moral structures presented in the previous section lend themselves quite naturally to justifications of private law's procedural rights-and-duties structure:[69] forms of private ordering allow us to create or exchange rights in relationships of mutual recognition and respect, while responses to right-violations can be seen as forms of moral address that highlight the fact that the violator wronged others, whose standing and authority to call the wrongdoer to account are solidified by private law. As our societies grow more impersonal, commercialised, and technologically-mediated, such relational structures become incredibly important.

Normally, the immediate beneficiaries of private law norms – the people whose basic interests figure centrally in their justification – have the exclusive

[66] Ronald Dworkin, *Justice for Hedgehogs* (Harvard University Press, 2013) 285–89, 300–03.

[67] See Raz, 'Being in the World' (n 33); Philip Pettit, 'The Capacity to Have Done Otherwise: An Agent-Centred View' in *Relating to Responsibility* (n 51) 21.

[68] Joseph Raz, 'Promises in Morality and Law' (1982) 95 *Harvard Law Review* 916.

[69] *See* Jason M Solomon, 'Equal Accountability Through Tort Law' (2009) 103 *Northwestern University Law Review* 1765; Stephen Darwall and Julian Darwall, 'Civil Recourse as Mutual Accountability' (2011) 39 *Florida State University Law Review* 17.

standing and authority to exercise, claim or enforce them: for instance, to enter a contract, claim that a certain nuisance must desist, or initiate litigation about a negligently caused harm. Judicial powers to grant declaratory, injunctive or compensatory orders, for example, can be exercised only if the right-holder exercised their power to call the alleged duty-bearer to account in court. In this sense, the right-holder controls the normative situation with the duty-bearer:[70] an aspect of rights that the Kantian will theory places at their centre.[71] This private authority, unlike state authority to enforce the law, need not aim to benefit the political collective or serve public goals: we do not see private law right-claiming as detached from the right-holder's interests. Right-holders can decide if, when and how to exercise or claim their rights; and they are completely within their rights if they decide to waive their rights or allow certain right-violations to go unanswered: something that we normally see them as better positioned than third parties or state agents to decide.[72]

The other side of the coin is that right-claims are addressed only at alleged duty-bearers, as reflected in the structure of litigation and the zero-sum nature of remedial decisions: whichever remedy resolves the right-holder's predicament must be extracted from or imposed on the duty-bearer.[73] Therefore, without an identifiable duty-bearer – and unlike the case with general constitutional rights – right-claims do not even 'get off the ground'.[74] From the duty-bearer's side, they are accountable for their conformity with private law norms only to the right-holder rather than to third parties or to the political collective. Now, private law can be seen as including the law-creation or enforcement activities of state agents, when they regulate relationships between private parties: for example, with regard to standard terms in insurance contracts or workplace safety.[75] I take no position on how to define private law in general (if that is even possible); but for the purpose of thinking about constitutional horizontality we should start with the cases that pose the strongest resistance: the problems of complexity, intrusion, crowding out, scrutiny and authority are weaker when it comes to regulation that does not recognise morally robust rights that are privately exercised and claimed.

[70] On this control, see also David Owens, 'The Roles of Rights' in Paul B Miller and John Oberdiek (eds), *Civil Wrongs and Justice in Private Law* (Oxford University Press, 2020) 3, 7–12.

[71] HLA Hart, 'Legal Rights' in *Essays on Bentham* (Oxford University Press, 1982) 162.

[72] Rebecca Stone, 'Private Liability Without Wrongdoing' (2023) 73 *University of Toronto Law Journal* 53.

[73] Jules L Coleman, *Risks and Wrongs* (Cambridge University Press, 1992) 286.

[74] John Gardner, 'Backward and Forward with Tort Law' in Joseph Keim Campbell, Michael O'Rourke and David Shier (eds), *Law and Social Justice* (The MIT Press, 2005) 255, 258–59.

[75] See Hanoch Dagan and Roy Kreitner, 'The Other Half of Regulatory Theory' (2020) 52 *Connecticut Law Review* 430.

3.4.1. Law and Morality

Technically, private law's procedural structure can tolerate direct horizontality or private attorney general models of norm-enforcement. However, and this is a main axis in this book, this procedural structure is inherently tied to moral principles that push back against these models and favour models that take more seriously the relational normative habitats within which private rights operate. Some legal theorists (say, with realist, economic or progressive leanings) have little patience for such claims: they see the use of morally-laden language in private law as a distraction from policy promotion (if not a form of deception).[76] My reply to such claims is not empirical: I can concede that some legal actors treat private law norms as mere price tags or as predictions of judicial sanction and concepts like rights, duties or wrongs as mere 'signposts' or 'placeholders' with no intrinsic moral weight.[77] But I reject the stronger claim that private law rights are purely formal or nominal from a moral perspective, in the sense that the only constraints on their possible content are practical or linguistic.[78] This stronger claim is not about the subjective perceptions of legal actors but about the objective nature of private law norms and the moral reasons or obligations that shape their possible content.[79]

In some areas of law, rights and duties may operate in a more detached manner: for example, complex corporate tax regulations or municipal health codes for pubs.[80] There are duties here (to pay taxes or store certain products in refrigerators), but they are owed to the public; and there are enforcement rights here, but they are not about their holder's well-being but about their ability to perform their institutional role. Moral principles underlie these norms as well, but they are consequentialist and instrumentalist and operate at a greater distance from the relational moral structures described in the previous section.

Things are different in private law. Even if its justified norms are not moral norms and their legal validity does not depend on their justification, they must still, to be good law, at least purport to obligate us not only legally but also morally; and as John Gardner explained, if legal norms aim to tell us what we *really* ought to do, they must be justified, shaped and applied as 'would-be moral obligations'.[81] This leaves room for the law to take prevailing attitudes towards its moral authority into account, to deviate from morality (even unjustifiably), to engage morality indirectly and implicitly, and to gradually turn to morality

[76] See generally Stephen A Smith, 'Taking Law Seriously' (2000) 50 *University of Toronto Law Journal* 241.

[77] Such a deflationary account of legal concepts was famously presented in Felix Cohen, 'Transcendental Nonsense and the Functional Approach' (1935) 35 *Columbia Law Review* 809.

[78] See Liam Murphy, 'Purely Formal Wrongs' in *Civil Wrongs and Justice in Private Law* (n 70) 19.

[79] Weinrib, *The Idea of Private Law* (n 3) 114 (referring to private law's 'normative roots').

[80] See also Duarte D'Almeida (n 5).

[81] John Gardner, 'Obligations and Outcomes in the Law of Torts' in *Relating to Responsibility* (n 51) 111, 121.

less frequently for guidance.[82] However, even if in some legal domains (like criminal law or tax law) morality pushes legal practices to focus on legally valid norms, in areas that are developed and applied more dynamically, like private law, the ties between law and morality are more porous and impose more visible constraints.[83] Thus, good private law rights and duties must be tethered to relational morality, at least in the sense that they deviate from it when it is also justified according to moral principles.

This means that claims about what private rights there should be, or how the constitution obligates private agents, cannot be purely legal or technical or rely on social conventions: they must rely on critical moral principles.[84] While the law cannot provide a correct answer to every question, including about constitutional horizontality (a position that Hart famously referred to as a 'noble dream'), we must still avoid seeing the law as completely malleable in this regard (a position that Hart referred to as a 'nightmare').[85] Authority and discretion must be exercised, but within moral limits – of the kind that theories of constitutional horizontality must explain.

Even if the constitution is superior in some senses to other legal norms, its interpretation and application must, to be morally authoritative, be sufficiently congruent with moral principles: even constitutional norms cannot go morally rogue. Therefore, there are strong moral pressures to carefully integrate the constitution's horizontal aspects within the normative fabric of private rights-and-duties relationships: within the relational structures described in the previous section. When the legal system grants private agents the standing to call others to account for failures to meet public standards of conduct whose justifications centre around interests of people in the claimant's position, it is difficult to escape the relational normativity of rights and questions about the limits of the responsibilities of duty-bearers towards particular right-holders. The idea is not that there is something natural or pre-political about such rights (regulation does not aim to simply mirror moral norms) but that the private law type of regulation is necessarily accompanied, shaped and constrained by relational moral principles.

3.4.2. Form and Substance

To be morally authoritative, constitutional horizontality must not only treat private rights and duties as robust norms rather than price tags, or ensure that

[82] Scott Hershovitz, *Law is a Moral Practice* (Harvard University Press, 2023) 16–18, 39, 27–28, 167.

[83] ibid 85–91.

[84] See Peter Cane, 'Rights in Private Law' in *Rights and Private Law* (n 49) 35, 52–53; Jean Thomas, 'The Elusive Third Way? The Role of Positive Morality in Recognizing Wrongs' (2023) 27 *Jerusalem Review of Legal Studies* 74, 84–87.

[85] HLA Hart, 'American Jurisprudence Through English Eyes: The Nightmare and the Noble Dream' (1976) 11 *Georgia Law Review* 969.

they effectively guide private agents, but also integrate them within relational normative structures. Constitutional horizontality reasoning must adequately connect the right-holder's interests and standing to the duty-bearer's responsibility and accountability – thereby following a 'pattern of argument' that is dominant in private law,[86] in which justifications for primary norms are often 'bilateral' and 'right-shaped'.[87]

Explosion. A railroad employee who helped a latecomer board a train gave him a push that made him drop a package – that happened to explode. The explosion caused heavy metal scales to fall on Mrs Palsgraf, who stood across the platform. The minority in the New York Court of Appeals held that the duty to take reasonable care when there is a foreseeable risk of physical harm to anyone (say, the latecomer) is owed to everyone (including Mrs Palsgraf). But Chief Justice Cardozo held, for the majority, that 'negligence, like risk, is a term of relation',[88] and therefore that even if a duty of care was breached it was not a duty owed to Mrs Palsgraf, whose harm was not a foreseeable outcome that the railroad employee should have made efforts to avoid. Highlighting the moral stakes, Cardozo added that unlike in criminal law, in tort law 'the plaintiff sues in her own right for a wrong personal to her':[89] we have tort law rights to be treated in certain ways – not for others to conduct themselves in certain ways.

Cardozo's ideas were warmly adopted by tort theorists who insist (largely against economic theories) that tort law's structure is rights-based and relational: as Ben Zipursky explains, this decision highlights a principle of 'substantive standing', which ties tort law's procedural structure to the kind of claims private agents can address at each other.[90] The *Explosion* case is interesting because while the company's conduct was sub-standard, and this resulted in harm to someone towards whom the company must act with due care, it was not the kind of failure to take the right-holder's interests seriously that amounts to a right violation. To take another example used by Zipursky, it is not enough for a seller to make a fraudulent statement to commit fraud: the inaccurate statement must not only be made to and reach a person but that person must actually rely on this statement before transacting with the seller.

Private law rights that sellers do not make fraudulent statements or do not act negligently, period, raise the problems of complexity, intrusion, crowding out, scrutiny and authority: they weaken the ties between the standing to call duty-bearers to account and their responsibilities not to injure claimants.

[86] Ernest J Weinrib, *Corrective Justice* (Oxford University Press, 2012) 10.

[87] Robert Stevens, 'Private Law and the Form of Reasons' in Andrew Robertson and James Goudkamp (eds), *Form and Substance in the Law of Obligations* (Hart Publishing, 2019) 119, 124.

[88] *Palsgraf v Long Island Railroad Co* 162 NE 99, 101 (1928).

[89] ibid 100–101.

[90] Benjamin C Zipursky, 'Substantive Standing, Civil Recourse, and Corrective Justice' (2011) 39 *Florida State University Law Review* 299, 301–04, 320–23.

Such general duties are more effective and justified as parts of public forms of regulation. This public–private distinction (in Cardozo's decision, between criminal law and tort law) is adopted not only by legal theorists. Darwall and Wallace, whose relational moral theories were mentioned above, also distinguish between a criminal paradigm under which wrongdoers are called to account by and on behalf of the community and a private law paradigm under which wrongdoers are called to account by and on behalf of individual agents.[91] The underlying idea is that duty-bearers are not obligated to bring about the best states of affairs (and it might actually wrong the right-holder to do so), but to treat the right-holders in certain ways. The justification of their actions is internal to their relationship with the right-holder.[92]

This idea brings the restrictive and choice-sensitive conception of responsibility to bear on private law.[93] The most visible expression of its influence is the distinction between general and special rights: the latter arise out of contingent transactions or relationships and tend to obligate only the parties to them (property rights are an exception, as they can have only the first but not the second feature).[94] Anglo-American private law, in the spirit of its common law heritage, is still reluctant to impose complex or affirmative duties to protect, aid or benefit (even in cases of easy rescue) absent well-defined forms of assumption of responsibility by the duty-bearer towards particular right-holders.[95]

The clearest case of an assumption of responsibility is a contract. One of the central goals of contract law's apparatus – for example, substantive norms like misrepresentation, mistake, duress or undue influence and interpretive norms that clarify vague terms or fill gaps – is to ensure the integrity of the choice of the parties to assume mutual legal obligations.[96] As we will see, in the special cases in which contractual obligations are imposed, it is on agents that assumed certain roles: for example, sellers cannot choose not to transact with customers because of certain prohibited grounds (say, race or sex). Additionally, contracts cannot obligate third parties; and, importantly, third parties only have the standing to call the contractual parties to account for breaches if the contract grants them this standing, regardless of how badly their interests will be or have been affected by the contract's breach.[97]

[91] Wallace (n 52) 98–100; Darwall, 'Bipolar Obligation' (n 54).

[92] See Paul Hurley, *Beyond Consequentialism* (Oxford University Press, 2009) 118–28, 144–50, 167–72.

[93] See John Oberdiek, 'It's Something Personal: On the Relationality of Duty and Civil Wrongs' in *Civil Wrongs and Justice in Private Law* (n 70) 301.

[94] Jeremy Waldron, *The Right to Private Property* (Oxford University Press, 1988) 106–24.

[95] Ripstein, *Private Wrongs* (n 3) 53–79; Benson, 'Misfeasance' (n 51).

[96] On the centrality of consent in the structure and basic doctrines of contract law, see Nancy S Kim, 'Relative Consent and Contract Law' (2017) 18 *Nevada Law Journal* 165. For critical claims in this regard, see Nathan B Oman, 'Reconsidering Contractual Consent' (2017) 83 *Brooklyn Law Review* 215.

[97] See, eg, the Contracts (Rights of Third Parties) Act 1999, s 1(1), (2); The Restatement (Second) of Contracts (American Law Institute, 1981) § 302, 304. See also Stephen A. Smith, 'Contracts for

In some areas of private law, the boundaries are more vague: for example, tort law, in which duties are imposed rather than voluntarily assumed.[98] The boundaries of general duties – such as not to batter, falsely imprison, or negligently cause physical harms – aim to ensure that adherence to them is intelligible and feasible. Tort law imposes affirmative, complex or demanding duties – not to negligently cause pure emotional or economic harms,[99] or not to cause harms regardless of fault,[100] for example – when the duty-bearer assumes extended responsibilities by performing certain roles on which people rely for protection, aid or beneficence. Much of tort law deals with this delicate interplay between agency and well-being.

Drunk Driving. On New Year's Eve of 1999, a drunk driver coming back from a house party drove his car into oncoming traffic and collided with another car, thereby killing one person and badly injuring three. One of the injured parties, who remained paralysed from the waist down, sued the hosts for negligently failing to prevent the driver from driving, despite his history of drunk driving and his clear state of intoxication. The Supreme Court of Canada rejected the claim.[101] It held that even though the driver's alcoholic tendencies and history of impaired driving were known to the hosts, they had no duties to protect third parties from his negligent driving after leaving the party. Exceptions to the rule that there are no affirmative duties are justified when agents attract patients to risks that they create or control, supervise and control vulnerable patients, or fulfil public roles or benefit from offering services to the public. But the hosts fall into none of these exceptions; and, therefore, there is no sufficient proximity between the parties to justify the imposition of positive duties. Importantly, the analysis does not rely on the fact that the hosts are not well-situated to prevent the harm (they are) or on some balance of interests of hosts, guests and third parties (the harms are quite devastating). Rather, the reasoning focuses on the agency and responsibility of the hosts to third parties, in terms of the creation of risks of harm or the assumption of responsibilities to alleviate risks.

Tort law, like private law more generally, does not treat agency and choice as impartial values that should be promoted or maximised. Rather, it engages

the Benefit of Third Parties: In Defence of the Third-Party Rule' (1997) 17 *Oxford Journal of Legal Studies* 643; JW Neyers, 'Explaining the Principled Exception to Privity of Contract' (2007) 52 *McGill Law Journal* 757.

[98] Even tort duties that expectedly follow an invitation to rely on the duty-bearer, such as duties not to negligently cause pure economic harms, remain distinct from voluntarily assumed contractual duties.

[99] See, eg, Dan B Dobbs, 'Undertakings and Special Relationships in Claims for Negligent Infliction of Emotional Distress' (2008) 50 *Arizona Law Review* 49; Peter Benson, 'The Problem with Pure Economic Loss' (2009) 60 *South California Law Review* 823.

[100] See, eg, Goldberg and Zipursky, *Recognizing Wrongs* (n 3) 190–92; John Gardner, 'Some Rule-of-Law Anxieties about Strict Liability in Private Law' in Lisa M Austin and Dennis Klimchuk (eds), *Private Law and the Rule of Law* (Oxford University Press, 2014) 207, 219.

[101] *Childs v Desormeaux* [2006] SCC 18.

rights and duties and constraints on their possible content from a qualitatively different perspective: it evaluates agency and choice to see when and how private agents can be burdened to serve other people's interests, as part of rights-and-duties relationships.[102] This does not mean that interests are irrelevant or that there is no balancing:[103] only that interests and balancing enter the picture in ways that are shaped by agency and choice within relationships. This also does not mean that our control of private law duties must be absolute: as noted above, and as we will see in later chapters when locating paths from the constitution to private law, the latter works with a normatively thick conception of responsibility,[104] more remote from moral disapprobation and closer to the impact our actions have on others.[105] While this leaves room for private law to resolve collective coordination problems related to the realisation of public goals by assigning responsibilities and duties, the mechanism offered by direct horizontality models is too crude and aggressive. As I add now, they fail to respond to the ways in which the structure and underlying values of private rights-and-duties relationships apply pressures on the norms regulating them to be strictly relational and therefore to push back against external normative influence.

3.5. STRICT RELATIONALITY

The influence exerted by the restrictive conception of responsibility on private law through its procedural structure pushes rights to be tightly paired with duties – and therefore to be specified, peremptory and strictly relational in terms of their focus on the relationship between the right-holder and the duty-bearer. If the loose relationality of constitutional rights expands their scopes towards private law, the strict relationality of private law rights pushes back against such forms of external influence. The metaphor of bipolarity, adopted most famously and forcefully by Ernest Weinrib,[106] captures these two sides of private law: it takes both rights and duties to close the normative circuit; and once the normative circuit is closed, it operates as a self-sufficient and largely closed system. Again, my claims in this regard are not empirical: private rights can and often do take more loosely relational forms – but it is important to engage constitutional horizontality by starting with the trickier cases.

[102] Victor Tadros, 'Secondary Duties' in *Civil Wrongs and Justice in Private Law* (n 70) 185, 200–05.
[103] On these concerns, see Gregory C Keating, 'Form and Substance in the "Private Law" of Torts' (2021) 14 *Journal of Tort Law* 45, 60–62.
[104] See, eg, John CP Goldberg and Benjamin C Zipursky, 'Tort Law and Moral Luck' (2007) 92 *Cornell Law Review* 1123.
[105] Honoré, *Responsibility and Fault* (n 36).
[106] Weinrib, *The Idea of Private Law* (n 3).

3.5.1. Specification

In the previous chapter, the generality of modern constitutional rights – the fact that they can pre-exist and shape the recognition of their correlating duties – was presented as an important step towards their horizontal expansion. Here, in thinking about the opposite normative forces of exclusion, we must first see how personal responsibility pushes private rights in the opposite direction: towards tight correlativity, in the spirit of the will theory of rights.

Necessity. After the Lake Erie Transportation Company finished unloading cargo to a dock owned by Vincent, the ship's captain refused to unmoor it because of an imminent storm. The storm smashed the ship against the dock, thereby causing it serious damage. The Supreme Court of Minnesota agreed that the captain's conduct was justified and added that Vincent had no right to refuse to allow an endangered ship to dock or to unmoor it and send it to a storm, but still held that the company had to compensate Vincent.[107]

While the facts of this case are quite unusual and other courts have ruled differently in similar cases,[108] this case became quite central in private law theory, and it is also echoed in the example, central in rights theory and presented in the previous chapter, about breaking into a secluded cabin to survive a storm. To reiterate, the specificationist holds that if the trespasser's or captain's actions are justified, the cabin or dock owner has no property rights in such cases of necessity; and the generalist holds that there can be rights to property in these cases, but that they are justifiably infringed rather than violated.

Does the *Necessity* case support the existence of a general property right, which people in peril should balance against their interests when considering which protective measures they can take? This issue is contested in property theory. What is important for us is not the state of the law in this or that jurisdiction but the moral pressures that this question exposes. The basic point here is that even if for certain purposes it is helpful to talk about a general private law right to property, to recognise such a right – or, for that matter, to physical integrity, freedom of expression, dignity or privacy – would be complex and burdensome, if we see the right as morally robust and accompanied by the relational normative structures within which rights operate. Such rights, which pre-exist and shape the allocation of duties raise the problems of complexity, intrusion, crowding out, scrutiny and authority.[109]

The problem with general private law rights, whose justified infringements leave a residue dealt with, for example, by compensation, is that such rights significantly strain the private duty-bearer's reasoning: in cases like *Necessity*,

[107] *Vincent v Lake Erie Transportation Co* 124 NW 221 (1910).

[108] See George C Christie, 'The Unwarranted Conclusions Drawn from Vincent v. Lake Erie Transportation Co. concerning the Defense of Necessity' (2006) 5 *Issues in Legal Scholarship* 7–9.

[109] Andrew Robertson, 'Justifying Liabilities and Duties' in Simone Degeling, Michael Crawford and Nicholas Tiverios (eds), *Justifying Private Rights* (Hart Publishing, 2021) 201, 202–05.

we do not and cannot expect the ship captain (or an aeroplane pilot who makes an emergency landing for that matter) to weigh the value of different properties to decide where and when to dock (or land) so as to best realise the general right,[110] as we would from state agents in similar regulatory scenarios. What guides duty-bearers in practice is a general interest in property, which they are not directly obligated to give proper weight to:[111] its partial realisation is not accompanied by the conflict-resolution devices that accompany general rights, like proportionality analysis in constitutional law. In this sense, necessity trumps rather than being balanced against the right to property.[112]

We might still have good reasons to avoid reducing property to a 'bundle' of independent rights, each applying against countless others:[113] for example, reducing information and deliberation costs. However, these reasons do not necessarily justify seeing property as a general right, claimable against other private agents. A general interest in property can underlie concrete and interdependent rights, whose connections are not merely contingent and instrumental.[114] The 'lumpiness' of this rights-cluster and its resistance to external scrutiny can decrease as we move from tangible to intangible forms of property.[115] All this can be maintained while holding that we have no single general private law right to property.

Private law rights are therefore rarely defined in general terms like property or physical integrity: the status of a right is normally ascribed to specific aspects of such terms, such as trespass or battery.[116] Values like property or physical integrity are too complex to be recognised as general private law rights, which apply universally; and private agents will rarely assume extended duties to others to realise the entire scopes of such values. In this context, rights really are peremptory conclusions of normative reasoning, reconciling beneficiary-centered values such as property, privacy or dignity with agent-centered values.[117] This reconciliation does not take the form of open-ended balancing. Rather, we engage the general values from a relational perspective

[110] Christie, 'The Unwarranted Conclusions' (n 108) 13–14.

[111] Peter Jaffey, 'Duties and Liabilities in Private Law' (2006) 12 *Legal Theory* 137, 146; Andrew Halpin, 'Rights, Duties, Liabilities, and Hohfeld' (2007) 13 *Legal Theory* 23, 31–34.

[112] Gregory C Keating, 'Property Right and Tortious Wrong in Vincent v. Lake Erie' (2005) 5 *Issues in Legal Scholarship* 1, 23, 27–32.

[113] Christopher M Newman, 'Using Things, Defining Property' in James Penner and Michael Otsuka (eds), *Property Theory: Legal and Political Perspectives* (Cambridge University Press, 2018) 69, 74.

[114] Jesse Wall, 'Taking the Bundle of Rights Seriously' (2019) 50 *Victoria University of Wellington Law Review*; JE Penner, *Property Rights* (Oxford University Press, 2020) 4–5, 11–15, 41–43, 48–51.

[115] Simon Douglas and Ben McFarlane, 'Defining Property Rights' in James Penner and Henry E Smith (eds), *Philosophical Foundations of Property Law* (Oxford University Press, 2013) 219, 240.

[116] RB Grantham and CEF Rickett, 'Property Rights as a Legally Significant Event' (2003) 62 *Cambridge Law Journal* 717, 737–38.

[117] John Oberdiek, 'Specifying Rights Out of Necessity' (2008) 28 *Oxford Journal of Legal Studies* 127, 135.

that searches for the overlapping areas of these values and the agency and choice of private agents. These values gain weight, in private law, only if we can point to the agent who is responsible to realise them. This means that when rights are recognised, their vectors already point towards particular duty-bearers: for example, dignity gains the force of a right once we centre on the wrong of defamation. In this sense, we do not reason from values to rights and then to duties but, with the specificationist, from values to rights and duties simultaneously – to an inseparable right–duty nexus.

This does not mean rights are just the 'analytical reflex' of the recognition of duties,[118] or that private law operates exclusively through 'duty-based reasoning'.[119] It is more accurate to say that private law rights and duties form perfectly correlating pairs but that the normative environment in which these pairs are shaped pushes legal actors 'to focus on the "duties" side of the equation'.[120] It is in this spirit that I read Patrick Atiyah's claim that English law has 'been more prone to start with duties, and to treat rights as the incidental flow-on from duties, rather than to start with rights and impose duties to protect those rights'.[121]

Neither rights nor duties have justificatory priority in private law: they form inseparable pairs. However, agent-centered considerations are more dominant in shaping these pairs; and, thus, Atiyah's complaint that beneficiary-centered considerations are often neglected,[122] or Gregory Keating's complaint that private law theories tend to focus on wrongs rather than rights,[123] are not entirely off the mark. To borrow Waldron's words, private law's approach to rights focuses more on how agency must be exercised (each agent is concerned mostly with keeping a clean personal slate) than on people's well-being.[124] To echo our discussion of moral paradigms in the first chapter, this account of rights expresses 'a particular aspect of moral personality: the active, practical, and assertive side of human life, as opposed to the passive, affective, or even pathological side', and 'principles of laissez-faire and minimalist theories of the state'.[125] While we will see that private law often deviates from this picture,

[118] Weinrib, *The Idea of Private Law* (n 3) 123–26.

[119] John CP Goldberg and Benjamin C Zipursky, 'The Moral of *Macpherson*' (1998) 146 *University of Pennsylvania Law Review* 1733, 1845.

[120] Tadros, 'Secondary Duties' (n 102) 198–99. See also Peter Cane, 'Rights in Private Law' in *Rights and Private Law* (n 49) 35, 43.

[121] PS Atiyah, *Pragmatism and Theory in English Law* (Stevens and Sons, 1987) 18. See also Neil MacCormick, *Legal Right and Social Democracy* (Oxford University Press, 1984) 223.

[122] Atiyah, *Pragmatism and Theory in English Law* (n 121) 21.

[123] Gregory C Keating, 'Duty or Right? A Comment on John Gardner's *From Personal Life to Private Law*' (2017) 15 *Jerusalem Review of Legal Studies* 152, 153–58.

[124] Waldron, *The Right to Private Property* (n 94) 76–77; Jeremy Waldron, 'Rights in Conflict' (1989) 99 *Ethics* 503, 505.

[125] Jeremy Waldron, 'Introduction' in Jeremy Waldron (ed), *Theories of Rights* (Oxford University Press, 1984) 1, 11. See also Thomas Nagel, 'Libertarianism Without Foundations' (1975) 85 *Yale Law Journal* 136, 143–44.

it still exerts a strong normative pull. To be effective and justified, large-scale reasons for regulation must respond to rather than ignore this pull – including its implications regarding the specification of rights.

3.5.2. Exclusion

The next and crucial step in the argument is to see how specified right–duty nexuses exclude or push back against constitutional reasons for regulation. These clusters include what Raz called 'exclusionary reasons': rather than providing a counterweight to first-order reasons, these are second-order reasons not to include certain first-order reasons in our deliberation;[126] for example, being too tired to weigh reasons for and against buying a car at the dealership has nothing to do with first-order reasons about the transaction but about the choice situation.

Darwall's description of the normative structure of moral relationships as a circle of interdependent concepts, to which there is no breaking into from the outside, conveys a similar idea:[127] we cannot just hold, for example, that someone has the standing to call another agent to account, without adequately tying their claims to neighbouring concepts such as interests, responsibility, accountability, injury, wrong, reactive attitudes, and remedies. The point is not to balance these concepts as values. Rather, justifications that do not fit within this relational structure gain no weight in our reasoning.

In this spirit, reasons external to private rights-and-duties relationships, including constitutional reasons, cannot be directly relied on to justify the recognition of horizontal legal rights and duties. There are second-order moral reasons, cemented in private law's foundations but exerting influence beyond it, to exclude such external justifications if they cannot be integrated within relational normative structures. As noted above, because the constitution must also take morality into account, the horizontal delineation of constitutional rights cannot ignore such second-order exclusionary reasons.

The problems of complexity, intrusion, crowding out, scrutiny and authority can only be resolved by taking the unique normativity of private rights seriously. Even law-creating state agents must take into account the ways in which rights operate in practice, on the ground: the ripple effects of direct reliance on constitutional reasons – interwoven with third-party interests and complex public goals – justify more nuanced forms of reasoning, which

[126] Joseph Raz, 'Postscript to the Second Edition: Rethinking Exclusionary Reasons' in *Practical Reason and Norms*, 2nd edn (Oxford University Press, 1999) 178, 185.

[127] I rely here on Darwall, *The Second-Person Standpoint* (n 52) 8, 12–13.

address the unique connections between the right-holder's interests and the duty-bearer's agency.

Therefore, it is difficult to justify an obligation to enter a contract because the duty-bearer has a good whose reallocation to the other party can promote a more egalitarian social distribution of goods; or absolving a poor person who negligently caused devastating physical harms to a rich person from paying compensation merely because of the regressive consequences of this remedial action. Such reasons for regulation are, again, in the wrong normative key, insofar as many private law rights-and-duties relationships are concerned.

What seems to bother many private law practitioners and theorists – like moral theorists criticising different versions of consequentialism – are forms of aggregation or systematisation between interactions. Private law does not impose duties to reduce contractual promise-breaking or negligent harms in society: only not to break our promises or to negligently harm others. It therefore resists what Scheffler called a 'maximizing rationality'.[128] While private law defines rights, it does not aim to maximise their exercise or minimise their violation.[129] Even if actions are defined as wrongs and have impartial disvalue, right-holders have the discretion about how to respond to them and duty-bearers are only obligated to avoid them. Third parties, whether public (such as judges) or private (such as insurers), might have reasons to respond to private law wrongs in certain ways, but these reasons do not have the status of primary duties of conduct owed to particular right-holders.[130]

As Weinrib notes, private law norms are elements in the right-holder's and the duty-bearer's 'immediate interaction as such',[131] and their justifications focus on their relationship.[132] They can still refer to states of affairs, such as ensuring timely delivery of goods or preventing certain harms to customers frequenting a bookstore.[133] Such duties can be demanding and ongoing: for example, employers can have duties to cover the costs of medical monitoring for employees negligently exposed to toxic substances, to try to prevent the increased risk of disease (that they created) from materialising.[134]

[128] Samuel Scheffler, 'Agent-Centered Restrictions, Rationality, and the Virtues' (1985) 94 *Mind* 409, 414.

[129] See PS Atiyah, 'The Practice of Promising' in *Promises, Morals and Law* (Oxford University Press, 1981) 138; Dan Priel, 'Tort Law for Cynics' (2014) 77 *Modern Law Review* 703, 718–20.

[130] Gardner, *From Personal Life to Private Law* (n 3) 108–10.

[131] Ernest Weinrib, 'The Insurance Justification and Private Law' (1985) 14 *Journal of Legal Studies* 681, 683.

[132] Ernest Weinrib, 'Deterrence and Corrective Justice' (2002) 50 *UCLA Law Review* 621, 624. See also Andrew Robertson, 'Constraints on Policy-Based Reasoning in Private Law' in Andrew Robertson and Tang Hang Wu (eds), *The Goals of Private Law* (Hart Publishing, 2009) 261; Nicholas J McBride, *The Humanity of Private Law – Part I: Explanation* (Hart Publishing, 2019) 40.

[133] Robertson, 'Justifying Liabilities and Duties' (n 109) 212.

[134] John CP Goldberg and Benjamin C Zipursky, 'Unrealized Torts' (2002) 88 *Virginia Law Review* 1625.

Such duties can also obligate to protect from third parties: for example, the owner of an apartment building can have a duty to keep the door locks in good condition, to prevent third parties from entering. However, and this is the important point, these duties do not involve balancing the interests of different right-holders: we will not say, for example, that the building owner can spend less money on the locks of a building with 20 tenants so that he can spend more money on the locks of a building with 50, or 200, tenants. We figure out the content of the duty in each owner–tenant relationship, engaged in relative isolation.

Therefore – again, unlike in constitutional law – the duty-bearer might have conflicting legal duties that cannot be discharged simultaneously, which would require proportionality analysis or some other version of rights-realisation reasoning on a social scale. If I expand my pub and incur more duties to more employees, I do not thereby owe less duties to the neighbours. This does not mean that consequentialist considerations about which activities should be permitted are irrelevant: in fact, they are inescapable.[135] Rather, the idea is that if a social activity is permitted by public law – building a pub in a residential neighbourhood, for example – the allocation of duties through private law will assume this background decision rather than keep reflecting on and developing it. We can switch between the perspectives – one of the main roles of constitutional horizontality is to say when and how – but once we go down the private law path, we adopt a relational perspective.

To summarise, the relationality of private law rights is not merely loose, in the sense that their correlative duties determine how we must or must not treat right-holders as opposed to how we must conduct ourselves in general.[136] In this loose sense, we can also talk about rights under public forms of regulation. In private law, relationality is stricter both in the sense that rights are claimed and enforced by their holders and in terms of the values that underlie and shape rights, which refer to the right-holder's relationship with the duty-bearer and therefore push towards specification and the exclusion of reasons for regulation that fail to address this relationship. The problem with direct horizontality models is that they are rather oblivious to these limitations, which might even be seen as shackles that constitutional horizontality must break. But we started seeing – and the next chapters will develop this point – that private law's relationality can also be seen as a morally justified response to the normative structure and underlying values of private rights-and-duties relationships. This relationality is necessary to reduce the problems of complexity, intrusion, crowding out, scrutiny and authority to reasonable dimensions.

[135] See Kenneth W Simons, 'Tort Negligence, Cost–Benefit Analysis, and Tradeoffs: A Closer Look at the Controversy' (2008) 41 *Loyola of Los Angeles Lew Review* 1171; John Oberdiek, *Imposing Risk* (Oxford University Press, 2017) 131–33.

[136] This loose form of relationality is adopted in Goldberg and Zipursky, *Recognizing Wrongs* (n 3) 92–93.

3.6. PRIVATE SPHERES

This chapter has built on the unique normativity and underlying values of private rights-and-duties relationships, largely in isolation from the political collective, to criticise direct horizontality. It is quite clear, though, and acknowledged even by private law theorists who see it as inherently strictly relational and isolated from distributive or policy goals, that private law has public aspects.[137] For example, its norms are created and disputes about them are often adjudicated by state agents. It is therefore important to emphasise, on the one hand, that the state is not out of the strictly relational picture presented in this chapter but in its background – and later chapters will gradually move it to the foreground, while building on the arguments made in this chapter; but, on the other hand, that while abstraction and simplification drive these arguments, they do capture basic aspects of private law and of constitutional horizontality.

Water Supply. In the second half of the nineteenth century, Bradford was one of the fastest-growing cities in Britain. After several decades in which it used water from a spring, fed by water flowing through Mr Pickles' land, he announced his plan to drain the water and attempt to mine flagstone. In response to claims that Mr Pickles had no property right to do so, the House of Lords ruled that he could do whatever he wanted with his land: even if the results were socially undesirable and even for selfish, malicious or vexatious reasons.[138]

This case, as Michael Taggart claimed, is not a mere museum piece: 'it remains an integral part of the common lawyers' private law mindset', that sees even weighty public goals, such as securing a sprawling city's water supply, as trumped by private rights.[139] This case captures, to the point of caricature, the narrow focus that private law's strict relationality can lead to. But the caricature is only part of the picture: after all, parliament may expropriate Mr Pickles' water rights through public law. Strictly relational private law rights are not natural or pre-political, and are not directed against the state in its regulatory capacity. The judges simply did not want to make such redistributive decisions themselves, by using common private law tools.[140] Their hesitations and the resulting institutional and substantive divisions of labour reflect the paradigmatic distinction that this chapter and the previous one described: between collective responsibility and social justice on the one hand, and personal responsibility and relational morality on the other. Even in crude forms, these distinctions cannot be ignored: to adequately understand and shape constitutional horizontality, we must expose and explain the sources of

[137] See Ernest J Weinrib, 'Adjudication and Public Values: Fiss's Critique of Corrective Justice' (1989) 39 *University of Toronto Law Journal* 1; Ernest J Weinrib, 'Private Law and Public Right' (2011) 61 *University of Toronto Law Journal* 191, 196–97.

[138] *Bradford v Pickles* [1895] AC 587.

[139] Michael Taggart, *Private Property and Abuse of Rights in Victorian England: The Story of Edward Pickles and the Bradford Water Supply* (Oxford University Press, 2002) 195–203.

[140] Waddams, *Dimensions of Private Law* (n 18) 212–15.

resistance to it in its most challenging forms. We cannot deny that at least as a matter of what we owe to our neighbours (well, perhaps not if they are cities), Mr Pickles at least had a point.

This case highlights, quite vividly, the fact that private law is part of the basic structure of society. It is a form of regulation through which the political collective allocates benefits and burdens. Against this background, direct horizontality is quite appealing. But this case also highlights private law's limitations as a regulatory tool: the fact that because private law relies on private norm-enforcement, some reasons for regulation are excluded from or marginalised in this segment of the regulatory process. The next chapters will show that this is important not only as a matter of relational morality but also as a matter of social and constitutional justice: taking the unique features of strictly relational rights seriously can help constitutional horizontality be more justified and effective. Cases like *Water Supply* should not lead us, therefore, to the conclusion that private law should be seen instead as a public form of regulation: we should allow the tension to inform our analysis. While the state does pursue many public goals by recognising rights that are exercised and enforced in private relationships, this pursuit, even when constitutionally-grounded, is limited by relational normative factors, touching the ways in which private rights empower and private right-based duties constrain.

3.6.1. Conservatism

Importantly, these arguments do not rely on or lead to simple and rigid forms of conservatism, which have been associated with common private law for centuries: it has been described as a domain that largely ignores the ability to bring about justified social states of affairs through regulation, and normally responds to large-scale normative concerns by evolving organically and incrementally, while remaining close to its existing moral trajectory.[141] These claims are often coupled with concerns about the competence and democratic legitimacy of the judiciary that, it is assumed, carries the mantle in developing private law;[142] and they are often underpinned by a largely Kantian vision of a compossible system of stable and negative rights, which do not require legal agents to resort to contested values in complex balancing procedures.[143]

[141] Weinrib, *The Idea of Private Law* (n 3) 13; Benjamin E Zipursky, 'Pragmatic Conceptualism' (2000) 6 *Legal Theory* 457, 468–69. See also FA Hayek, *Law, Legislation, and Liberty: Volume 2 – The Mirage of Social Justice* (Routledge, 1982) 24–25; Frederick Schauer, *Thinking Like a Lawyer* (Harvard University Press, 2009) 105, 116–17.

[142] See, eg, Ross Grantham and Darryn Jensen, 'The Proper Role of Policy in Private Law Adjudication' (2018) 68 *University of Toronto Law Journal* 187, 197–98.

[143] Nigel E Simmonds, 'Rights at the Cutting Edge' in *A Debate Over Rights: Philosophical Enquiries* (Oxford University Press, 1998) 113, 117–18, 135–36, 176–86; Hillel Steiner, 'Working Rights' in *A Debate Over Rights* (ibid) 233, 264–74.

Theories that follow these lines have been criticised for portraying private law as libertarian,[144] regressive,[145] anachronistic,[146] and isolated from the rest of the regulatory system.[147] As a matter of fact, all state branches are involved in private law's development as a set of goal-oriented regulatory tools, which aim to influence social structures and distributive patterns – and for good moral reasons. The appearance of strict relationality results from the fact that beneficiary-centered values can be realised only when tied to a duty-bearer's agency, and the fact that over time such values get buried under layers of strictly relational doctrines, which become 'entrenched and ossified' and relatively immune to influence by external considerations.[148] But the fact remains that these layers can always be peeled off – and leaving them where they are is a policy choice that must be substantively justified. Tying private law's resistance to constitutional horizontality to its relational form leaves room for such normative processes.[149]

While the main point of constitutional horizontality is to apply normative pressure to 'entrenched and ossified' norms, thereby pushing them towards social justice, it must be accepted that private law is inherently limited as a form of regulation: it not only leaves central activities of entitlement creation or exchange and calling to account to private agents,[150] but is also, because of this procedural feature, subjected to substantive limitations of its possible content. The important distinctions in this regard are not about the values that underlie private law or constitutional law but about the normative structure of their right-norms; and, therefore, these limits also apply when constitutional law expands horizontally by recognising private rights and duties.

A good example of the constraining force of this normative structure is the tortification of discrimination law in the United States: the process through which federal courts have, over decades, subordinated its promotion of equality to the requirement that duties be grounded in their bearers' responsibilities to the right-holders to whom the duty-bearer is accountable.[151] For example, legislatively-created employer duties not to be motivated by biases (even if they

[144] Stephen R Perry, 'Professor Weinrib's Formalism:The Not-so-empty Sepulchre' (1993) 16 *Harvard Journal of Law & Public Policy* 597, 603–07; Dan Priel, 'The Political Origins of English Private Law' (2013) 4 *Journal of Law & Society* 481, 502–07.

[145] George P Fletcher, 'Corrective Justice for Moderns' (1993) 106 *Harvard Law Review* 1658, 1668.

[146] Gregory C Keating, 'Personal Inviolability and "Private Law"' (2007) 1 *Journal of Tort Law*.

[147] TT Arvind and Joanna Gray, 'The Limits of Technocracy: Private Law's Future in the Regulatory State' in *Private Law in the 21st Century* (n 43) 237, 238.

[148] Schauer, *Thinking Like a Lawyer* (n 141) 15–16, 106. See also Hugh Collins, *Regulating Contracts* (Oxford University Press, 1999) 35, 38, 52.

[149] See also Donal Nolan and Andrew Robertson, 'Rights and Private Law' in *Rights and Private Law* (n 49) 1, 2–7, 26.

[150] Benjamin C Zipursky, 'The Inner Morality of Private Law' (2013) 58 *American Journal of Jurisprudence* 27, 36–42.

[151] Tom Kohavi, 'Discrimination Law as Private Law' (forthcoming) *Albany Law Review*.

are not but-for causes of adverse decisions) were applied in a restricted manner; and causation requirements were imposed on duties that the legislature did not explicitly exempt from this general tort principle, which was seen as applying in discrimination law as well. When it comes to more complex duties, such as to accommodate disability or prevent harassment, judges have made efforts to ensure that the burdens are reasonable – again often by finding nooks and crannies in legislation through which tort principles can enter. Similarly, judges in the United Kingdom have treated the proportionality component in employment legislation, such as duties against indirect discrimination, as a categorical threshold requirement that employers can meet relatively easily by pointing at business objectives, whose importance is not thoroughly scrutinised from a broader perspective.[152] It has been claimed, more generally, that even when discrimination law fails to promote equality, it tends to avoid imposing duties on new categories of agents towards new categories of beneficiaries or complex duties weakly tied to personal responsibility.[153] This shows that even the evolution and application of policy-infused domains like discrimination law are shaped by the inherent relationality of private rights and duties and their ties to the restrictive notion of responsibility. This is a crucial point for understanding the nature and limits of constitutional horizontality.

3.6.2. The State

So far, I have been talking about the state in its regulatory or political function. However, the state is often a private law right-holder or duty-bearer: it can own property, enter contracts, and negligently harm, for example. I should therefore add that despite the fact that I am not making any definitive claims here about the nature or scope of private law, there is something odd about treating the state's rights or duties as 'private': after all, both the interests that justify rights and the responsibilities to discharge duties are collective.

When thinking about what the state owes to us as a private law duty-bearer, it makes little sense to rely on the strictly relational apparatus that draws its force from the restrictive conception of personal responsibility – and may even prove morally wrong. As Scheffler noted, we should be careful not to engage moral concepts outside the adequate domains of their normative extension.[154] Stelios Tofaris and Sandy Steel claim, for example, that the justifications for not imposing tort duties of care in cases of pure omissions are much weaker when applied

[152] Aaron Baker, 'Proportionality and Employment Discrimination in the UK' (2008) 37 *Industrial Law Journal* 305.

[153] Colm O'Cinneide, 'New Directions Needed: Exponential Equalities and the Limits of Equality Law' in Shreya Atrey and Sandra Fredman (eds), *Exponential Inequalities: Equality Law in Times of Crisis* (Oxford University Press, 2023) 123.

[154] Samuel Scheffler, 'Morality and Reasonable Partiality' in *Equality and Tradition: Questions of Value in Moral and Political Theory* (Oxford University Press, 2012) 41, 69–72.

to the state and especially to institutions like the police, which are tasked with preventing harms to vulnerable individuals.[155] It could be claimed that public agents can only do what they are legally authorised to do, and positive duties can therefore be imposed on them only when legislation recognises certain overarching powers that must be exercised reasonably – and in this sense, even positive state duties of care are still special rather than general.[156] However, when delineating these special duties (we will see in later chapters that this is often where the action is when it comes to constitutional horizontality), the restrictive conception does much less work than it does when it comes to private agents: we ask questions about the purpose of legislation, the structural or allocative roles of public agents, and their ability to realise social justice principles. We can see this in discrimination law: private (and often statutory) anti-discrimination duties are about the terms of one-to-one interactions, which involve dialogical normative processes, while public (and often constitutional) anti-discrimination duties are about social conditions and general justifications – and in this sense, the related wrongs of discrimination are also different.[157]

Things are trickier when it comes to the state as a private law right-holder. The agency and responsibility of private agents as duty-bearers are not irrelevant in their relationships with the state. Negligence or contract breaches are not excused if they result in harms to state interests: first, because they can also result in harms to people in their non-official capacity – for example, if I negligently injure a police officer; second, because even when it comes to pure public interests, we are responsible and accountable as duty-bearers for the exercise of our agency. If there is a difference, it is that in such cases there is more leeway to take policy reasons into account when delineating private responsibilities and liabilities. For example, if a poor person negligently harms public property, it is easier to justify limiting the amount of compensation – while engaging the case from a redistributive perspective.

I will touch on such cases in later chapters. The important point, at this stage, is that for the purpose of thinking about constitutional horizontality, we can treat cases in which the state is a private law right-holder or duty-bearer as marginal. It is preferable, from an explanatory perspective, to go back to the state after we have clarified the challenge in more complex cases, in which there is stronger resistance to the influence of constitutional reasons.

[155] Stelios Tofaris and Sandy Steel, 'Negligence Liability for Omissions and the Police' (2016) 75 *Cambridge Law Journal* 128.

[156] Tom Cornford, 'The Negligence Liability of Public Authorities for Omissions' (2019) 78 *Cambridge Law Journal* 545.

[157] Anthony Sangiuliano, 'Can There Be a Unified Doctrine of Anti-discrimination in Canada?' (2022) 18 *Journal of Law and Equality* 1.

3.7. CONCLUSION

This chapter started by highlighting the moral deficiencies of direct constitutional horizontality, which struggles to adequately integrate constitutional reasons within private rights-and-duties relationships because it cannot compute their unique normativity. This chapter drew, in this regard, from criticisms of consequentialist moral theories and of instrumentalist private law theories. It highlighted the ways in which private law's procedural structure invites relational morality to shape and constrain its evolution and therefore the substance of its norms: for instance, the limits of contracting or duties not to harm. It was shown that even if the political collective is present in private law in many ways, it is both descriptively inaccurate and morally problematic to say that private agents make or contest rights-claims against each other on the collective's behalf. In this sense, private law is not and should not be 'public law in disguise';[158] and the political collective's presence in it must remain more nuanced.

Direct horizontality is problematic in this regard not only in terms of feasibility but also because it crudely politicises private legal rights-and-duties relationships. It ignores the ways in which private rights invite expectations and therefore blame – and how the proliferation of agents authorised to call us to account for our actions in the name of the political collective would change workplaces, university seminars, family homes, and other private relationships, associations and practices. Because it threatens to erode or distort values internal to such social spheres, in which the state is less directly involved, direct horizontality also threatens to diminish the force and value of private rights, and therefore also their ability to realise constitutional rights.

Direct horizontality fails to acknowledge not only the dramatic implications of the large-scale teleological normativity of constitutional rights, but also the ability of relational private law principles to contribute to the effectiveness and justification of constitutional horizontality. Direct horizontality effectively establishes a parallel track of legal evolution, that both ignores and intrudes into private law. The problem here is not merely the failure to take advantage of centuries of attempts to do what constitutional horizontality tries to do, even if less ambitiously: to realise public values through the regulation of private relationships. It is also that private law expresses forms of reasoning that focus on what we owe to each other directly, which constitutional reasoning cannot merely borrow or imitate. The imposition of constitutional private duties, distinct from private law, will therefore not only leave many private law domains undisturbed, but also fail to harness private law's relational principles.[159]

[158] Green (n 4).

[159] Edward Béchard-Torres, 'Social Rights and Transformative Private Law' (2023) 60 *Osgoode Hall Law Journal* 375, 391–92.

Now, these claims are provisional, in two important senses. First, private law is not entirely strictly relational: as we will see in later chapters, there are, for example, abstract standards that respond to public goals (like duty in negligence law or good faith in contract law), aggregative devices like class actions, and heavy involvement of regulatory public bodies. I presented strict relationality as a structural rather than substantive starting point with the aim of leaving room for further questions about its ability to accommodate constitutional reasons, in what might be described as private law's margins – without reducing reasoning about these margins to open-ended forms of policy calculations. I will claim that moving from the core to the margins allows us to devise more principled reasoning structures.

The second way in which my claims are provisional is that they leave room for direct horizontality in some special cases. Burdening private agents with constitutional and strictly relational duties not to torture or enslave, for example, seems quite justified. Duties to protect people from torture or enslavement are more problematic, but they can also be justified in special relationships.[160] Direct horizontality can therefore remain in our toolbox. The problem with it is as a general model: by working only from the top-down, it lacks the tools to say when it is justified and when it is not. For this, we need theories of constitutional horizontality that can take more seriously the normativity of private rights-and-duties relationships.

Importantly, narrowing the scopes of constitutional rights in terms of the agents that they obligate – holding that they obligate primarily and preliminarily the political collective – need not reduce their scopes in terms of actions and activities. On the contrary, this narrowing facilitates their expansion in terms of actions and activities: it allows us to bring additional aspects of beneficiary-centered values like privacy, equality or dignity to bear on private relationships. Somewhat counterintuitively, it can contribute to the effectiveness of constitutional horizontality. Indirect models of horizontality, to which the next chapters turn, rely on this possibility to offer regulatory avenues that make better use of private law's resources.

[160] This is a possible reading of the 13th Amendment to the Constitution of the United States, according to which 'neither slavery nor involuntary servitude … shall exist within the United States …'.

4

Pluralistic Realisation

4.1. FROM DELINEATION TO REALISATION

THE PREVIOUS TWO chapters dealt with the horizontal delineation of constitutional rights. It was claimed that their scopes can be horizontally wide in terms of the actions and activities that they address, which can also be private, but not in terms of the agents that they obligate to respond to such actions and activities, who are normally public. But delineation is only half of the picture. The recognition of general and complex rights means that more actions and activities are constitutionally evaluated to separate justified infringements from unjustified violations.[1] This process offers no neat solutions: to properly realise such rights in sub-constitutional law, we must regularly resolve normative conflicts that involve competing reasons for regulation.

The underlying premise of the common constitutional model is that rights are not absolute: they may be realised only partly. It is reflected in the recognition of rights alongside 'limitations clauses' determining the conditions for their infringement.[2] These clauses are often applied through a series of tests referred to as 'proportionality analysis': in general terms, first, the reviewed action or activity must pursue legitimate public goals; second, the action or activity must be suitable to pursue these goals; third, there must not be actions or activities that can pursue these goals with similar effectiveness while having a smaller adverse impact on the right; finally, the benefits of the action or activity in terms of the promotion of public goals must exceed the burdens in terms of their adverse impact on the affected rights.[3]

It is therefore misleading to talk about general constitutional rights as trumps or as having categorical priority.[4] Because they are not fully specified, their scopes

[1] Kai Möller, 'Proportionality and Rights Inflation' in Grant Huscroft, Bradley W Miller and Grégoire Webber (eds), *Proportionality and the Rule of Law: Rights, Justification, Reasoning* (Cambridge University Press, 2014) 155; Jeff King, *Judging Social Rights* (Cambridge University Press, 2012) 193–98.

[2] Limitations clauses can be general (eg, Article 36 of the Constitution of South Africa (1996); Article 1 of the Canadian Charter of Rights and Freedoms (1982)) or specific (eg, Article 8(2) of the European Convention on Human Rights (1950)). See generally Aharon Barak, *Proportionality: Constitutional Rights and Their Limitations* (Cambridge University Press, 2012) 80–82, 262–77.

[3] Barak, *Proportionality* (n 2); Grant Huscroft, Bradley W Miller and Grégoire Webber, 'Introduction' in *Proportionality and the Rule of Law* (n 1) 1.

[4] See generally Andrei Marmor, 'On the Limits of Rights' (1997) 16 *Law and Philosophy* 1.

include reasons that can be defeated but still require the duty-bearer's ongoing attention and care.[5] It is also misleading to talk about the second stage of constitutional rights-based reasoning as being about the ex-post judicial evaluation of adverse actions or activities. Judicial scrutiny also addresses forward-looking constitutional principles that guide and constrain rights realisation, and touch not only isolated actions or activities but also the large-scale impact of regulation – including the concerns, discussed in the previous chapter, about complexity, intrusion, crowding out, scrutiny and authority.

These issues often arise in litigation. For example, a private law defendant can reply to a claimant by holding that the norms on which their allegations are founded are unconstitutional: in *Eviction*, for example, a tenant claimed that her right to respect for home justified subjecting a company's right to take possession of her home to substantive fairness tests, not recognised in private law.[6] Alternatively, a claimant could hold that a defendant should be held liable according to a new cause of action, whose non-recognition is unconstitutional. For example, supermodel Naomi Campbell claimed that a tabloid that published photographs of her leaving a Narcotics Anonymous meeting and articles exposing her ongoing treatment should be held liable according to a new tort protecting her privacy.[7] Both defensive and offensive constitutional horizontality claims raise concerns endemic to litigation that the next chapter addresses. But the horizontal aspects of constitutional rights obligate duty-bearers regardless of actual right-claims. Even if such claims are regularly made in litigation – which remains central for elucidating and developing constitutional norms – duty-bearers must constantly strive to realise constitutional rights to a justified extent. For example, a legislative committee might recommend the abolition or recognition of private law norms, while grounding its claims in the unconstitutionality of the current legal regime.

This means that before getting to the features of claims or decisions about constitutional horizontality by particular agents in specific institutional settings, we should address the features of reasons and duties to realise rights: the ways in which constitutional rights constrain and guide regulatory activities, while being reconciled with competing reasons for regulation. This chapter zeroes in on this issue by showing how indirect horizontality – which sees mostly state agents as obligated to realise constitutional rights, but also in private spheres – can alleviate the problems of direct horizontality. However, it adds that indirect horizontality models can be too strong if they construe realisation reasoning as overly consequentialist: if they fail to create sufficient distance from direct models and therefore raise similar (even if more nuanced) concerns. The problem, I will claim, is that such models do not take seriously the predicament of moral

[5] See Leif Wenar, 'The Value of Rights' in Joseph Keim Campbell, Michael O'Rourke, and David Shier (eds), *Law and Social Justice* (MIT Press, 2005) 179, 187–88.

[6] *McDonald v McDonald* [2016] UKSC 28.

[7] *Campbell v MGN Ltd* [2004] UKHL 22.

pluralism. I will present this predicament and explain how a contractualist approach to realisation reasoning can help us respond to it by leaving more room for relational reasons for regulation.

4.2. GOING INDIRECT

Indirect models of constitutional horizontality come in many shapes and forms. Their shared principle is that constitutional rights obligate mostly state agents (*contra* direct horizontality), but that these obligations also address private actions and activities (*contra* traditional verticality). State agents must therefore shape and apply private law norms in ways that adequately realise constitutional rights – in the spirit of the interest theory, according to which rights entail 'waves of duties'.[8] These models echo the shift in moral philosophy from consequentialist theories that target individual actions to consequentialist theories that target social institutions or systems of rules: a move that responds to criticisms of consequentialism as a decision procedure – but not as a standard of evaluation, from which such procedures can be derived.[9]

This indirect structure licenses the recognition of complex and conflicting norms whose realisation requires abilities and resources that private agents lack.[10] As Henry Shue noted in the human rights context, 'isolated and uncoordinated efforts by individuals are materially wasteful and can be psychologically oppressive to no good purpose': while 'indirect duties could be more demanding than direct duties', the 'institutions established for the purpose of coordinating individual responses' can constitute an important 'psychological buffer'.[11] This buffer can improve the effectiveness and justification of constitutional horizontality practices. It allows indirect models to avoid the isolation of the private from the public by exposing more social spheres to constitutional rights influence, without subordinating the private to the public, as the burdens placed on private agents are carefully filtered by public agents.

The idea of indirect horizontality originated in the *Boycott* case, mentioned in the first chapter, in which the German Constitutional Court recognised the 'radiating effect' of constitutional rights. Different versions of indirect horizontality later appeared, for example, in decisions of the European Court of Human Rights (unsurprisingly, given its exclusive jurisdiction over states) and the supreme courts of Canada and the United Kingdom. While my arguments

[8] Jeremy Waldron, 'Rights in Conflict' (1989) 99 *Ethics* 503, 509–12.

[9] David O Brink, 'Utilitarian Morality and the Personal Point of View' (1986) 86 *Journal of Philosophy* 417; Paul Hurley, *Beyond Consequentialism* (Oxford University Press, 2009) 36–46. See generally Brad Hooker, 'Rule Consequentialism' in Edward N Zalta and Uri Nodelman (eds), *The Stanford Encyclopedia of Philosophy* (Spring 2023).

[10] Contra Onora O'Neill, 'The Dark Side of Human Rights' (2005) 81 *International Affairs* 427, 436.

[11] Henry Shue, 'Mediating Duties' (1988) 98 *Ethics* 687, 696–97.

do not depend on this trend, there are claims in the literature that liberal legal systems are moving away from verticality and direct horizontality, towards indirect horizontality.[12] What is more important for us are the intrinsic normative features of indirect models, which can often, as I will claim in the following chapters, better respond to the challenge of horizontality.

4.2.1. Normative Triangles

Under indirect models, state failures to properly regulate private actions or activities can violate constitutional rights, even if such actions or activities cannot. Because constitutional duties can be imposed on any state agent, questions arise about the distinction between direct and indirect models when the latter see judges as obligated to realise constitutional rights and private agents as empowered to claim that judges must create new private law rights in private disputes.[13] A somewhat technical way of describing the difference is that while direct horizontality entails private constitutional duties, indirect horizontality entails private law duties. This has implications for the relations between state agents: if judicial decisions are made at the constitutional level, it will often be more difficult for later administrative or legislative decisions to contradict them. But the more important differences for us touch the relationships between private agents, where the buffer of state regulation can alleviate the problems of complexity, intrusion, crowding out, scrutiny and authority. To explain the nature of this buffer, we must first see how private relationships are regulated by a triadic cluster of legal norms under indirect models.

Discrimination. In the first chapter, I mentioned the case of a Colorado bakery owner who refused to sell a wedding cake to gay customers, because gay marriage conflicted with his Christian beliefs.[14] The Supreme Court of the United States held that there was no unlawful discrimination, while largely ignoring the competing rights to equality and freedom of religion, focusing instead on the hostile and non-neutral conduct of the state of Colorado towards the baker. Compare this with the approach of the Supreme Court of the United Kingdom in a case dealing with the religiously-grounded refusal of owners of a guesthouse to provide a double room to a gay couple. The Court adopted an indirect approach, holding that 'while both parties can assert their rights against the state', they 'cannot assert their rights directly against' each

[12] Johan van der Walt, *The Horizontal Effect Revolution and the Question of Sovereignty* (de Gruyter, 2014) 3–4; Jud Mathews, *Extending Rights' Reach* (Oxford University Press, 2018) 4–6.

[13] Nick Friedman, 'The South African Common Law and the Constitution: Revisiting Horizontality' (2014) 30 *South African Journal on Human Rights* 63, 70–74; Mattias Kumm and Victor Ferreres Comella, 'What Is So Special about Constitutional Rights in Private Litigation?' in Andras Sajó and Renata Uitz (eds), *The Constitution in Private Relations: Expanding Constitutionalism* (Eleven International Publishing, 2005) 241, 252–56.

[14] *Masterpiece Cakeshop v Colorado Civil Rights Commission* 584 US 617 (2018).

other; and that the claims against the state do not focus on each party's separate relationship with the state but on a balance of the owners' right to freedom of religion and the couple's rights to equality.[15] This triangular structure reappeared in the Court's decision about a religiously-grounded refusal of a baking company to supply a cake with the message 'support gay marriage': the decisive factor in reading the relevant legislation was that the objection was to the message on the cake and not to the buyer's identity – a factor that touches the relationship of the parties, rather than the relationship between the baker and the state (as in the United States).[16] Importantly, this relational focus does not mean that the state drops completely out of the picture.

Fertility Treatment.[17] A woman started fertility treatments with her partner before her ovaries were removed. The relationship broke down before the embryos were implanted. The partner wanted to exercise his right to have them destroyed, which was formalised in a consent form signed at the clinic, in line with the United Kingdom's Human Fertilisation and Embryology Act 1990. The woman claimed that the partner's legal power to withdraw his consent violated her Convention right to respect for private and family life. The European Court of Human Rights noted that while the domestic courts saw the case as being about state interference with the woman's right, it is actually about the state's duties to balance between the rights of both parties – to become or not to become a parent – and public interests, such as the importance of consent and legal clarity and certainty. It was held that the local legal regime did strike this balance, and was therefore compatible with the parties' Convention rights.

We see in these cases a triadic normative structure comprised not only of each private party's private law rights and duties but also of their constitutional rights and the state's correlating duties – that, importantly, obligate it to respond to the constitutionally important features of the regulated private relationship. Private law reasoning often ignores the public sides of the triangle.[18] But when the state regulates the actions and activities of private agents, it cannot see them only as, say, parents, employers, tenants or consumers. It must see them as citizens as well: as members of the political collective, who are not only constitutional right-holders but also potential bearers of indirect burdens to realise constitutional rights. The other side of the coin is that once we recognise that the state is regularly involved in private law relationships, even if latently, we can unburden private agents of the direct and demanding burdens associated with constitutional rights realisation.

[15] *Bull v Hall* [2013] UKSC 73, para 5.

[16] *Lee v Ashers Baking Company Ltd and others* [2018] UKSC 49, para 56 (Lady Hale).

[17] *Evans v UK*, App no 6339/05 (ECtHR, 10 April 2007).

[18] See Stephen A Smith, 'The Rights of Private Law' in Andrew Robertson and Tang Hang Wu (eds), *The Goals of Private Law* (Hart Publishing, 2009) 113, 141.

4.2.2. Reasoning in the Shadow of the Constitution

Indirect horizontality models do not see private agents as obligated to engage in constitutional reasoning, like state agents. Rather, they see private agents as having imperfect moral duties to consider how their responsibilities as members of the political collective can be integrated with their personal responsibilities – which is the state's role.[19] This attempt to avoid the pitfalls of traditional verticality and direct horizontality creates strong normative tensions.

Caricature. Delivery men working in a company set up a trade union. A caricature of the human resources manager being sexually gratified by other employees who testified in favour of the company in a legal dispute about working conditions appeared on the cover of the union's newsletter. The company dismissed the delivery men. The European Court of Human Rights recognised their rights to ridicule their bosses and co-workers in a newsletter distributed and displayed on the company's premises, but also the bosses' and co-workers' rights to respect, dignity and reputation. The balance of these rights, it was held, supports the private law rule permitting the dismissal.[20]

Tensions arise because private agents must also take into account constitutionally protected interests, such as dignity and freedom of expression. In this sense, they contribute to constitutional rights-realisation not only in public roles, such as voters, but also in private roles, such as co-workers. Their personal responsibilities are altered by the inclusion of the interests of other private agents within the scopes of constitutional rights, even if our expectations from public and private agents remain different – if public agents must address additional complexities, such as structural threats to these interests.

It is the state's role to ensure that private reasoning does not become so complex and demanding that it creates the problems of direct horizontality. There are no hard and fast rules here. In some private spheres (such as the workplace), private reasoning can be quite burdensome, reflecting the normative significance and structure of the regulated relationships; in others, private reasoning will be more limited. Indirect models risk a collapse into direct horizontality if we focus on the products of legal reasoning: on what private agents end up owing to other private agents. However, as noted in the previous chapter, the problems with direct horizontality touch not only the burdens of abiding by settled primary norms, but also the burdens of navigating complex constitutional norms to figure out our legal duties and being held accountable in this regard in private social spheres. Under indirect models, private agents are not responsible for private law's development,[21] not even in the sense of trying to speculate what

[19] See Elizabeth Kahn, 'Beyond Claim-Rights: Social Structure, Collectivization, and Human Rights' (2020) 52 *Journal of Social Philosophy*.

[20] *Sanchez v Spain*, App no 28955/06 (ECtHR, 12 September 2011).

[21] See also Gonçalo de Almeida Ribeiro, 'The Effects of Fundamental Rights in Private Disputes' in Hugh Collins (ed), *European Contract Law and the Charter of Fundamental Rights* (Intersentia, 2018) 242–46.

would have been the legal arrangements had public agents fulfilled their constitutional duties. Under indirect models, claims that private law should change are directed only at state agents, who must consider relational reasons like reliance, intimacy or trust, and the open texture of legal norms.

There are important differences between law and morality in this regard. In law, agents need not engage in what JJC Smart labelled 'rule worship': ignoring good reasons for breaking rules, to preserve their indirect consequentialist value as part of a system of regulation.[22] Indirect horizontal approaches do not ask private agents to follow rules blindly: rather, they ask them to rely on state agents who constantly evaluate and recalibrate rules. While this creates a complex challenge for private or public reasoning under regulatory practices, facing this challenge is a step forward, compared to the rigidity of traditional verticality and direct horizontality.

4.3. STRONG INDIRECT EFFECT

I said above that indirect models come in different shapes and forms. For the sake of simplicity, I will distinguish between strong and weak models. Their distinctions are qualitative and multifaceted. They cannot be clearly separated based on a single normative feature. In crude terms, strong indirect models claim that state agents have positive and comprehensive rights-based duties to bring about constitutionally-justified states of affairs through private law, while weak indirect models claim that the related duties of state agents are imperfect because the horizontal dimensions of constitutional rights constrain and guide as open-ended values.

Under this distinction, weak models can also justify private law's creation or change – a function often ascribed only to strong models, while labelling private law's mere application or interpretation as weak horizontality.[23] My focus is on the constitutional input rather than the private law output – specifically, the nature and structure of horizontality reasoning. Whether this reasoning ends in law creation or interpretation lies further downstream from the problems that I identify with strong models, which also apply to mere interpretation (and with weak models, which can also apply to law creation). The focus on the input is more inclusive as it allows us to focus on the relations between different reasons for horizontal rights realisation before touching the authorities and obligations of particular state agents in this regard.

The rest of this chapter presents and criticises an idealised version of the strong indirect model. I start by explaining its consequentialist approach to constitutional rights realisation in general. Then, I explain how the consequentialisation

[22] 'Extreme and Restricted Utilitarianism' (1956) 6 *Philosophical Quarterly* 344, 349.

[23] eg, Gautam Bhatia, *Horizontal Rights: An Institutional Approach* (Hart Publishing, 2023) 49.

of relational normative factors leads to a conception of constitutional horizontality under which relational reasons for regulation are ignored, eroded or distorted – both in public reasoning and in private reasoning.

4.3.1. Optimisation

The starting point of strong indirect models is that the constitution has normative priority in the legal hierarchy of norms. Therefore, when thinking about the realisation of constitutional rights, we must follow the constitution's prescriptions until they run out. The important factor in this regard is that while proportionality analysis – which dominates realisation reasoning under the common model – leaves room for non-constitutional and relational reasons for regulation, it pulls them towards consequentialist terrain. While there are basic deontological thresholds that the legitimate purpose test establishes (for example, infringements cannot be racist or sexist), realisation reasoning is comprehensive, in the sense of taking into account the interests of all affected members of the political collective (and, potentially, of non-members as well).[24] Any infringement's benefits in terms of the pursuit of legitimate public goals must outweigh its costs in terms of the values that underlie affected rights. For example, a defamation tort's contribution to the protection of privacy must outweigh the costs of limiting freedom of expression.

At this point, the teleological foundations of general constitutional rights enter the picture. It can be held that if the values underlying these rights relate to social conditions and states of affairs, their partial realisation must be better in terms of social conditions or states of affairs. It need not be held that constitutional rights provide all the required normative information – that private law is just their further horizontal elaboration.[25] It also need not be held that we can turn to non-constitutional (say, relational) reasons only after we have satisfied all the reasons for regulation derived from constitutional rights. Rather, even if constitutional rights run out at some point and are agnostic about some regulatory questions, and even if they can be only partly realised, the fact that justifications for their infringements must, so the thought goes, be in the normative key of values like autonomy, equality or privacy, pulls realisation reasoning to consequentialist terrain. Such values set the terms in which other

[24] See generally Frederick Schauer, 'Balancing, Subsumption, and the Constraining Role of Legal Text' (2010) 4 *Law and Ethics of Human Rights* 34; George Pavlakos, 'Constitutional Rights, Balancing and the Structure of Autonomy' (2011) 24 *Canadian Journal of Law and Jurisprudence* 129.

[25] See generally Mattias Kumm, 'Who is Afraid of the Total Constitution? Constitutional Rights as Principles and the Constitutionalization of Private Law' (2006) 7 *German Law Journal* 341; Hugh Collins, 'The Constitutionalization of European Private Law as a Path to Social Justice?' in Hans-W Micklitz (ed), *The Many Concepts of Social Justice in European Private Law* (Edward Elgar Publishing, 2011) 133, 136–39, 142.

reasons join the action, because the latter must outweigh the former; and these terms refer, in this context, to how basic interests are realised by the state in different social conditions or states of affairs.

The idea is not necessarily to maximise the values underlying constitutional rights, if this even makes sense, given their complexity and interdependence.[26] It is enough to take us down the consequentialist path to hold, with Robert Alexy, that rights should be optimised – extended as much as possible.[27] Alexy's approach expresses German constitutional principles, at least in horizontality cases.[28] The basic idea is that conflicts involving general rights (principles, in Alexy's terms) are resolved by making ordinal or qualitative (rather than cardinal or quantitative) distinctions that attach idealised degrees of weight to the affected rights, the extent of their societal realisation, and the reliability of our information.[29] Three features of this realisation model are important for us: first, all reasons for regulation that pass the legitimate purpose threshold test are weighed; second, these reasons are weighed by comparing their likely regulatory consequences – rights should cover as much ground as possible in terms of social conditions and states of affairs; and third, regulatory decisions leave no open questions or normative residue, in the sense that we reach the 'optimal' or 'best' result in particular regulatory contexts – for example, if freedom of expression should not be extended to additional forms of speech.

4.3.2. Consequentialisation

The idea of optimisation has far-reaching horizontal implications. Basically, to introduce relational or small-scale reasons for regulation into constitutional realisation reasoning, these reasons must be reshaped so that they address social conditions or states of affairs; or, to use a term from moral theory, 'consequentialised'.[30] The idea is that the state – as an impartial regulator – should consider not only reductions in tangible aspects of well-being, but also normative features of actions: for example, states of affairs can be worse because they were brought about by negligent acts, contract violations,

[26] George Letsas, 'Rescuing Proportionality' in Rowan Cruft, S Matthew Liao and Massimo Renzo (eds), *Philosophical Foundations of Human Rights* (Oxford University Press, 2015) 316, 324–28.

[27] Robert Alexy, *A Theory of Constitutional Rights* (Julian Rivers tr, Oxford University Press, 2002) 47–48.

[28] Niels Petersen, 'Alexy and the "German" Model of Proportionality' (2020) 21 *German Law Journal* 163.

[29] Robert Alexy, 'On Balancing and Subsumption: A Structural Comparison' (2003) 16 *Ratio Juris* 433; Robert Alexy, *Law's Ideal Dimension* (Oxford University Press, 2021) 121–32, 154–74.

[30] See David McNaughton and Piers Rawling, 'Agent-Relativity and the Doing-Happening Distinction' (1991) 63 *Philosophical Studies* 167, 168. See also Campbell Brown, 'Consequentialize This' (2011) 121 *Ethics* 749; Paul Hurley, 'Consequentializing and Deontologizing: Clogging the Consequentialist Vacuum' in Mark Timmons, *Oxford Studies in Normative Ethics, Volume 3* (Oxford University Press, 2013) 123.

or discrimination.[31] Thus, it could be held, for example, that while contractual promise-keeping is of value, this value should not be promoted by inducing private agents to make more promises, to ensure that other agents keep their promises, or to break their promises if it allows more promises to be kept.[32] The state aims to create optimal contractual practices – but its account of what is optimal is informed by relational normative factors.

The role of relational factors in realisation reasoning is subsidiary: they gain weight only to the extent that they form parts of social conditions or states of affairs. Much like the twister taking Dorothy from Kansas to Oz, consequentialisation takes the relational rights, values and principles underlying private law from their natural habitat in private interactions to complex regulatory systems. They are consequentialised so that we can evaluate the ways and extent to which we realise constitutional rights in society.

Defamation. An Alabama jury awarded high damages to a police commissioner, Sullivan, for the libellous description of his alleged civil rights abuses in the New York Times. The decision spurred a wave of lawsuits by officials against media outlets, threatening to use tort law to stifle civil rights dissent, freedom of the press, and public debate. The Supreme Court of the United States found the decision to constitute state action (coming close to indirect horizontality); and held that to avoid violating the constitutional right to freedom of expression, libel against public officials must be made with 'actual malice': either with knowledge of the statement's falsity or with reckless disregard to its potential falsity.[33] This constitutional principle did not respond to the direct interaction of newspapers and public officials. Rather, values like dignity, privacy and freedom of expression were engaged from a political perspective, focusing on democratic debate and dissent and public accountability.

This case put defamation law (and neighbouring areas like privacy law) on strong indirect horizontality paths. The normative force of the First Amendment in the United States not only led to the labelling of many forms of expression (such as publishing the names of rape victims or protests at funerals) as matters of public concern, but also instilled in judges deep concerns about limiting expression. Thus, priority is often given to agents over their victims: not because of the moral nature of their relationships, or of a direct reconciliation of their rights, but because strong expression rights, the thought goes, create valuable social conditions.[34] In this sense, the importance of *New York Times v Sullivan* lies not in the rule adopted, but in its justifications.

[31] See Amartya Sen, 'Consequential Evaluation and Practical Reason' (2000) 97 *Journal of Philosophy* 477, 487–94; Derek Parfit, *On What Matters: Volume One* (Oxford University Press, 2011) 373–74.

[32] Hurley, 'Consequentializing and Deontologizing' (n 30) 127–31.

[33] *New York Times v Sullivan* 376 US 254 (1964).

[34] Kirsty Hughes and Neil M Richards, 'The Atlantic Divide on Privacy and Free Speech' in Andrew T Kenyon (ed), *Comparative Defamation and Privacy Law* (Cambridge University Press, 2016) 164.

Strong indirect models need not hold that there is one 'super value' (utility, for instance) to which all values collapse. Rather, it is enough that we can engage in processes that make values compatible[35] or locate them on a single normative scale:[36] for instance, a qualitative scale on which regulatory options are ranked according to the ways in which they realise constitutional rights and competing public goals.[37] Thus, in *Defamation* cases, we can make qualitative distinctions between the implications of legal norms on public debate and democratic institutions. By locating all reasons for regulation on a single scale, we ensure that there are no areas of legal regulation immune from constitutional scrutiny.

Indirect Discrimination. A factory in the United States adopted a company policy that required a high-school diploma or the passing of certain tests as a condition of employment or promotion – which had a disproportionate effect on African-Americans. The Supreme Court held that while there was no discriminatory intent, the policy was discriminatory because there was no business justification for these requirements.[38] In their attempts to justify such duties against indirect discrimination, theorists extended the notion of discrimination away from interactions and relational concepts like intent, blame or responsibility, towards the interests and needs of vulnerable persons, as seen from a broader perspective.[39] When asking what discrimination is, they placed more weight on what we need it to be to bring about the best social conditions or states of affairs in terms of social equality. There are no discontinuities here between the relational wrong and the large-scale prescriptions entailed by the value of equality. Duties under discrimination law should therefore be placed on any agent that can increase social equality, and the limits of these duties must be shaped by a balancing of the rights of all affected parties.[40]

Gautam Bhatia claims, in a similar spirit, that constitutional rights should entail private duties when the position of a private agent within a normative institution (such as employment) creates a power disparity that enables them to violate the rights of other private agents.[41] Power and vulnerability are not

[35] Ronald Dworkin, 'Do Liberal Values Conflict?' in Mark Lilla, Ronald Dworkin and Robert Silvers (eds), *The Legacy of Isaiah Berlin* (New York Review Books, 2001) 73.

[36] Matthew Adler, 'Law and Incommensurability: Introduction' (1998) 146 *University of Pennsylvania Law Review* 1169.

[37] See Virgilio Afonso Da Silva, 'Comparing the Incommensurable: Constitutional Principles, Balancing and Rational Decision' (2011) 31 *Oxford Journal of Legal Studies* 273, 280–83.

[38] *Griggs v Duke Power Co* 401 US 424 (1971).

[39] See, for example, the essays in Hugh Collins and Tarunabh Khaitan (eds), *Foundations of Indirect Discrimination Law* (Hart Publishing, 2018).

[40] Sandra Fredman, 'Equality Law: Labour Law or an Autonomous Field?' in Alan Bogg, Cathryn Costello, ACL Davies and Jeremias Prassl (eds), *The Autonomy of Labour Law* (Hart Publishing, 2015) 257.

[41] Bhatia (n 23) 87–92. For a similar approach, see also Eleni Frantziou, *The Horizontal Effect of Fundamental Rights in the European Union: A Constitutional Analysis* (Oxford University Press, 2019) 165–70.

strictly relational but form parts of social structures,[42] and wrongs consist in the impact of patterns of conduct rather than isolated actions.[43] Under this approach, the wrong in discrimination – even in direct forms, such as refusals to sell houses to black people – is that it manifests and solidifies institutions of social subordination, which the collective is committed to eradicate.[44] This approach takes a broad view of responsibility, which tracks factors addressing complex social structures rather than relational choices or actions.

Privacy. I mentioned the case in which supermodel Naomi Campbell claimed that publications about her Narcotics Anonymous meetings and ongoing treatment violated her right to privacy. A House of Lords majority found in her favour.[45] While English law did not recognise a tort of invasion of privacy, a balance of privacy, freedom of expression, and public interests justified stretching the 'breach of confidence' tort beyond direct relationships to cover the relationship in this case. This introduced proportionality analysis into the relationship between the publisher and Campbell. Lord Hope noted that when courts review the publisher's decision, they must ask 'whether publication of the material pursues a legitimate aim and whether the benefits that will be achieved by its publication are proportionate to the harm that may be done by the interference with the right to privacy'.[46] Thus, a focus on the contribution to public debate, which is also a feature of similar decisions by the European Court of Human Rights,[47] can take us quite close to direct horizontality and to private engagement in complex constitutional reasoning.

4.4. MORAL PLURALISM

Strong indirect models do not obligate private agents to realise constitutional rights or obligate state agents to ignore relational values, but they pull private rights-and-duties relationships and their regulation in these directions. Relational normative factors figure in realisation reasoning merely as components of patterns of conduct, social structures, or states of affairs. This affects both public reasoning about and private reasoning within these relationships. This section holds that the main problem in this regard is the inadequate recognition of moral pluralism by strong indirect models: they fail to recognise discontinuities and qualitative distinctions that afflict the normative universe,[48] and therefore also constitutional rights realisation reasoning.

[42] Bhatia (n 23) 92–97, 120–29.

[43] ibid 100, 127.

[44] ibid 124, 207.

[45] *Campbell v MGN Ltd* [2004] UKHL 22.

[46] ibid para 113. Lord Caswell joined Lord Hope's opinion in this regard (ibid para 167).

[47] eg, *Von Hannover v Germany (No 2)*, App no. 40660/08 (ECtHR, 7 February 2012).

[48] Isaiah Berlin, 'Two Concepts of Liberty' in *Liberty* (Henry Hardy ed, Oxford University Press, 2016) 166, 212–17. See also Elinor Mason, 'Value Pluralism' in Edward N Zalta and Uri Nodelman (eds), *The Stanford Encyclopedia of Philosophy* (Summer 2023).

My concern is not that normative systematisation through consequentialisation is never possible or desirable, nor that constitutional rights and relational rights, values and principles are always incomparable. It is that having state agents engage these relational factors from a large-scale teleological perspective comes at prices that we must not ignore.[49] This perspective is not morally neutral, and it has practical implications even as an evaluative framework.[50]

Now, obviously, realisation reasoning must take consequences into account: the states of affairs brought about by private law norms must influence decisions about their change, creation or abolition.[51] One of the central justifications for constitutional horizontality is that private law must answer questions about the social conditions or structures it creates and the states of affairs it brings about and their implications for constitutional rights.

However, we must be careful about how we pose these questions to private law, thereby exposing its deep relational features to systematic and goal-oriented scrutiny. Strong indirect models call for constant, direct and crude forms of teleological reasoning that often come quite close to consequentialism. They drag relational normative factors 'kicking and screaming to the tribunal of justice', to borrow Waldron's words.[52] Criticisms of this failure to recognise the sensitivity of private law's deep structural features to large-scale scrutiny are often made by private law theorists who voice concerns about how its instrumentalisation under economic theories ignores its inherent rights-based relationality. I share their concerns, even if I see the values that private law serves as going beyond relational values like negative freedom or civil recourse. My concerns are therefore not about this or that substantive value but about the reasoning structure that strong indirect models bring to bear on private law, which reduce the effectiveness and justification of the regulation of private relationships, associations and practices – not only in terms of relational values but also in terms of the values underlying constitutional rights.

4.4.1. Public Reasoning

The first problem with strong indirect models is that they increase the risk that state agents will ignore or distort relational normative factors when reasoning about the creation, change or abolition of private law rights and duties. The problem

[49] Peter Schaber, 'Are There Insolvable Moral Conflicts?' in Peter Baumann and Monica Betzler (eds), *Practical Conflicts: New Philosophical Essays* (Cambridge University Press, 2004) 279, 285–89.

[50] S Andrew Schroeder, 'Consequentializing and its Consequences' (2017) 117 *Philosophical Studies* 1475.

[51] Rawls claimed, in a similar vein, that 'all ethical doctrines worth our attention take consequences into account in judging rightness' (John Rawls, *A Theory of Justice* (rev edn, Harvard University Press, 1999) 26).

[52] Jeremy Waldron, 'The Primacy of Justice' (2003) 9 *Legal Theory* 269, 272.

arises because state agents are obligated to give weight to relational factors only if they are located within the scope of a constitutional right. If not, neglecting them may be wrong but will wrong no specific individual. Because working out the requirements of constitutional rights is complex and demanding, and because relational factors play a merely negative role as potential justifications for rights infringements, it is quite easy to ignore them. Crucially, even if relational factors do find a home within the scopes of constitutional rights, and there are therefore more robust duties to engage them, they are engaged as parts of social structures, practices or institutions.

What are likely to go missing are the interdependent normative components of private rights-and-duties relationships: claims, expectations, responsibilities, predispositions, attitudes, and so on. Normative reasoning is path-dependent and compartmentalised, in the sense that whether we start by focusing on agency or on beneficence makes certain conclusions more likely.[53] If we start in the 'consequentialist circle', to borrow Paul Hurley's term, we are drawn to see relational factors as parts of or as responses to states of affairs.[54] Criticisms in this spirit were directed not only at economic private law theories, which reduce rights and duties to malleable regulatory tools, and at consequentialist moral theories, which see individuals as obligated to bring about the best states of affairs, but also at Rawls's political theory that focuses on allocations of benefits and burdens through social institutions.[55]

Take *Discrimination* as an example. When thinking about the clash between the service provider's religious or expressive liberties and the gay customer's dignity, we must pay attention to social patterns of repression or the economic structures of markets. However, we must also consider factors intrinsic to particular interactions – for example, the seller's assumption of responsibility towards the customer, and the customer's resulting reliance, expectations and vulnerabilities. If the justification for private duties not to discriminate is merely that private agents can contribute effectively to the collective project of realising social patterns of equality, there might be no wrong, say, in forms of workplace harassment that do not have negative impacts on job opportunities,[56] or in refusals to provide services to gay or black customers if there are other

[53] See Kurt Gray and Chelsea Schein, 'Two Minds Vs. Two Philosophies' (2012) 3 *Review of Philosophy and Psychology* 405. See also FM Kamm, 'Moral Intuitions, Cognitive Psychology, and the Harming-versus-Not-Aiding Distinction' (1998) 108 *Ethics* 463.

[54] Paul Edward Hurley, 'Exiting the Consequentialist Circle: Two Senses of Bringing it About' (2019) 60 *Analytic Philosophy* 130, 131.

[55] See Samuel Scheffler, 'Responsibility, Reactive Attitudes, and Liberalism in Philosophy and Politics' (1992) 21 *Philosophy & Public Affairs* 299; Thomas W Pogge, 'The Problems with Contractarian-Consequentialist Ways of Assessing Social Institutions' (1995) 12 *Social Philosophy and Policy* 241; Arthur Ripstein, 'The Division of Responsibility and the Law of Tort' (2004) 72 *Fordham Law Review* 1811, 1820–29.

[56] eg, Richard Thompson Ford, 'Bias in the Air: Rethinking Employment Discrimination Law' (2014) 66 *Stanford Law Review* 1381, 1403–05, 1412.

willing service-providers.[57] The problem is not merely the inadequate scope of legal duties, which will leave some forms of wrongful misconduct unregulated, such as isolated incidents of harassment or refusals to provide services. The problem is deeper and touches legal evolution: if the ties between private law rights and duties and their neighbouring relational moral norms are ad hoc and weak, it becomes more difficult to ensure its legitimacy, force and value – which depend on its integration within relational normative structures, whose ties to relational morality are unbreakable.

These claims are not novel. They form a basic feature of debates about moral pluralism. From this perspective, these tensions and translation difficulties are not contingent or pathological problems – and do not represent a failure of moral reasoning. Even a morally-sensitive supercomputer will struggle to translate relational factors to consequentialist factors. The nature of human life, imagination and thought is such that we face tragic moral conflicts. To ignore or distort normative factors to avoid such conflicts, as Isaiah Berlin noted, is 'either self-deceit or deliberate hypocrisy'.[58] The best we can do is engage each factor in its own terms and normative environment – which requires a principled system of priority, exclusion, and reconciliation rules – and exercise reasoned discretion that takes into account the changing features of the state and society when slowly developing our normative systems.

Constitutional horizontality brings these tensions to a boiling point, and strong indirect models struggle to alleviate them. They ignore the fact that realisation reasoning often involves less systematic (or 'statistical')[59] forms of evaluation and reasoning, which engage relational factors on their own terms and in their normative habitat. This results in deficiencies not only in terms of congruence with relational morality but also in terms of the ability to realise constitutional rights through the regulation of private relations. Take contract law as an example. It obviously has important social benefits. But the normativity of particular agreements or obligations is strictly relational and relies on notions like power, expectations, reliance and trust – whose understanding must address them as a coherent whole and in their relational context.[60] Trust, for example, is not something that states can create in a calculated sequence of top-down regulatory moves. This implies that we will fail to create the best practice of contractual agreements – or to realise constitutional rights through it – if we adopt a purely consequentialist perspective.

[57] eg, Nathan B Oman, '*Doux Commerce*, Religion, and the Limits of Antidiscrimination Law' (2017) 92 *Indiana Law Review* 693, 717–20.

[58] Berlin (n 48) 216.

[59] Thomas Nagel, *The View from Nowhere* (Oxford University Press, 1986) 166, 177. See also Berys Gaut, 'Rag-bags, Disputes and Moral Pluralism' (1999) 11 *Utilitas* 37.

[60] See Stephen Darwall, 'Demystifying Promises' in Hanoch Sheinman (ed), *Promises and Agreements: Philosophical Essays* (Oxford University Press, 2011) 255.

This can even result in regulatory backfire that harms constitutional rights. Take, for example, *Indirect Discrimination*, which touches the congruence between small-scale allocative decisions and social equality: for example, hiring requirements that unjustifiably exclude single parents or minorities. While the dominance of responsibility and blame in private relationships can easily distract state agents, when shaping private rights and duties, from systematic aspects of social inequality,[61] the problem in our context is that even if state agents can identify all relevant factors, top-down attempts to integrate them within rights-and-duties relationships by stretching the definition of discrimination as a wrong in the hope of creating around it relational structures of responsibility and blame are likely to fail.[62] As Michael Selmi claimed, the focus of indirect discrimination law on distributive patterns rather than on responsibility has weakened its regulatory impact:[63] 'the desire to avoid blameworthiness misunderstood the crucial role blame plays in fostering a willingness to remedy discrimination',[64] and robbed discrimination law of moral principles that can guide its evolution while drawing support from legal actors.[65] If we try to promote equality by imposing right-based duties on private agents, we must justify more than social allocations of costs and benefits.[66]

4.4.2. Private Reasoning

A related and more nuanced problem is that the reasoning of state agents under strong indirect models – even if it identifies all the relevant factors and reaches the correct substantive result – can distort private reasoning about how to exercise and conform with private law norms, and therefore the ways in which private agents abide by relational morality. This moral conformity is important not only because it can contribute to the realisation of the values that underlie constitutional rights but also because while the constitution sits at the apex of the legal system, it is not the only source of standards for its moral evaluation

[61] Iris Marion Young, *Responsibility for Justice* (Oxford University Press, 2011) 113–22; Sandra Fredman, 'Direct and Indirect Discrimination: Is There Still a Divide?' in *Foundations of Indirect Discrimination Law* (n 39) 31, 47–50.

[62] Jeremy Waldron, 'Indirect Discrimination' in Stephen Guest and Alan Milne (eds), *Equality and Discrimination: Essays in Freedom and Justice* (F Steiner, 1985) 83. See also Samuel R Bagenstos, 'The Structural Turn and the Limits of Antidiscrimination Law' (2006) 94 *California Law Review* 1, 34–47.

[63] Michael Selmi, 'Was the Disparate Impact Theory a Mistake?' (2006) 53 *UCLA Law Review* 701; Michael Selmi, 'Indirect Discrimination and the Anti-Discrimination Mandate' in Deborah Hellman and Sophia Moreau (eds), *Philosophical Foundations of Discrimination Law* (Oxford University Press, 2013) 250, 254–55.

[64] Selmi, 'Was the Disparate Impact Theory a Mistake?' (n 63) 773.

[65] Selmi, 'Indirect Discrimination' (n 63) 257; Sophia Moreau, 'The Moral Seriousness of Indirect Discrimination' in *Foundations of Indirect Discrimination Law* (n 39) 123, 128.

[66] See also Tristin K Green, 'A Structural Approach as Antidiscrimination Mandate: Locating Employer Wrong' (2007) 60 *Vanderbilt Law Review* 849, 871–73.

and therefore of its legitimacy. Much of the value of constitutional horizontality depends on its ability to realise, express, specify or develop relational morality – or, if there are good reasons to deviate from it, at least leave room for private agents to be guided by and follow it.[67] The problem is that when coupling private law's discursive features with the far-reaching prescriptions of general constitutional rights, there is a serious risk in strong indirect reasoning of spillovers from public to private reasoning, which will reintroduce the problems of complexity, intrusion, crowding out, scrutiny and authority.

Two underlying factors are important in this regard. First, the processes through which state agents shape private law are relatively transparent: while some degree of opacity is desirable and inevitable, it cannot and must not be absolute – and not only for democratic reasons:[68] because private law regularly evolves through judicial decisions, in which creation and application are fused together, we cannot separate its norms from the reasons that justify them, chart a course for their evolution, and tie them to neighbouring norms.[69]

Second, the exercise of private law rights or conformity with private law duties are not just a series of isolated, self-centered and technical choices: we must internalise these norms, reflect on their features, adjust them with norms from neighbouring domains (say, morality or religion), consider their impact on others from their perspective, and self-monitor and modify our conduct.[70] Private law rights empower their holders and constrain duty-bearers not only by erecting rigid boundaries;[71] rather, as Dworkin noted, more generally, there is an 'interplay between law and morals in ordinary practical life, even when no lawsuit is in prospect and each citizen is judge for and of himself'.[72] In this sense, private law norms operate through normative processes that are not limited to their linguistic content, but also touch their public justifications,[73] which prime us to engage reasons that are not included in any narrow definition of the norm itself. Think, for example, about how contracts induce us to reflect on promises and torts on people's dignity or bodily integrity, regardless of the exact details

[67] Seana Valentine Shiffrin, 'The Divergence of Contract and Promise' (2007) 120 *Harvard Law Review* 708.

[68] Even if we could create a strict separation between the norms applying to state agents and the norms applying to individuals (Meir Dan-Cohen, 'Decision Rules and Conduct Rules: On Acoustic Separation in Criminal Law' (1984) 97 *Harvard Law Review* 625), doing so might result in what Williams referred to as 'government house utilitarianism': see Bernard Williams, 'Theory and Prejudice' in *Ethics and the Limits of Philosophy* (Routledge, 2006) 94, 108.

[69] Ernest J Weinrib, *Reciprocal Freedom: Private Law and Public Right* (Oxford University Press, 2022) 204–26.

[70] Jeremy Waldron, 'Vagueness and the Guidance of Action' in Andrei Marmor and Scott Soames (eds), *Philosophical Foundations of Language in the Law* (Oxford University Press, 2011) 58, 65.

[71] For a similar point, see Avihay Dorfman, 'Foreseeability as Re-Cognition' (2014) 59 *American Journal of Jurisprudence* 163.

[72] Ronald Dworkin, 'The Common Law' in *Law's Empire* (Harvard University Press, 1986) 275, 300–01. See also Ronald Dworkin, 'Liberal Community' (1989) 77 *California Law Review* 479, 502–04.

[73] Dan Priel, 'Jurisprudence and Psychology' in Maksymilian Del Mar (ed), *New Waves in Philosophy of Law* (Palgrave Macmillan, 2011) 77, 88.

of contract or tort norms. This idea that law's authority is not binary and is affected by the kind of reasons that justify particular norms is a basic constitutional feature of the common law tradition.[74] This idea is important for us because constitutional horizontality, as already noted, is not merely about legal validity but also about the recognition of effective and justified norms.

This normative pressure especially strong regarding private law rights and duties. As noted in the previous chapter, while in some areas of law (say, tax law) norms can be engaged in a detached manner as technical requirements or prices, there is something inescapably moral in a system of norms that regulate private rights-and-duties relationships. Even if such norms are adopted for instrumental and goal-oriented reasons, with time, if things work well, they become embedded in the normative fabric of the relationships that they regulate.[75] Therefore, their normative force and value also depend on their ability to operate as morally robust rights and duties within such relationships.

The problem with strong indirect horizontality, in this regard, is that if private law rights and duties operate effectively, their moral echoes feed back into private relationships; and if their justifications are goal-oriented or consequentialist, these justifications shape the ways in which private agents exercise powers, claim rights and abide by duties – and therefore the rest of the normative fabric of the private relationships in which they operate. If state reasoning about private law focuses on how private agents can be conscripted to bring about better states of affairs, the problems of complexity, intrusion, crowding out, scrutiny and authority resurface – not only when private agents devise strategies for litigation or receive legal advice, but also when they consider how to conduct themselves in private relationships.

For example, even if state agents identify all the relevant reasons for and against a right against discrimination, and even if they adopt an all-things-considered justified norm, if their reasoning is openly consequentialist or political, problems are likely to emerge over time. The problems with discrimination law described above – its struggles to evolve effectively and justifiably while harnessing support – also result from failures in this deeper normative level. They result not only from how state agents reason but also from how norms are received by private agents. The fact that private law rights and duties are painted in political or instrumentalist colours harms their integration within private relationships as robust and morally-grounded norms. If hotel managers see their duties not to discriminate against gay couples as a political attempt to realise distributive patterns on a social scale, or if news editors and reporters see their duties as rooted in commitments to the market of ideas and political accountability rather than also to the dignity or privacy of the subjects of their

[74] David Dyzenhaus and Michael Taggart, 'Reasoned Decisions and Legal Theory' in Douglas E Edlin (ed), *Common Law Theory* (Cambridge University Press, 2007) 134, 152.

[75] See also John Gardner, *From Personal Life to Private Law* (Oxford University Press, 2018) 8–9.

reports – if duties are not about what private duty-bearers owe to private right-holders – these norms lose much of their force and value.

Strong indirect horizontality will not always result in such problems, and it is difficult to figure out exactly when it will, given the normative intricacy of private relationships and their interdependence with moral, cultural, economic and other factors. The ripple effects of legal norms and their underlying justifications are often complex and unexpected. Take, for example, what is often labelled 'defensive medicine': the technical, formal, and often unnecessary adherence to expansive rules by medical practitioners in response to medical malpractice norms. Over-regulation is often criticised in this regard for increasing financial costs or unnecessary medical procedures,[76] but there are also more normative harms, to the attitudes and habits that constitute doctor–patient relationships: alleviating these harms requires qualitatively different and inherently relational forms of reasoning, which could not be translated to consequentialist terms without losing their basic features, thereby distorting not only public regulatory reasoning, but also private relational reasoning.

It is not enough for state agents to properly identify relational factors – they must positively protect them at the point of application from competing forms of reasoning – grounded in, for example, profit-oriented or liability-adverse motivations. Such preferential treatment is at odds with strong indirect models, which locate all reasons for regulation on a single scale, referring to the realisation of beneficiary-centered values in society. Technical or superficial changes to strong indirect models cannot solve this problem. It goes down to the perspective from which they engage regulatory questions and their conception of the state as an agent that we trust to arrange things so that we treat each other fairly.[77] This account of the state often underlies criticisms of indirect models by theorists advocating more direct models, who raise concerns about the lack of attention to the effective integration of constitutional rights into private relationships, with their intricate patterns of motivations, attitudes, dispositions, claims, expectations, reliance, responsibility, accountability, respect, wrongs and remedies. However, as we will see, this criticism does not afflict all indirect horizontality models.

4.5. SOCIAL AND LOCAL JUSTICE

To pave the way forward, and elucidate the shortcomings of strong indirect horizontality models, the rest of this chapter goes back to the contractualist framework. We already addressed the focus of Rawls's social justice theory on the basic structure of society: on the one hand, it aims to ensure – against the

[76] See, eg, Michael D Frakes, 'The Surprising Relevance of Medical Malpractice Law' (2015) 82 *University of Chicago Law Review* 317.

[77] See Jürgen Habermas, 'Paradigms of Law' (1996) 17 *Cardozo Law Review* 771, 779.

libertarian reduction of the political to the relational – that social justice is realised effectively by basic institutions; on the other hand – against the utilitarian subordination of the relational to the political – it leaves room for private relationships, associations and practices.[78] These motivations combine to justify social justice's indirect horizontal effect. Rawls claimed, against the libertarian, that social justice constrains all basic institutions – for example, we enjoy our constitutional rights even as family members:[79] 'if the so-called private sphere is a space alleged to be exempt from justice, then there is no such thing' as social justice holds 'in and through all so-called domains'.[80] However, against the utilitarian, social justice does not apply directly to private actions within basic institutions: 'the principles of political justice are applied … directly to the basic structure and indirectly to the associations within it'.[81] Social justice does not obligate private agents directly: they cannot violate it through their private actions or activities since it must be further specified through basic institutions in terms of more concrete norms, notably legal ones.[82]

The philosophical debate about private law's subjection to social or distributive justice principles can be framed as a debate about whether it is part of the basic structure of society (a matter on which Rawls was somewhat ambiguous).[83] It is tempting to justify private law's subjection to social justice principles by showing that it is as much a part of the basic structure as domains like tax law.[84] It could then be replied that because private law operates against the background of public institutions that attain and sustain social justice, it can hold individuals responsible for their actions towards particular others without recourse to structural or allocative considerations.[85] This debate is important, but we should resist the temptation to reduce it to the binary question of whether private law is 'in' or 'out' of the basic structure.[86] We must not assume that if private law is in, social justice applies to it fully and uniformly; or that if

[78] John Rawls, *Political Liberalism*, 2nd edn (Columbia University Press, 2005) 267–69. See also Samuel Scheffler, 'The Division of Moral Labour: Egalitarian Liberalism as Moral Pluralism' (2005) 79 *Proceedings of the Aristotelian Society* 229, 239–40; Samuel Freeman, 'The Basic Structure of Society as the Primary Subject of Justice' in Jon Mandle and David A Reidy (eds), *A Companion to Rawls* (John Wiley & Sons, 2014) 88, 99–101.

[79] John Rawls, *Justice as Fairness: A Restatement* (Erin Kelly ed, Harvard University Press, 2001) 164.

[80] ibid 164.

[81] ibid 166.

[82] Rawls, *Political Liberalism* (n 78) 267–68; Samuel Scheffler, 'Distributive Justice, the Basic Structure and the Place of Private Law' (2015) 35 *Oxford Journal of Legal Studies* 213, 220–21, 234.

[83] See Scheffler, 'Distributive Justice' (n 82) 217–22.

[84] Kevin A Kordana and David H Tabachnick, 'On Belling the Cat: Rawls and Tort as Corrective Justice' (2006) 92 *Virginia Law Review* 1279.

[85] Arthur Ripstein, 'Private Order and Public Justice: Kant and Rawls' (2006) 92 *Virginia Law Review* 1391; Arthur Ripstein, *Private Wrongs* (Harvard University Press, 2016) 290–95. See also Stephen Perry, 'Ripstein, Rawls, and Responsibility' (2004) 72 *Fordham Law Review* 1845; William Lucy, *Philosophy of Private Law* (Oxford University Press, 2007) 355–57.

[86] See generally Kok-Chor Tan, *Justice, Institutions, and Luck* (Oxford University Press, 2012) 37–38; Miriam Ronzoni, 'What Makes a Basic Structure Just?' (2008) 14 *Res Publica* 203.

it is out, it is entirely isolated from social justice. As Rawls noted, to allow the basic structure to sustain social justice in response to changing conditions – for example, new medical procedures, family structures, or practices of workplace surveillance – we must not define its boundaries too sharply or rigidly.[87]

Citizens have general duties, as part of the collective, to create and support just institutions.[88] In non-ideal circumstances, these duties could be translated into individual moral or even constitutional duties to respond to social justice directly. But in moderately justified and effective legal systems, it is usually state agents that are obligated to respond to complex patterns of private actions and activities through forms of regulation that are effective (*contra* libertarianism) without being too onerous (*contra* utilitarianism).[89] Then, the important questions are not about whether social justice influences private law but about how it does.

The problem of constitutional horizontality arises within Rawls's social justice scheme because constitutional rights go wherever the basic structure goes.[90] My goal in discussing this scheme is not exegetical. It is encouraging that the trend towards indirect horizontality converges with ideas of one of the most prominent political philosophers of the last century. But my focus is not on what Rawls claimed and why – and, anyway, he did not address constitutional horizontality, and his account of constitutional rights is quite thin. My goal in building on Rawls is to shed light on the nature and force of certain moral principles, starting with the distinction between social justice and more local forms of justice – and moving to the idea of sequencing our reasoning about the realisation of justice in society.

4.5.1. Local Justice and the Four-Stage Sequence

The principles of justice that regulate the political collective's actions with regard to the basic structure are principles of social justice. They are about what 'we the people' owe to members of the collective in terms of how basic institutions attain and sustain social justice. The justifications of such principles are political, as they touch foundational features of the normative scheme through which we organise ourselves as a society, such as the electoral system, mandatory education, relations of church and state, and the role of organised labour.

[87] Rawls, *Justice as Fairness* (n 79) 12. See also Scheffler, 'Distributive Justice' (n 82) 216–17.

[88] Rawls, *A Theory of Justice* (n 51) 93–101, 293–301; Rawls, *Political Liberalism* (n 78) 199–200, 440.

[89] See Kok-Chor (n 86) 44–47; Anthony Townsend Kronman, 'Contract Law and Distributive Justice' (1980) 89 *Yale Law Journal* 472, 501; Thomas W Pogge, 'On the Site of Distributive Justice: Reflections on Cohen and Murphy' (1998) 29 *Philosophy and Public Affairs* 137, 164–66; Thomas Porter, 'The Division of Moral Labour and the Basic Structure Restriction' (2009) 8 *Political Philosophy & Economics* 173.

[90] Frank I Michelman, *Constitutional Essentials: On the Constitutional Theory of Political Liberalism* (Oxford University Press, 2022) 188–90.

The unique roles of social justice are elucidated when it is distinguished from 'local justice': the principles 'followed directly by associations and institutions within the basic structure'.[91] Rawls did not elaborate on local justice, but noted that 'in general, principles for the basic structure constrain (or limit), but not determine uniquely, the suitable principles of local justice':[92] for example, religious associations cannot burn heretics, universities cannot discriminate against minority members, and parents cannot prevent medical care for their children. Such constraints are contextual and shaped by the 'nature and role of the association, group, or relation at hand'.[93] They express the categorical priority of social justice, grounded in its unique ability to identify deep problems with how the basic structure operates over time, in ways that go above and beyond relational morality and local justice (for example, how private activities exacerbate patterns of inequality or distort the democratic process).

That social justice constrains but does not determine local justice reflects the fact that social justice is not definitive of justice in the liberal state – both because social justice is not comprehensive and detailed enough to guide individual conduct and its regulation, and because some moral principles, while qualitatively different (that is, not subsumed under social justice), have important roles to play in less political settings.[94] Therefore, while social justice must constrain and influence private law rights-and-duties relationships, it lacks the details or proclivity to fully determine all private law norms.[95] As Scheffler adds, social justice leaves room for values that focus on how we treat people in our 'moral neighbourhood':[96] relational values that express a qualitatively different form of moral engagement.[97]

Importantly, Rawls not only affirms moral pluralism by recognising the qualitative independence of local justice, but also – and this also pushes back against utilitarianism – points towards a strategy for accommodating this pluralism.[98] Rawls was concerned that normative theories or systems with no clear priority rules or methods of resolving conflicts between competing principles will have to resort to unprincipled ad hoc decisions grounded in intuitions.[99] This concern

[91] Rawls, *Justice as Fairness* (n 79) 11 (referring to John Elster, *Local Justice: How Institutions Allocate Scarce Goods and Necessary Burdens* (Russell Sage Foundation, 1992)).

[92] ibid.

[93] ibid 164.

[94] The claims that social justice is comprehensive and exclusive are made in David Blankfein-Tabachnick and Kevin A Kordana, 'On Rawlsian Contractualism and the Private Law' (2022) 108 *Virginia Law Review* 265, 278–86. See also GA Cohen, 'Introduction' in *Rescuing Justice and Equality* (Harvard University Press, 2008) 1, 3–4; Colin M Macleod, 'Applying Justice as Fairness to Institutions' in Jon Mandle and David A Reidy (eds), *A Companion to Rawls* (Wiley & Sons, 2014) 164, 168–69.

[95] But see Freeman, 'The Basic Structure of Society' (n 78) 91.

[96] Scheffler, 'The Division of Moral Labour' (n 78) 231–34.

[97] Samuel Scheffler, 'Projects, Relationships, and Reasons' in RJ Wallace (ed), *Reason and Value: Themes from the Moral Philosophy of Joseph Raz* (Oxford University Press, 2004) 247, 252, 257–58.

[98] Scheffler, 'The Division of Moral Labour' (n 78) 248.

[99] Rawls, *A Theory of Justice* (n 51) 34.

underlies the priority of social justice in certain contexts and a reasoning structure under which it is unpacked and applied to institutions.

The realisation of social justice is dealt with in a somewhat neglected part of Rawls's theory: a four-stage sequence in which the 'veil of ignorance' is gradually lifted and additional information becomes available to the deliberating parties.[100] Like the original position, these stages are expository devices. Each stage represents a normative perspective from which we evaluate the basic structure. The transition between the stages builds on their nature and limits to elucidate and structure our reasoning, thereby accommodating moral pluralism. As we proceed from the original position to constitutional, legislative and application stages, we also face reasons that are not distributive or structural and involve other standpoints. As we will see, these stages also shed light on the horizontal realisation of constitutional rights.

After the original position, in which the principles of justice (of basic liberties, equal opportunities, and equality of basic goods unless inequalities serve the worse-off) are adopted, comes a constitutional stage. The social justice principle of basic liberties and institutional considerations are translated into a system of foundational norms. The process of rights-delineation, as noted in chapter 2, operates at this high level of abstraction, asking about how basic interests are likely to fare under different institutions and practices that the constitution shapes. The constitutional stage does not deal with the effective realisation of rights – a topic that requires more contextual and detailed reasoning and further considerations: rather, this stage merely aims to adopt the constitution 'most likely to lead to just and effective legislation'.[101]

Reasoning about the realisation of constitutional rights is therefore more at home in the legislative stage, in which idealised legislators weigh economic, cultural and other factors that were not dealt with in the previous stages.[102] While constitutional rights are firmly rooted in social justice, their realisation through sub-constitutional law also requires engagement of local justice considerations: rights-realisation reasoning must respond to the ways in which individuals can and should adhere to both local and social justice in private relationships, associations or practices. As noted above, this is so not only because the realisation of social justice should be effective, but also because to be justified it cannot be imperialistic. For example, the equality principles must leave room for justified forms of private ordering[103] and the 'values expressed by free

[100] Rawls, *Justice as Fairness* (n 79) 48; Rawls, *Political Liberalism* (n 78) 397–99. See also Macleod (n 94).

[101] Rawls, *Political Liberalism* (n 78) 336. See also Jeremy Waldron, 'Socioeconomic Rights and Theories of Justice' (2011) 48 *San Diego Law Review* 773, 794–95.

[102] Rawls, *A Theory of Justice* (n 51) 174–75.

[103] Rawls, *Political Liberalism* (n 78) 283.

and fair agreements';[104] and members of associations like churches or universities need not necessarily have political rights with regard to their operation.[105]

The legal scheme created in the legislative stage – including norms that reconcile constitutional rights and competing reasons for regulation – is applied to specific cases in the final stage of the sequence by administrative agents, judges, and private agents in their own affairs. At this stage, we have room, for example, for corrective justice principles, which respond to actions that harm legitimate entitlements in relative isolation from the principles of social justice, which establish entitlements from a broader perspective (thus, even if we strive to promote equality, we might still find it justified to hold a poor private agent liable for negligently damaging the car of a wealthy person).[106] Relational local justice principles can therefore justify decisions about specific allocations of goods and burdens in the room left for them by principles of social justice, which is often quite extensive given the many ways in which the political collective can pursue social justice through the basic structure over time.

We will get back to the application stage in the next chapter. At this point, our focus is on the distinction between the constitutional and the legislative stages, which serves as a springboard to move beyond strong indirect models. These models ignore qualitative distinctions between the aims, perspectives and structures of the delineation and realisation of constitutional rights as normative activities. The four-stage sequence helps us see that realisation is a separate normative activity. While constitutional realisation reasoning relies on the existence of a system of constitutional rights, they are delineated from a more abstract, systematic and teleological perspective. Realisation reasoning is more contextual and therefore leaves more room for relational reasons for regulation to operate in their own terms and closer to their natural habitat.

Strong indirect models are too close to direct horizontality, in the sense that they try to derive concrete deontic implications directly from balancing exercises within a beneficiary-centered system of rights:[107] for example, by requiring journalists in cases like *Privacy* to reconcile moral considerations on a social scale. The response to this system's under-specification is to translate normative data from relational systems; but while this translation is justified with regard to the delineation of constitutional rights, it causes deep problems when it comes to their realisation. This is true not only regarding the more traditional areas of private law, such as intentional torts or interpersonal agreements, but also in private law's more novel and policy-oriented periphery – for example, as we started seeing, in discrimination law. I will further unpack this claim by

[104] Rawls, *A Theory of Justice* (n 51) 53–54.

[105] Rawls, *Justice as Fairness* (n 79) 10–11.

[106] Stephen R Perry, 'On the Relationship Between Corrective and Distributive Justice' in Jeremy Horder (ed), *Oxford Essays in Jurisprudence* (Oxford University Press, 2000) 237, 238–44; Steven Walt, 'Eliminating Corrective Justice' (2006) 92 *Virginia Law Review* 1311.

[107] On this problem, see Roderick Bagshaw, 'Privacy and Tort Design' in Katja S Ziegler (ed), *Human Rights and Private Law: Privacy as Autonomy* (Hart Publishing, 2007) 79, 85–90.

distinguishing between the structural principles that can and should dominate delineation reasoning and the allocative principles that can and should dominate realisation reasoning.

4.5.2. What We Owe to Each Other

Every rights-realisation decision must reconcile competing interests, even when evaluating the infringement of a right against public goals that serve diffuse interests: for example, when evaluating voting procedures, police authorities, limits on recreational drug use, or mandatory education requirements. But because, in horizontal realisation cases, justifications for infringements lie in the interests of agents with whom the right-holder can or does interact, it is even clearer that there is a moral relationship between them, constituted by their conflicting claims. Because we are discussing general norms, these parties occupy idealised standpoints: for example, journalists and public figures or drivers and pedestrians. But a relationship still exists, and it is more direct than the relationship between parties with claims about the basic structure or the delineation of constitutional rights. Private law is generally part of the basic structure, but it is not only about what we owe to each other as members of political collectives through public institutions. It also concerns what we owe to each other as participants in private relationships, associations and practices. This distinction between types of justificatory relationships has important implications for horizontal realisation reasoning.

Scanlon's contractualist theory sheds light on this distinction. It complements Rawls's theory – particularly, at the legislative stage – because it is less political and more relational, in three basic ways:[108] it is about what we owe to each other as individuals; it models moral reasoning on a hypothetical conversation between individuals, in the sense that it is wrong to follow a principle that we cannot justify to an affected party; and it relies on a relationship of mutual recognition and respect as an ideal that shapes the structure of justification and motivates adherence to moral principles, which we follow not just out of a general sense of duty but because we value standing in justified relationships with other moral agents. These relationships need not involve familiarity or history: compliance with moral principles can realise a valuable way of relating to others in any 'context of potential interaction structured by legitimate

[108] See Thomas Scanlon, *What We Owe to Each Other* (Harvard University Press, 1998) 155–56, 189–91; Rahul Kumar, 'Contractualism on the Shoal of Aggregation' in R Jay Wallace, Rahul Kumar and Samuel Freeman (eds), *Reasons and Recognition: Essays on the Philosophy of T.M. Scanlon* (Oxford University Press, 2011) 129, 136–38.

expectations',[109] even with strangers. This form of moral reasoning is therefore relational rather than relationship-based.[110]

Even with respect to strangers, there are important differences between dynamic distributions of goods and burdens to members of the political collective through the basic structure, and the allocations of limited bundles of goods and burdens through particular institutions or practices, such as car manufacturing or sports. Rawls distinguished, in this regard, between distributive justice – on which his theory focuses – and allocative justice.[111] Choices between legal regimes – say, between criminal sanctions, tort duties to compensate for harms regardless of fault, and tort duties not to harm negligently – must reconcile distributive-structural claims of citizens against the political collective but also more directly conflicting allocative claims of the targets or beneficiaries of regulation. For example, driving speed limits can be justified, in this allocative sense, if drivers cannot justify more lenient rules to pedestrians as part of relationships of recognition and respect between them (even if they never met and never will). The one-to-one comparison of claims allows this reasoning structure to accommodate deontological principles: for example, constraints on gravely harming one person to cause slight pleasure to millions are justified because each beneficiary cannot reject the victim's stronger claim relative to them.[112]

In the senses above, Scanlon's scheme is more relational than Rawls's. However, its suitability for realisation reasoning results from the fact that it is still general and systematic (and thus echoes basic consequentialist themes). It does not focus on specific people affected by specific actions but on the general standpoints of everyone affected by moral principles for the regulation of society,[113] including members of future generations (for instance, when thinking about environmental harms).[114] We reason about 'what the social world will be like',[115] or 'how there is reason to want people in general to go about deciding what to do',[116] thereby considering the probable consequences of the adoption of general principles.[117] Objections may therefore concern not only

[109] Rahul Kumar, 'Defending the Moral Moderate' (2000) 28 *Philosophy & Public Affairs* 275, 286. See also R Jay Wallace, *The Moral Nexus* (Princeton University Press, 2019) 136–43, 195.

[110] On this distinction see Samuel Scheffler, 'Morality and Reasonable Partiality' in *Equality and Tradition: Questions of Value in Moral and Political Theory* (Oxford University Press, 2012) 41, 56–68.

[111] Rawls, *Justice as Fairness* (n 79) 50.

[112] Kumar, 'Defending the Moral Moderate' (n 109).

[113] Scanlon, *What We Owe to Each Other* (n 108) 195, 202. See also Jeffrey Brand-Ballard, 'Contractualism and Deontic Restrictions' (2004) 114 *Ethics* 269; Julian Jonker, 'Contractualist Justification and the Direction of a Duty' (2019) 25 *Legal Theory* 200; Jussi Suikkanen, 'Hooker's Rule-Consequentialism and Scanlon's Contractualism – A Re-evaluation' (2022) 35 *Ratio* 261, 270–72.

[114] Rahul Kumar, 'Risking Future Generations' (2018) 21 *Ethical Theory and Moral Practice* 245.

[115] Kumar, 'Defending the Moral Moderate' (n 109) 295–96.

[116] Scanlon, *What We Owe to Each Other* (n 108) 153–54.

[117] ibid 203; Kumar, 'Contractualism on the Shoal of Aggregation' (n 108) 133–35.

the direct results of actions but also the social patterns of actions they permit or demand: for instance, the psychological burdens of constant self-monitoring.[118] Aggregation, in turn, while not sufficient to reject principles, is permissible when competing claims are similar enough: for example, if we can save only one of two groups facing similar risks of harm, it is justified to save the bigger group; and, interestingly, a failure to follow such aggregative decision procedures when they are adequate wrongs all affected parties – even those who happen to benefit from them (say, if they belong to the smaller group of claimants), because the duty to follow the justified principle is owed to all affected parties.[119]

Given these features, it is unsurprising that Scanlon's scheme has been described as a 'characterization of morality in public policy choice',[120] as 'quasi institutional',[121] and as 'legislative' rather than interpersonal – and therefore as suitable for reasoning about collective obligations and the recognition of legal rights.[122] The questions dealt with by utilising Scanlon's scheme are often at the level of generality dealt with by constitutional rights realisation reasoning: for instance, exempting ambulances from traffic rules, permitting air travel or the sale of certain products, distributing vaccines, building schools or research facilities, or placing additives in groundwater.[123]

While the details of Scanlon's scheme diverge from proportionality analysis, it illuminates the possibility of a better balance between generality and relationality, on which indirect horizontality models can rely. It justifies the systematicity of realisation reasoning: standing in relationships of recognition and respect with all affected parties obligates us to accept the results of such fair reasoning structures, and even aggregation if the competing claims are similar. It also leaves room within this structure for relational considerations. The one-to-one comparison of claims on a social scale does not focus on the isolated relationships of homogenous citizens with the state. Rather, because the legitimacy of realisation reasoning also relies on recognition and respect between citizens as private agents, it might have to take into consideration the unique features of their relationships – as is often the case when thinking about which private law rights and duties to adopt. This careful interplay between relationality and

[118] Kumar, 'Defending the Moral Moderate' (n 109) 304–07.

[119] Kumar, 'Contractualism on the Shoal of Aggregation' (n 108) 142, 146; TM Scanlon, 'Contractualism and Justification' in Markus Stepanians and Michael Frauchiger (eds), *Reason, Justification, and Contractualism: Themes from Scanlon* (de Gruyter, 2021) 17, 31–32.

[120] Aaron James, 'Contractualism's (Not So) Slippery Slope' (2012) 18 *Legal Theory* 263, 289.

[121] Andrew Lister, 'Contractualist Alternatives to the Veil of Ignorance' (2023) 31 *Journal of Political Philosophy* 177, 188.

[122] Liam Murphy, 'Nonlegislative Justification' in Jeff McMahan, Tim Campbell, James Goodrich and Ketan Ramakrishnan (eds), *Principles and Persons: The Legacy of Derek Parfit* (Oxford University Press, 2021) 247, 258, 260, 267.

[123] See, eg, Kumar, 'Contractualism on the Shoal of Aggregation' (n 108) 148–49; James, 'Contractualism's (Not So) Slippery Slope' (n 120) 272–73; Rahul Kumar, 'Risking and Wronging' (2015) 43 *Philosophy & Public Affairs* 27, 32–35; Johann Frick, 'Contractualism and Social Risk' (2015) 43 *Philosophy & Public Affairs* 175, 181–82.

generality – and the fact that this allocative form of reasoning complements Rawls's more political and distributive scheme – can help us structure horizontal realisation reasoning in ways that avoid the pitfalls of strong indirect models, by distinguishing delineation from realisation reasoning and making room in the latter for contextual and relational reasons for regulation. Thus, the next section argues that Rawls's and Scanlon's contractualisms justify priority and reconciliation principles: both upstream between structural and allocative reasons and downstream with strictly relational reasons. These principles will be further developed in the next chapters, but even in their crude forms they can further highlight the deficiencies of strong indirect models.

4.6. REALISATION REASONING

Allocative reasoning can evaluate not only the direct results of legal norms (say, whether they effectively prohibit actions that amount to subordination or exploitation), but also the social patterns of conduct that they permit, prohibit or require:[124] for example, whether they impose heavy psychological burdens of constant self-monitoring to figure out if we should benefit others.[125] In this sense, allocative reasoning occupies an intermediate level of generality, between distributions through the basic structure and the specific details of rights and duties within private relationships, associations and practices. This intermediate level of reasoning can integrate systematicity and relationality. For example, when thinking about replacing tort law with public insurance, we must compare distributive claims about effective compensation for injuries and relational claims about the potential erosion of our sense of agency and the notion that we owe it to others, as moral agents, to treat them fairly.[126]

Against crude consequentialist approaches, this does not mean that realisation reasoning must aggregate interests and needs while treating right-holders as receptacles of value.[127] The benefit to one person as a source of valid claims does not cancel claims about the burdens imposed on others. Respect for right-holders does not require setting aside the interests and claims of others: respect can be shown by how the right-holder's interests are taken into account by the duty-bearer.[128] This means that direct and indirect relationships of recognition

[124] Scanlon, 'Contractualism and Justification' (n 119) 24.

[125] Kumar, 'Defending the Moral Moderate' (n 109) 304–07.

[126] David Enoch, 'Tort Liability and Taking Responsibility' in John Oberdiek (ed), *Philosophical Foundations of the Law of Torts* (Oxford University Press, 2014) 250. See also Scott Hershovitz, 'Treating Wrongs as Wrongs: An Expressive Argument for Tort Law' (2017) 10 *Journal of Tort Law* 405.

[127] See generally Alastair Norcross, 'Two Dogmas of Deontology: Aggregation, Rights, and the Separateness of Persons' (2009) 26 *Social Philosophy and Policy* 76, 77–78; Richard Yetter Chappell, 'Value Receptacles' (2015) 49 *Noûs* 322.

[128] Simon Cabulea May, 'Moral Status and the Direction of Duties' (2012) 123 *Ethics* 113, 124.

and respect with the potential beneficiaries of legal regulation can shape and constrain constitutional realisation reasoning. While sometimes (say, in some areas of private law) we exercise and claim rights as dissociated individuals, in constitutional law we do so as associated citizens. It is a failure of disrespect towards other members of the political collective to expect their interests to be set aside when considering how to realise our constitutional rights.[129]

The justification for systematicity in realisation reasoning relies, therefore, not only on the unique nature of the state as an agent or on the legitimacy of distributing justified shares of burdens of realising collective responsibilities to the collective's members. Rather, when the state limits journalistic speech to protect the dignity of celebrities, limits a seller's freedom of contract to protect underaged customers or obligates employers to accommodate disabled employees, it also draws legitimacy from the moral relationships between these types of duty-bearers and these types of right-holders. Importantly, this moral support is conditional: it comes only if the state takes seriously certain moral priority and reconciliation principles.

4.6.1. Second-Order Reasons and Contextualism

The fundamental normative challenge for horizontal realisation reasoning, not only from the contractualist perspective but also from sophisticated consequentialist perspectives,[130] is how to properly engage and realise relational values such as recognition, respect, consent, intimacy, trust, foreseeability or reasonableness within systematic and general forms of reasoning. Strong indirect models, I claimed, pull too strongly towards the latter end of the spectrum. Scanlon's focus on mediated moral relationships of recognition and respect is helpful because it opens the door for second-order reasons and therefore for contextualism and relationality.

The first step is adding second-order reasons. As noted above, if first-order reasons are for or against certain courses of conduct, second-order reasons are about when and how to engage first-order reasons: that is, about the choice situation.[131] For example, we might have good first-order reasons to purchase a new car from a certain dealership, but second-order reasons not to do so at a certain time because we are too tired to evaluate the transaction's details. Similarly, in the legal context, there could be substantive first-order reasons for certain reforms but institutional second-order reasons about the authority or

[129] Rowan Cruft, *Human Rights, Ownership, and the Individual* (Oxford University Press, 2019) 78–79.

[130] Philip Pettit, 'The Inescapability of Consequentialism' in Ulrike Heuer and Gerald Lang (eds), *Luck, Value, and Commitment: Themes from the Ethics of Bernard Williams* (Oxford University Press, 2012) 41, 44–47.

[131] See Ruth Chang, 'Putting Together Morality and Well-Being' in *Practical Conflicts* (n 49) 118, 140–47.

expertise of different agents or rule of law second-order reasons about legal stability that determine when and how to engage first-order reasons.

Exclusionary reasons, not to even weigh or engage certain first-order reasons, are basic second-order reasons.[132] For example, it could be held that judges should not decide political issues, as they fall in the legislature's province. Closer to our topic, and as noted in chapter 2, exclusionary reasons shape the relational structure of private rights-and-duties relationships: there are reasons not to expose private relationships, associations and practices to certain types of external influence. For example, the unique normativity and underlying values of academic activities can justify not subjecting them to constant political scrutiny in an attempt to evaluate their promotion of social equality, even if reform in this regard is generally justified.

Exclusionary reasons make room for contextualism: the reasons that we engage can focus on the special normative and factual features of the problem. Philosophers from Aristotle to Berlin presented contextualism as part of the solution to problems of comparability in conditions of moral pluralism: conflicts between liberty and equality, for example, cannot be resolved in the abstract by appealing to a general formula, but only in the context of particular cases – say, discrimination in hiring decisions.[133] The resolution of such conflicts remains under-generalised, in the sense that we do not try to locate them in a broader normative scheme whose parts are fully consistent.[134] We do not approach them with a general solution that we apply to them, nor do we leave them with one. In the constitutional context, this means that constitutional rights maintain their general form. They keep conflicting and overlapping at the constitutional level. Their conflicts are resolved only at the sub-constitutional level, through norms that could be regularly changed – for example, if we decide that we must better reconcile freedom of speech and dignity in defamation law.[135]

This implies that relational reasons, touching the normativity and underlying values of private rights-and-duties relationships, get a say about when and how they will be engaged from broader normative perspectives and placed under the weight of constitutional rights that refer to social conditions or states of affairs. In this sense, the superiority of constitutional rights is not exhibited

[132] Joseph Raz, *Practical Reason and Norms* (Oxford University Press, 1999) 182–86. See also Iddo Porat, 'The Dual Model of Balancing' (2005) 27 *Cardozo Law Review* 1393.

[133] Thomas Nagel, 'The Fragmentation of Value' in *Mortal Questions* (Cambridge University Press, 2012) 128, 135; George Crowder, 'Pluralism, Relativism, and Liberalism' in Joshua L Cherniss and Steven B Smith (eds), *The Cambridge Companion to Isaiah Berlin* (Cambridge University Press, 2018) 229, 237–40.

[134] Cass R Sunstein, 'Incompletely Theorized Agreements' (1995) 108 *Harvard Law Review* 1733; Vladislava Stoyanova, 'Common Law Tort of Negligence as a Tool for Deconstructing Positive Obligations under the European Convention on Human Rights' (2020) 24 *International Journal of Human Rights* 632, 638–41.

[135] Barak, *Proportionality* (n 2) 37–44; Da Silva (n 37) 285–92. See also Samantha Besson, 'Human Rights in Relation' in Stijn Smet and Eva Brems (eds), *When Human Rights Clash at the European Court of Human Rights: Conflict or Harmony?* (Oxford University Press, 2017) 23, 29–30.

in each interaction with non-constitutional reasons for regulation, but in more nuanced ways and over time: in how they shape legal regulation as an ongoing and dynamic process – and in the structure of realisation reasoning. Relational second-order reasons can therefore justify using judicial tools that allow the gradual realisation of rights: for example, using soft interpretive methods, giving limited remedies or entering into dialogue with other state agents.[136] This restraint aligns with the culture of justification and the rule of law because second-order reasons can be engaged in principled and transparent ways: even if we cannot reduce them to simple rules, we can present qualitative priority or reconciliation rules that address all relevant factors;[137] and, as importantly, we can incrementally devise more stable and structured principles.

Surveillance.[138] An employer monitored and recorded his employee's online correspondence with his brother and fiancée, which broke the employer's rule prohibiting the use of work computers for personal purposes, leading to the employee's dismissal. Rather than offering a general formula for evaluating privacy invasions by employers, the European Court of Human Rights reduced the level of generality by engaging relational factors closer to their natural habitat.[139] It asked, for example: was the employee informed about the nature and extent of monitoring? Why were the measures taken? Were less intrusive measures available? It found that the right to privacy was violated by the local private law regime's failure to prevent such forms of workplace surveillance, but the result could have been different given other answers to such questions and others. The choice situation was limited to particular aspects of the right to privacy – not to be dismissed after certain forms of surveillance – while ignoring many other complex reasons for regulation.[140] This particular aspect of the general right to privacy was, in a way, 'relationalised': it does not deal with social conditions or states of affairs, such as the protection of privacy at the workplace in general, but with a limited relational pattern. Importantly, such localised and relational aspects of constitutional rights can be reconciled with relational moral elements such as subordination, intimacy or trust, without consequentialising them.

Of course, a balance must constantly be struck between particularity and generality. Different aspects of the right to privacy, for example, must exhibit a strong degree of coherence and integrity, tied to the right's basic features. However, progress can also be made by focusing on relational factors such as disrespect or reliance, rather than societal concerns about threats to privacy in the workplace – even if the latter cannot be completely ignored. When it comes to some decisions, the best we can and should do is contain the tensions by

[136] King (n 1) 289–303.
[137] Cass R Sunstein, *Legal Reasoning and Political Conflict* (Oxford University Press, 1998) 136–47.
[138] *Bărbulescu v Romania*, App no 61496/08 (ECtHR, 5 September 2017).
[139] Samantha Besson, 'Human Rights in Relation' in *When Human Rights Clash* (n 135) 23.
[140] See also Da Silva (n 37).

relying on methods of reasoning, like analogy – long employed in the common law – that are more particularised and nuanced.

4.6.2. Priority and Reconciliation Principles

The contextualism created by second-order reasons allows us to adopt priority and reconciliation rules in horizontal realisation reasoning. I make two claims in this regard. First, structural and allocative reasons take priority in reasoning about the adoption of legal regimes, even if the evaluation of private law regimes from structural or allocative perspectives must rely on relational reasons without crudely consequentialising them. Second, if it is justified to adopt private law regimes, structural and allocative reasons about their details must be diluted and integrated with relational reasons, which determine when and how large-scale reasons can influence rights-and-duties relationships justifiably and effectively. This structure will be further developed as we proceed. At this point, we focus on how it allows us to adopt indirect forms of realisation reasoning that can accommodate moral pluralism better than strong indirect models.

Upstream decisions. We start with the priority of structural and allocative reasons. Clearly, we cannot isolate the legal regulation of private relationships, associations or practices from the basic structure or from allocative patterns: mutual recognition and respect require state agents to consider moral inputs from the standpoints of all affected individuals. While private agents might lack the standing to call other private agents to account as co-citizens or participants in allocative institutions and practices, the state must consider all structural and allocative objections to its activities. This means that individual objections to legal regulation cannot reject structural or allocative facets of the moral universe as irrelevant, even if they rarely form independent parts of extra-legal private relationships.

This entails a certain priority for structural and allocative reasons in horizontal realisation decisions. Social justice has priority with regard to decisions not to recognise private law regimes when they raise moral concerns from the structural perspective: for example, if the enforcement of contracts contributes to social patterns of inequality (such as contracts alienating basic rights without robust consent); or if protections of reputation in defamation law (such as the rights of political figures against journalists) short-circuit the democratic process. Allocative reasoning that focuses on more direct relationships under institutions or practices and relational reasoning that focuses on rights-and-duties relationships are often blind to such structural factors, which social justice is equipped to identify.

Allocative reasons can justify not recognising private law regimes when a person's claim, even if they are not a party to a regulated relationship, association or practice, is morally stronger than the claims that justify this recognition. For example, it might be justified to criminally prohibit certain forms of risk-creation,[141] or to offer reliable public insurance coverage for certain injuries,[142] rather than to adopt a tort regime; and it might be justified not to enforce duly agreed parenthood contracts because of potential harmful impacts on children.[143] Relational reasoning is inadequate in such cases because it focuses on what one party owes to another in the limited context of rights-and-duties relationships, while often ignoring harms to third parties, social conditions and ripple effects, and regulatory alternatives.

When it comes to upstream structural and allocative reasons, large-scale and systematic reasoning is not only permitted but required. Of course, there are constraints on such forms of reasoning as well. For example, to prevent historical or social contingencies from shaping the principles of social justice, Rawls placed deliberating parties behind a 'veil of ignorance'. Scanlon, in turn, relied on the method of one-to-one comparison and allowed aggregation only when competing individual claims are morally similar. My goal here is not to justify these particular methods of reasoning, but only to highlight the kind of arguments that must figure in upstream realisation decisions.

This takes us to the limitations of structural and allocative reasons, even in the genuine domains of their application. To evaluate structural or allocative claims that, for example, tort law or parts of it should be replaced by public insurance, or that some types of contracts should not be enforced, we must be able to figure out how tort law or contract law regimes operate in the relevant contexts. We still focus on the basic structure or on regulatory regimes, and in this sense we engage private rights-and-duties relationships from the outside. However, we do not consequentialise them, because the Rawlsian and Scanlonian frameworks are both internally more nuanced and externally more limited in scope, and therefore leave room for contextualism and relationality.

This is easier to see in the Rawlsian context. Relational values can form part of principles of social justice or constitutional rights if they are justified in the original position (or any equivalent reasoning scheme) or at the constitutional delineation stage. It seems reasonable that some aspects of the rights we find in private law – for instance, prohibited forms of treatment and the powers to contract or own property – will form parts of principles of social justice and constitutional rights. However, they will obligate only the state, and their details will have to be filled at the later legislative and application stages, while relying on more specific information and on relational principles of local justice.

[141] John Oberdiek, *Imposing Risk* (Oxford University Press, 2017) 137–50.

[142] Christopher J Robinette, 'Harmonizing Wrongs and Compensation' (2021) 80 *Maryland Law Review* 343.

[143] Gregg Strauss, 'Parentage Agreements are not Contracts' (2022) 90(6) *Fordham Law Review* 2645, 2663–72.

Scanlon's framework is a little murkier in this regard. Scanlon noted that he addresses a kind of moral wrongness that need not involve right-violations.[144] In this sense, his scheme operates upstream from rights-and-duties relationships. However, as Wallace adds, relational moral elements such as claims or wrongdoing still have a place in this scheme.[145] The starting point here is that the force of moral reasons is determined by their nature as claims made within moral relationships. When these relationships involve rights and directed duties – for instance, between contractual parties or between drivers and pedestrians – allocative claims must, to figure out what mutual recognition and respect require, explore their relational normativity, which is comprised of interconnected concepts such as claims, standing, responsibility, accountability, blame and remedies. Consider tort law's different responses to agents that performed similar actions with different results: two agents drove carelessly, but only the one that hit a pedestrian will be liable to pay compensation. Tort regimes that leave room for such forms of luck are justified only if the claims of unlucky drivers are weaker than competing claims – say, of pedestrians. It is important, however, when evaluating claims in this regard, to consider the situation not only in allocative terms (such as the amount of compensation paid) but also in more relational terms: for example, the accountability of drivers to pedestrians and the latter's legitimate expectations – and the difficulties of using tort law to regulate mere risk-creation. Thus, while structural and allocative reasons have a certain priority in upstream decisions about whether to adopt private law regimes, for which relational reasons are too short-sighted, the latter still have roles to play in the comparison of structural and allocative reasons – roles that strong indirect models have difficulties computing.

Downstream decisions. The limitations of structural and allocative reasons – and thus of strong indirect models – are even more visible in downstream decisions, about the details of rights-and-duties relationships. The systematicity and generality of these reasons do not entail that they are unlimited in scope – they do not cover the entire moral domain. We saw that Rawls leaves room for local justice while Scanlon leaves room for rights and directed duties. The converse of this limited scope is that structural or allocative claims that particular private law regimes should be adopted are subordinated, in downstream decisions, to relational reasons – which determine when and how structural and allocative reasons can and should be integrated within rights-and-duties relationships without creating the problems of complexity, intrusion, crowding out, scrutiny and authority. To put it in the terms used above, even when there are strong first-order structural or allocative reasons for private law's creation or change, second-order reasons can justify contextualism in downstream decisions, and therefore a focus on and a certain priority to more relational reasons.

[144] TM Scanlon, 'Reply to Leif Wenar' (2013) 10 *Journal of Moral Philosophy* 400, 403, 405.
[145] Wallace (n 109) 184–88.

Private law must effectively empower right-holders to control the normative situation and call duty-bearers to account while upholding their own interests; and ensure that duty-bearers' responsibilities, even when legally shaped, do not extend beyond the scope of their agency, as it manifests itself in the relationship with the right-holder. Such relational normative structures must express recognition and respect to ground legitimate claims, reactive attitudes, and remedies. The place and weight of large-scale reasons within these normative structures depend on how they tap into and connect their constitutive components – for two main reasons. First, this dependence ensures that large-scale reasons do not overstep their domains, thereby deputising right-holders as private attorneys general and enlisting duty-bearers as cogs in the state's institutional apparatus. Private law empowers us to engage with others consensually and to call them to account for wronging us – not for failures to act in socially desirable ways: for example, to vote, recycle, promote equality, or act with due care. Others are not accountable to us for such failures, which do not justify personal reactive attitudes (though they might justify such attitudes from an impersonal standpoint) or entitle us to remedies (from apologies to compensation). Second, even if it could be justified to shape private law norms in light of large-scale reasons, they often lack the normative resources to say when and how, because they operate at a distance from – and therefore cannot compute the fine details of – private rights-and-duties relationships. The issue lies not with the values underlying structural or allocative claims, but with their systematicity and generality. Such reasons must therefore rely on more relational reasons. This is the mirror image of the weakness and merely indirect roles of relational reasons in upstream decisions. By giving each type of reason priority in its endemic environment, we are able to engage them on their own terms while preventing them from distorting or obscuring each other.

State agents are therefore under strong moral pressure to pursue structural and allocative goals through private law only within the parameters that the relationality of rights and duties entails. The idea is not that such goals become important only if they cross certain thresholds of weight,[146] after all strictly relational reasons have been satisfied,[147] or if they fit in some complex consequentialist scheme.[148] Rather, we engage such goals from a qualitatively different normative perspective. If we find relational paths to be insufficient from structural or allocative perspectives, we may have reasons to forsake or revise our structural, allocative, or relational principles – as part of an ongoing and dynamic attempt to reach reflective equilibrium. But we have good reasons to start with the priority of relationality in downstream decision.

[146] On thresholds, see Larry Alexander, 'Deontology at the Threshold' (2000) 37 *San Diego Law Review* 893.

[147] On lexical priority, see Jeremy Waldron, 'Rights in Conflict' (1989) 99 *Ethics* 503, 513.

[148] On such forms of consequentialism, see Hooker (n 9).

This creates a filtering mechanism: large-scale reasons must be justified and integrated within rights-and-duties relationships. Because this mechanism is grounded in private law's value as a regulatory tool rather than in the structure of litigation or the limited law-making authority of judges, it also pushes back against strong forms of horizontality in non-judicial arenas. The reasons to create congruence between private law and relational structures draw their force from the ways in which rights and duties operate in practice. These reasons, therefore, should structure horizontal realisation reasoning – including in its common proportionality variant. This does not amount to a significant structural change: we still compare the claims of all affected parties and can even resort to aggregation when they are similar. It also need not amount to a deep substantive change: the scheme of priority and reconciliation principles presented above expresses the teleological logic of proportionality, as it holds the promise of better horizontal rights realisation over time.

The problem with strong indirect models is that they employ only structural – or at their most relational moments, allocative – forms of reasoning. Thus, they largely ignore the dependence of realisation through private law on normative resources that the optimising and beneficiary-centered normativity of general constitutional rights lacks. To say that when judges recognise new private law rights, they directly apply the constitution,[149] misses this point and fails to take advantage of the contextualism that indirect models offer.[150] An important aspect of private law norms and claims, is their ability to rely on latent moral values without acting as mere placeholders for consequentialist reasons.[151] For example, even if liberty and equality struggle to resolve concrete discrimination cases, they can still be helpful in unpacking and extending the principles adopted in earlier legal cases;[152] but their contribution depends on their operation in a well-specified relational context.

In this spirit, in a *Discrimination* case decided by the Supreme Court of the United Kingdom, Lady Hale found the decisive factor to be that the objection to providing a cake saying 'support gay marriage' was not to the customer's sexual orientation or political opinions, but to the message itself: no customer would be sold that specific cake and gay customers can buy other cakes.[153] This reasoning, while tied to structural and allocative reasons, is relational, because it does not take issue with the baker's objection to gay couples unless it is causally connected

[149] See Nick Friedman, 'The South African Common Law and the Constitution: Revisiting Horizontality' (2014) 30 *South African Journal on Human Rights* 63, 70–73.

[150] See Mathews (n 12) 6.

[151] Bernard Williams, 'Afterword: What Has Philosophy to Learn from Tort Law?' in David G Owen (ed), *Philosophical Foundations of Tort Law* (Clarendon Press, 1995) 487, 489.

[152] Chris McConnacie, 'Human Dignity, "Unfair Discrimination", and Guidance' (2014) 34 *Oxford Journal of Legal Studies* 609.

[153] *Lee v Ashers Baking Company Ltd* [2018] UKSC 49, paras 34, 47.

to direct discriminatory actions: a connection that exists, for example, when a seller refuses to provide a room with a double bed to a gay couple, because here the good coincides more tightly with the protected trait.[154] The result here does not rely on a large-scale balancing of the duty-bearer's freedom – that their 'publicness' affects – and their ability to promote equality.[155] Rather, such reasons form parts of more relational forms of reasoning, even when they take into account the broader social context. Take, for example, the holding of the European Court of Human Rights that the United Kingdom failed to protect the rights of employees to manifest their religion by sanctioning an employer's prohibition, as part of a dress code, of wearing religious symbols.[156] It is not enough to approach this issue by focusing on the importance of religious liberty in society or even on the dangers posed by employers to this liberty. Constitutional rights realisation reasoning must take into account the unique features of rights-and-duties relationships between employers and employees in specific types of workplaces – including their structural and allocative features (for instance, if they are integral to guaranteeing equal opportunity in society). The important point is that many horizontal realisation decisions operate at this more relational level of generality, for which strong indirect models leave little room. As we will see in the next chapter, this does not require neglecting large-scale reasons for regulation or proportionality analysis – merley locating them within a more nuanced reasoning framework.

4.7. CONCLUSION

This chapter took us from the delineation to the realisation of the horizontal dimensions of constitutional rights. It presented the temptation to adopt strong indirect models in response to the teleological orientation of general constitutional rights.[157] However, it claimed that such models ignore, erode or distort relational reasons by failing to take moral pluralism seriously: they ignore qualitative distinctions between structural, allocative and relational reasons, and second-order reasons to adopt priority and reconciliation rules that allow each type of reason to operate in its natural normative habitat.

Constitutional and human rights lawyers are often less concerned about these issues, which seem to be about private law's autonomy or integrity. But as we started seeing, disharmony in horizontal realisation reasoning will often lead

[154] *Bull v Hall* [2013] UKSC 73. See also Eugenio Velasco Ibarra, 'Lee v Ashers Baking Company Ltd and Others: The Inapplicability of Discrimination Law to an Illusory Conflict of Rights' (2023) 83 *Modern Law Review* 190.

[155] Contra Tarunabh Khaitan, *A Theory of Discrimination Law* (Oxford University Press, 2015) 200.

[156] *Eweida v United Kingdom* [2013] ECHR 37.

[157] This temptation is even greater in legal systems where the highest court does not decide private law cases, which could explain the attractiveness of strong indirect models for civil law systems.

to less effective and justified results in terms of constitutional rights realisation. Thus, not only private lawyers have good reasons to find more nuanced indirect horizontality models. Such models must appreciate, as Nagel noted, that some reasons are not merely incompatible in the sense that they cannot be realised simultaneously, but are in direct opposition in the sense that they condemn each other.[158] However, as Nagel adds, we can develop nuanced forms of reconciliation, whose aim is not 'to deny pluralism but to encompass it in a system that permits conflicts to be adjudicated without the triumph of one master value'.[159] This chapter takes this advice seriously. Nonetheless, adopting this nuanced and pluralistic approach also raises the spectre of fragmentation and conservatism in constitutional horizontality practices. The next chapter addresses this concern, while criticising weak indirect horizontality models.

[158] Thomas Nagel, 'Pluralism and Coherence' in *The Legacy of Isaiah Berlin* (n 35) 105, 106–07.
[159] ibid 109–10.

5

Realisation as Regulation

5.1. INTRODUCTION

THE PREVIOUS CHAPTER shifted the focus from the delineation of constitutional rights to their realisation, and from direct models that similarly obligate both public and private agents to indirect models that obligate primarily public agents, but also regarding private actions and activities. It argued that strong indirect models, which give realisation reasoning consequentialist features, reintroduce the problems of direct horizontality, because they do not take seriously the predicament of moral pluralism and qualitative distinctions between reasons for regulation: specifically, the priority of structural and allocative reasons in upstream decisions about the adoption of regulatory regimes and the need to integrate such reasons with relational reasons in downstream decisions about the details of private law regimes.

This chapter continues to develop this realisation reasoning framework. In many ways, it mirrors the previous chapter. It addresses weak indirect models, which see qualitative distinctions between reasons for regulation as grounds to separate private law from social justice and constitutional rights, thereby reintroducing the problems of traditional verticality. Interestingly, while strong indirect models rely on widely shared premises in constitutional and human rights theory about the adequacy of proportionality analysis, weak indirect models rely on widely shared premises in private law theory about its incremental and autonomous evolution.

This chapter argues that while the normative structure and underlying values of private rights-and-duties relationships justify discontinuities between private law and constitutional rights, weak indirect models fail to provide substantive justifications for these discontinuities and therefore construe them as too rigid and fail to reconcile all relevant reasons for regulation. They ignore the fact that private law not only identifies responsibilities in response to relational inputs like consent or causation but also assigns responsibilities in response to structural and allocative reasons for regulation. In this sense, there are strong and dynamic ties between private law's operation and evolution and the system of constitutional rights. While relational reasons have a priority in downstream decisions about the details of rights-and-duties relationships, these reasons must, to meet the constitution's demands, respond to structural and allocative reasons effectively and justifiably.

The chapter further explores how structural and allocative reasons can and should influence private law rights-and-duties relationships without creating the pitfalls of strong indirect models. The bottom line is that this task is familiar: in many ways, the common law has addressed this challenge for centuries – albeit often slowly and without sufficient integration of judicial principles with legislative and administrative inputs. I will finally touch, in this regard, on the unique limitations of litigation and adjudication with regard to constitutional horizontality. I will claim that the best way to deal with these limitations is not to isolate adjudication from constitutional horizontality but to see the latter as a collaborative regulatory practice.

This chapter unfolds in the following order. The next section presents an idealised version of weak indirect models, following basic features of their adoption in the United Kingdom and Canada. The following sections highlight the prescriptive deficiency of these models by distinguishing between the identification and the assignment of responsibilities, and explaining why assignments are necessary components of the horizontal realisation of constitutional rights. Finally, the chapter locates both identifications and assignments in a normatively rich conception of common law evolution, which relies on the collaborative effort of all state branches.

5.2. WEAK INDIRECT EFFECT

Like strong indirect models, weak indirect models see constitutional rights as shaping private law without obligating private agents. However, unlike strong indirect models, weak models recognise qualitative distinctions between large-scale 'policy' reasons and 'principled' relational reasons for horizontal rights realisation. Weak indirect models accept a certain priority of structural and allocative reasons in upstream reasoning about the adoption of private law regimes – in decisions considered political and policy-driven. However, they hold that once such regimes are up and running, the details of their ongoing operation are not constrained by constitutional rights. Rather, the values underlying those rights join the rich ensemble of values that shape private law's evolution through the common law development of relational principles.

The resulting institutional division of labour – upstream legislative choices are driven largely by policy reasons while downstream judicial decisions operate within private law's relational structure – reflects basic reasons of democratic legitimacy, separation of powers, and the rule of law. But it also accommodates moral pluralism by bringing different regulatory perspectives to bear on the process of horizontal realisation. It expresses the idea that private law cannot evolve in a purely top-down manner: to borrow Charles Fried's words, policy reasons 'descend from on high but stop some twenty feet above the ground' – from there, we must work from within private law 'to complete this structure of ideals and values, to bring it down to earth'.[1] This point applies not only to explanations of private law but also to prescriptions about its evolution so that it aligns more closely with constitutional rights. It is reflected in the claim made in the previous chapter, that structural and allocative reasons must be integrated with relational reasons to shape private rights-and-duties relationships.

5.2.1. From Rights to Values

The crucial move for weak indirect models is the transformation of constitutional rights into values in the context of private law's operation and incremental evolution.[2] This does not mean that these rights become entirely indifferent to private actions, which would effectively revert back to traditional verticality. Equality can still entail prescriptions about private discrimination, privacy regarding workplace surveillance, and dignity concerning defamation. These prescriptions can constrain, as duties, upstream decisions about the adoption or abolition of private law regimes. However, once such regimes are in place, constitutional rights guide by entailing imperfect duties with soft edges. Failures to realise these rights when interpreting legislation or developing the common law are wrong, but do not wrong any right-holder in particular.[3]

This transformation of rights into values originates in the seminal *Boycott* case, mentioned in the first chapter. In that case, the German Constitutional Court distinguished between the 'subjective' dimensions of constitutional rights as claimable rights against the state and their 'objective' dimensions as values whose 'radiating effect' influences the interpretation, application and development of all areas of law.[4] Traces of this approach can also be found in South Africa.[5] But this model found fuller expression in Canada.[6]

Defamation. After allegations made at a press conference on behalf of the Church of Scientology against Hill, a Crown attorney, proved groundless, the attorney sued for defamation. Lower courts imposed on the church liabilities for aggravated and punitive damages. The church appealed, claiming that the

[1] Charles Fried, 'Artificial Reason of the Law or: What Lawyers Know' (1981) 60 *Texas Law Review* 35, 57.

[2] See Robert Alexy, *A Theory of Constitutional Rights* (Julian Rivers tr, Oxford University Press, 2002) 355–59; Gonçalo de Almeida Ribeiro, 'The Effects of Fundamental Rights in Private Disputes' in Hugh Collins (ed), *European Contract Law and the Charter of Fundamental Rights* (Intersentia, 2018) 219, 235–38.

[3] See Anton Fagan, 'Determining the Stakes: Binding and Non-binding Bills of Rights' in Daniel Friedmann and Daphne Barak-Erez (eds), *Human Rights in Private Law* (Hart Publishing, 2001) 73.

[4] 7 BVerfGE 198 (15 January 1958). See also Jud Mathews, *Extending Rights' Reach* (Oxford University Press, 2018) 49–56.

[5] Stu Woolman, 'The Amazing, Vanishing Bill of Rights' (2007) 124 *South African Law Journal* 762.

[6] Mathews (n 4) 175, 180–83.

common law failed to adequately protect the constitutional right to freedom of expression. Building on an earlier seminal decision,[7] the Supreme Court of Canada held that 'the party challenging the common law cannot allege that the common law violates a Charter right because, quite simply, Charter rights do not exist in the absence of state action. The most that the private litigant can do is argue that the common law is inconsistent with Charter values' – values that do not ground duties, but 'provide the guidelines for any modification to the common law which the court feels is necessary'.[8] This gave the Court the leeway to uphold the lower courts' decisions and reject the claim that the common law should be changed to give additional protection to freedom of expression – for example, by adopting the 'actual malice' standard, mentioned in the previous chapter (requiring the duty-bearer to have knowledge of or show reckless disregard for their statement's falsity).[9]

A weak indirect model was also adopted, though less explicitly, in the United Kingdom. The Human Rights Act 1998 requires judges to interpret primary and subordinate legislation compatibly with rights recognised by the European Convention on Human Rights;[10] and if this is impossible, to issue a declaration of incompatibility, which does not affect the validity of the legal norm.[11] The Act emphasises that actions or failures to act by all public authorities, including courts, must be compatible with the Convention rights, except failures to introduce or pass primary legislation or make remedial orders.[12] It could be claimed that the Act goes further than Canadian jurisprudence by obligating judges to act compatibly with Convention rights. However, the Act explicitly imposes only interpretive duties on judges, which is important when combined with the fact that the Act imposes no duties to legislate, reflecting the foundational constitutional principle of parliamentary sovereignty.

This has led to much confusion and debate about the nature of the Act's horizontal influence, with theoretical claims ranging from direct horizontality to weak indirect horizontality. Gavin Phillipson and Alexander Williams offer a forceful and morally robust account of the Act's horizontal aspects, sensitive to judicial principles and trends: they claim that judges are obligated and not merely empowered to develop the common law compatibly with Convention rights, yet only incrementally.[13] Because this incrementalism constraint does not derive from individual rights but from constitutional principles such as

[7] *Retail, Wholesale and Department Store Union, Local 580 v Dolphin Delivery Ltd* [1986] 2 SCR 573.

[8] *Hill v Church of Scientology of Toronto* [1995] 2 SCR 1130, paras 95, 97.

[9] See ch 4, n 33.

[10] Article 3 (referring to the European Convention for the Protection of Human Rights and Fundamental Freedoms (4 November 1950) 213 UNTS 221).

[11] Article 4.

[12] Article 6.

[13] Gavin Phillipson and Alexander Williams, 'Horizontal Effect and the Constitutional Constraint' (2011) 74 *Modern Law Review* 878.

parliamentary sovereignty, the separation of powers, and the rule of law (which the Act does not deviate from), this weak model treats judicial obligations as largely imperfect.[14] Rights are simply overridden if judges cannot realise them incrementally. If there are no existing private law precedents or principles to develop, or if there are contrary ones, the hands of judges are tied.[15]

Thus, under weak indirect models, judges engage in full constitutional scrutiny of private law only to evaluate the choices of non-judicial state agents. For example, in Canada, it was held that the repeal of an act that facilitated collective bargaining between farm workers and their employers unfairly left this group of employees unprotected by labour law.[16] In the United Kingdom, it was held that the heterosexual definition of a spouse in the Rent Act 1977 offered inadequate protection to the right to private life and home of the homosexual spouse of a deceased statutory tenant, as it failed to protect him against eviction by a private landlord.[17] In both cases, it was the constitutional goal of ensuring equal legislative protection that was decisive: had there been no legislation, the decisions would have been more circumscribed.

The restricted nature of judicial rights realisation under the weak indirect model is demonstrated by the *Privacy* case, mentioned above, touching Naomi Campbell's claim that tabloid publications about her Narcotics Anonymous meetings violated her right to privacy. The House of Lords held that the Human Rights Act does not create a right against invasion of privacy but only obligates courts to interpret existing private law rights to see if they can better protect this interest.[18] Building on a balance between the values of privacy and freedom of expression, the tort right against 'breach of confidence' was stretched beyond direct relations to cover the tabloid's actions. Thus, while common private law is not immune to constitutional scrutiny, this scrutiny is limited: it is confined to the conceptual structure of existing doctrine. This structure reflects deep undercurrents in the theory of private law.

5.2.2. Private Law Traditionalism

In the previous chapter, I located the roots of strong indirect models in deep undercurrents in constitutional and human rights thinking regarding the aptitude of proportionality analysis for realisation reasoning. Here, I want to shed light on weak indirect models by locating their roots in deep undercurrents in private law theory. As explained in chapter 3, traditional private law theories

[14] ibid 888–90.
[15] ibid 907–09.
[16] *Dunmore v Ontario (Attorney General)* [2001] 3 SCR 1016.
[17] *Ghaidan v Godin-Mendoza* [2004] UKHL 30.
[18] *Campbell v MGN Ltd* [2004] UKHL 22. See also Hugh Collins, 'Private Law, Fundamental Rights, and the Rule of Law' (2008) 121 *West Virginia Law Review* 1, 16–17.

highlight its relationality, largely in response to instrumentalist theories, which see it as a set of malleable regulatory tools. The idea that private law is developed mostly by judges, who have discretion about how to accommodate constitutional values, alleviates deep concerns among theorists and practitioners about private law's corruption by external influence.

In this picture, the interactions between political and relational reasons for horizontal rights realisation are brief and shallow. Relational reasons have limited and indirect upstream influence: for example, highlighting the structural or allocative importance of contracting or safety from certain risks in different social spheres. This often leads to the prioritisation of large-scale policy considerations. For example, many prominent tort theorists regard whether to replace tort law with forms of public insurance as a question falling within the political domain and thus as largely guided by policy reasons.[19]

Sometimes this lethargy flows downstream as well. For example, leading tort theorists John Goldberg and Ben Zipursky hold that tort law's normative structure and basic concepts must be understood in light of the principle of civil recourse for legal wrongs.[20] However, because their approach is positivistic (the force of tort norms derives solely from their legal validity), it lacks the capacity to ensure that tort law's evolution preserves its nature as a system of morally robust rights and duties.[21] At most, their theory limits policy reasoning in judicial decisions, which they see as merely elucidating tort law's relational norms and principles.[22] From a legislative perspective, relational reasons merely shed light on tort law's basic features and possible pathologies.[23] These reasons may ultimately be overridden by policy reasons (which can, for example, justify replacing tort law with public insurance).[24]

Many private law theorists, however, are less permissive. Although they may not regard relational moral principles as constraining upstream reasoning about whether to adopt private law regimes, they see these principles as dominating the operation and evolution of these regimes. They argue not only that policy reasons have little to say about the finer details of private law rights-and-duties

[19] See Jules L Coleman, *Risks and Wrongs* (Cambridge University Press, 1992) 402–03; Ernest J Weinrib, *The Idea of Private Law*, 2nd edn (Oxford University Press, 2012) 24–25, 210; Arthur Ripstein, *Private Wrongs* (Harvard University Press, 2016) 292–94.

[20] John CP Goldberg and Benjamin C Zipursky, *Recognizing Wrongs* (Harvard University Press, 2020).

[21] Jean Thomas, 'The Elusive Third Way? The Role of Positive Morality in Recognizing Wrongs' (2023) 27 *Jerusalem Review of Legal Studies* 74, 80–87; Timothy Borgerson, 'The Weakness of Relationality as a Unifying Concept in Tort' (2023) 68 *American Journal of Jurisprudence* 131, 134–40.

[22] Goldberg and Zipursky, *Recognizing Wrongs* (n 20) 239–40, 279–80. For a similar approach, see Felipe Jimenez, 'A Formalist Theory of Contract Law Adjudication' (2020) 5 *Utah Law Review* 1121.

[23] Goldberg and Zipursky, *Recognizing Wrongs* (n 20) 271. See also John CP Goldberg and Benjamin C Zipursky, 'Legal Wrongs Between the Prescriptive and the Positive: Replies to Commentators on Recognizing Wrongs' (2023) 27 *Jerusalem Review of Legal Studies* 99.

[24] John CP Goldberg and Benjamin C Zipursky, 'Replies to Commentators' (2022) 41 *Law and Philosophy* 127 n 5.

relationships – about concepts like consent, intention or causation – but that such concepts are inherently independent of structural and allocative reasons.[25] At most, policy reasons may indirectly inform relational reasoning: for example, by indicating when certain acts do not amount to contractual consent or constitute an unreasonable risk imposition because of power disparities between the parties (say, between a landlord and a tenant).

Donal Nolan, for example, argued that English negligence law and human rights law serve qualitatively different purposes – neither of which takes priority because the Human Rights Act is not defined as constitutional higher law;[26] and that a 'process of convergence would serve to distort the law of negligence both by undermining established principles' (e.g., causation requirements or the distinction between acts and omissions) 'and by introducing alien concepts'.[27] These disparities allow for, at most, limited cross-influence: for example, the refinement of shared concepts such as basic interests.[28]

Similarly, Arthur Ripstein argued that public law can create normative conditions that allow tort law to hold private agents responsible for their actions without recourse to the policy goals that shape public law.[29] Such recourse would deviate from tort law's organising moral principle, that no person is in charge of another in terms of the innate rights to body and property, which limits the scope of our responsibilities and duties to others.[30] Duties to aid or protect, which were not voluntarily assumed, can therefore be imposed only by what are seen as public law domains: indirectly by domains like tax law and directly by domains like criminal law[31] or discrimination law.[32]

Ernest Weinrib's theory is helpful here, as he makes a serious effort to integrate traditional private law theory and constitutional horizontality. His theory's organising principle is the bipolar structure of relationships between people as the doer and the sufferer of private law wrongs.[33] The legitimacy of judicial decisions depends not only on their fit with existing doctrine, but also 'on the fairness and coherence of the connection that the judge's reasoning forges between the normative position of the particular plaintiff and that

[25] See, eg, Robert Stevens, *Torts and Rights* (Oxford University Press, 2014) 306–19.

[26] Donal Nolan, 'Negligence and Human Rights Law: The Case for Separate Development' (2013) 76 *Modern Law Review* 286, 293–98.

[27] ibid 302.

[28] ibid 313–19.

[29] Ripstein, *Private Wrongs* (n 19) 290–95.

[30] ibid 69–70. For a similar approach, see Martín Hevia, *Reasonableness and Responsibility: A Theory of Contract Law* (Springer, 2013) 56–59.

[31] Arthur Ripstein, 'Three Duties to Rescue: Moral, Civil, and Criminal' (2000) 19 *Law and Philosophy* 751.

[32] Arthur Ripstein, 'Private Authority and the Role of Rights: A Reply' (2016) 14 *Jerusalem Review of Legal Studies* 64, 82–85.

[33] Ernest J Weinrib, *Corrective Justice* (Oxford University Press, 2012) 41, 69–79; Ernest J Weinrib, *Reciprocal Freedom: Private Law and Public Right* (Oxford University Press, 2022) 1–12.

of the particular defendant'.[34] Private law's bipolar structure therefore limits its evolution, in the sense that the justifications of rights and duties must be inherently – that is, pre-legally – correlative.[35]

Weinrib sees room within this framework for constitutional rights to shape the translation of dignity and equal freedom into private law norms and principles:[36] these values serve as additional sources in the processes of rendering private law terms more determinate, which judges must take into account when developing private law – potentially, even if it means revising or abolishing existing norms or principles.[37] However, although Weinrib at times approaches a strong indirect position (for example, in terms of the duties placed on judges to develop private law or to resolve rights conflicts by relying on proportionality tests),[38] his approach is still largely weak. The important factor here is that constitutional rights that entail structural or allocative demands gain no weight in private law reasoning, because these demands are inconsistent with private law's focus on negative duties,[39] and 'do not connect the beneficiaries of the right to any particular private party'.[40] The most private law can ask of private agents with regard to such constitutional rights is to allow the state to realise them and not to impair their ongoing exercise or enjoyment.[41]

Eviction. A lower court in South Africa authorised the eviction of a public school operating on private property during the school year, after the responsible state agent failed to reach an agreement with the owner about payment for the property's use. The Constitutional Court held that the lower court did not properly consider the constitutional right of the students to basic education and the correlating constitutional duty of the property owner. It suspended the eviction until the public body ensured that the students could attend alternative schools, thereby deviating from the common law rule that placed no such limits on the right to evict.[42]

Weinrib sees this case as reflecting the principle that while public agents have positive duties to realise constitutional rights – such as ensuring that students have available school venues – private agents have only derivative negative duties – not to diminish the enjoyment or exercise of constitutional rights. In this case, the property owner was obligated not to impair the state's efforts to secure basic education[43] (and in a similar case, a property owner was obligated not to evict illegal occupiers if the eviction would render them homeless).[44]

[34] Weinrib, *Reciprocal Freedom* (n 33) 140.
[35] ibid 19–20, 27.
[36] ibid 121–23.
[37] ibid 131–48.
[38] ibid 178.
[39] ibid 152.
[40] ibid 159.
[41] ibid 149–51, 156–60.
[42] *Governing Body of the Juma Musjid Primary School v Essay NO* [2011] ZACC 13.
[43] ibid paras 58–60.
[44] *City of Johannesburg v Blue Moonlight Properties 39 (Pty) Ltd* [2011] ZACC 33.

In a similar spirit, although Weinrib argued that discrimination can be recognised as a tort if the constitution changes the social meaning of certain insults to one's dignity,[45] this value will struggle to justify, within this framework, affirmative duties to accommodate the needs of disabled employees or to protect employees from harassment by customers – and will do even less work when thinking about complex structural issues such as gentrification. This limitation, crucially, is not grounded in a balance of the rights of the parties or in systematic arguments about social structures or states of affairs. Rather, it reflects the subordination of constitutional horizontality to what are perceived as private law's structural limitations.

Thus, what started as an institutional division of labour – large-scale private law reform falling within the jurisdiction of legislatures, with judges merely developing private law while focusing on relational principles – turns into a softening of the edges and a weakening of the force of constitutional rights.[46] This transformation – treating rights as values that entail imperfect duties regarding judicial decisions to apply or develop private law – prioritises private law's relational structure and existing principles and doctrines over the structural and allocative reasons for horizontal realisation entailed by constitutional rights. Occasionally, non-judicial agents will engage in policy-driven private law reform. But much of the action, as reflected in traditional private law theory, takes place in judicial decisions; and here, the progress towards accommodating the constitution's requirements is incremental and often even circuitous.

5.3. IDENTIFYING RESPONSIBILITIES

Weak indirect models have many benefits. However, they are still limited in terms of fulfilling the progressive potential of constitutional horizontality. They reintroduce some of the problems of traditional verticality and overly rigid public–private distinctions, because their responses to the predicament of moral pluralism are merely side-effects of democratic, institutional and rule of law concerns: they do not fully and deeply reconcile structural, allocative and relational reasons for horizontal rights realisation.

One problem, in this regard, is that weak indirect models say little about upstream decisions – in practice, seeing these decisions as unconstrained political or policy choices. The principle of legislative supremacy carries great weight in common law legal systems, but constitutional horizontality is a process

[45] Lorraine E Weinrib and Ernest J Weinrib, 'Constitutional Values and Private Law in Canada' in *Human Rights in Private Law* (n 3) 43, 65–66.

[46] It should be noted that similar results could be reached by seeing constitutional rights as focused on internal features of regulated relationships with the right-holder: see Kai Möller, 'Dworkin's Theory of Rights in the Age of Proportionality' (2018) 12 *Law & Ethics of Human Rights* 281, 293.

directed not only at courts. Relational reasons for regulation – including second-order reasons touching the nature of private relationships, associations and practices – should also be properly engaged in legislative and administrative settings, even if, as explained in the previous chapter, this must occur in the context of more systematic reasoning.

A second and more significant problem arises downstream, in the shaping of private law rights-and-duties relationships. Weak indirect models ignore many political aspects of private law's evolution and their interactions with the relational aspects of its operation. They construe the qualitative distinctions between political and relational reasons as too rigid. To expose and explain this problem, this section adds that private law evolves not merely incrementally by identifying responsibilities in response to relational factors such as consent or causation. Rather, private law also evolves by assigning responsibilities in a regulatory and systematic manner. Weak indirect models lack the tools to address such assignments because they rigidly separate between public and private and between political and relational reasons for regulation.

5.3.1. Passive Regulation

A basic distinction exists between identifications and assignments of responsibility.[47] While identifications merely reveal that agents *are* responsible because of how their actions fit within an authoritative normative scheme (for example, a dinner guest is responsible to pay for a vase they broke), assignments change a normative scheme to *make* agents responsible (for example, a dinner guest is responsible to bring wine in response to the host's request). Assignments determine 'who is best doing what and seeing to what, and hence answering for what'.[48] Thus, if identifications are correct or incorrect, assignments are justified or unjustified.

Identifications are a basic function of private law. They can be remedial (say, awarding compensation) or substantive (say, determining whether an action falls within an existing duty). In both cases, they involve discretion and authority. However, they fit judicial reasoning because they present judicial decisions as merely revealing existing responsibilities by relying on norms recognised by law as it is, even if only latently and implicitly. Goldberg and Zipursky describe tort law's evolution in this spirit: 'even when new torts emerge, it is usually

[47] See David Miller, *National Responsibility and Global Justice* (Oxford University Press, 2007) 83–86.

[48] John Gardner, 'The Negligence Standard: Political Not Metaphysical' (2017) 80 *Modern Law Review* 1, 11–12. See also Robert Goodin, 'Social Welfare as a Collective Social Responsibility' in *Social Welfare and Individual Responsibility: For and Against* (Cambridge University Press, 1998) 97, 150.

because courts have come to realise that a pattern of liability imposed under recognised torts implicitly identifies a new wrong'.[49]

Such judicial identifications respond quite well to the voluntaristic concerns that animate the restrictive conception of personal responsibility – which, as discussed in chapter 3, applies pressure on private law to preserve strong congruence between each agent's choices and their responsibilities to others. Weak indirect models pair this conception of responsibility with circumscribed and rigid accounts of private law adjudication and evolution.

We see traces of this fusion in Kantian approaches, which limit private law's reach by giving strong priority to substantive relational principles (for instance, that no person is in charge of another) or to formal relational structures (for instance, the strict correlativity of rights and duties). In *Eviction*, we saw that Weinrib only goes so far as to hold private agents obligated not to impair the exercise or enjoyment of constitutional rights – there, to a school venue – the realisation of which remains primarily the state's responsibility. The assignment of structural or allocative responsibilities to property owners, for example, seems to be beyond private law's reach, even if it is necessary to solve social coordination problems and guarantee basic interests.

We can also see traces of this rigidity in Thomas's theory, which grounds moral claims for the recognition of new private law rights in a skeletal account of public law rights.[50] Thomas emphasises the importance of structuring this process in a principled manner,[51] and offers the following principle: only when a substantial degree of dependence exists in private relationships – when the right-holder's need or vulnerability are caused or exacerbated by the duty-bearer's voluntary undertaking – can rights that apply between citizens and the state be recognised by private law.[52] Because duties track choices, we cannot be burdened even with duties of easy rescue: for example, we can be burdened with duties to save children drowning in ponds only if we created this risk (say, by building a pond). If our undertaking produces goods, our duties can be merely procedural: for instance, hospitals cannot be obligated to admit patients but only to treat admitted patients in certain ways.[53] Only threats to existing goods – say, polluting water sources – can justify the imposition of substantive duties.

Thomas's focus on undertakings reflects the common law tradition of imposing complex duties – for example, not to discriminate – on business ventures that exercise significant market power and offer basic goods or services to the public.

[49] Goldberg and Zipursky, *Recognizing Wrongs* (n 20) 239–40. On how new torts are 'found', see also Anita Bernstein, 'How to Make a New Tort: Three Paradoxes' (1997) 75 *Texas Law Review* 1539, 1545.

[50] Jean Thomas, *Public Rights, Private Relations* (Oxford University Press, 2015).

[51] ibid 131–38.

[52] ibid 188–98.

[53] ibid 223–27.

The underlying principle, as Ammon Reichman notes, is that when private agents enter professions, for instance, they assume duties to potential customers, including duties not to discriminate on certain grounds. While 'profession' is treated as a status, and therefore as not completely private and malleable, the normative content of such statuses is determined by societal (non-legal) normative factors: that is, by 'certain expectations which flow directly from the *raison d'être* of the profession'.[54]

Weinrib, Thomas and Reichman express deep common law principles, touching second-order reasons addressing judicial authority and rule of law ideals such as intelligibility and stability. In this spirit, Thomas holds that private agents must be able to figure out independently which duties rights directed against them entail.[55] Relying on how goods are produced or on how professions are perceived limits judicial discretion and simplifies private reasoning. It presents private law as if it merely identifies responsibilities within the societal normative scheme.

One obvious problem in this regard is that societal morality or conceptions of goods or roles can go wrong – and, historically, often have. A deeper problem is that even critical morality can be conflicted or underdetermined with regard to what we owe to each other, especially when it comes to structural and allocative problems, whose resolution requires social coordination.[56] There are social activities that we struggle to get morally right absent legal deliberation and coordination: for example, journalism, banking, or driving. Therefore, to realise constitutional rights horizontally, private law must have the capacity – that I will claim below that it often exercises – to shape the normative conceptions and features of undertakings and professions and their attached legal responsibilities.

This problem is echoed in criticisms of Thomas's horizontality theory. Gautam Bhatia notes that it ignores broader societal factors: in fact, wrongness can result not from direct dependency or control of goods, but from how interactions align with larger social patterns (say, how restrictive covenants reflect patterns of discrimination); and, additionally, it is often difficult to say that private agents 'create' goods (for example, medical treatment) given the supportive social, political and legal structures.[57] Similarly, Mark Tushnet notes that Thomas ignores the ability to justifiably and effectively develop common law concepts that refer to undertakings, such as common carrier, in response to public goals or to structural and allocative concerns.[58]

[54] Amnon Reichman, 'Professional Status and the Freedom to Contract: Toward a Common Law Duty of Non-Discrimination' (2001) 14 *Canadian Journal of Law and Jurisprudence* 79, 119.

[55] Thomas, *Public Rights, Private Relations* (n 50) 147. See also ibid 33–41.

[56] Tony Honoré, 'The Dependence of Morality on Law' (1993) 13 *Oxford Journal of Legal Studies* 1.

[57] Gautam Bhatia, *Horizontal Rights: An Institutional Approach* (Hart Publishing, 2023) 80–82.

[58] Mark Tushnet, 'Public Rights, Private Relations' (2016) 7 *Jurisprudence* 355, 363–64.

5.3.2. The Limits of Identifications

Private law can be pushed in progressive directions even if we rely on the limited tool of responsibility identification, if we enrich the background against which choices or actions in private relationships are evaluated. For example, we can treat certain forms of discrimination as tortious negligence[59] or as intentional infliction of emotional distress;[60] tie affirmative duties of restitution that private agents cannot avoid being burdened with (in mistaken payment cases, for example) to their personal responsibility;[61] or subject contract terms to norms like honesty, trust, exploitation, or unconscionability through the principle of good faith.[62] As Hugh Collins adds, rather than bringing social justice to bear directly on private relationships, associations and practices, we can identify within them moral responsibilities that respond to social justice on their own terms: for example, to enrich contractual agreements with principles reflecting the organisational normative features of the workplace.[63]

An ambitious attempt in this regard was made by Hanoch Dagan and Avihay Dorfman. They see relational justice principles of reciprocal respect for self-determination and substantive equality, implicit in private law, as guiding its evolution.[64] Relying on these values (rather than strictly relational values like mutual independence) enables them to explain demanding and complex private law norms that address structural and allocative concerns by tying these norms to the personal responsibilities of private agents toward particular others: for example, employer duties to make the workplace inclusive of their employees' needs and landlord duties not to discriminate against tenants or buyers.[65] Dagan and Dorfman's approach is important because it appreciates the importance of systematic justification for private law's evolution, framed within a process of reaching reflective equilibrium: they therefore treat private law as it currently is as having no inherent moral authority but as merely illuminating our considered judgements and principles about the normative frameworks that can and should regulate private relations.[66]

[59] Sophia Moreau, 'Discrimination as Negligence' (2010) 40 *Canadian Journal of Philosophy* 123.

[60] Martha Chamallas, 'Discrimination and Outrage: The Migration From Civil Rights to Tort Law' (2007) 48 *William & Mary Law Review* 2115.

[61] Kit Barker, 'The Nature of Responsibility for Gain: Gain, Harm, and Keeping the Lid on Pandora's Box' in Robert Chambers, Charles Mitchell and James Penner (eds), *Philosophical Foundations of Unjust Enrichment* (Oxford University Press, 2009) 146, 162–71.

[62] Hugh Collins, 'Implied Terms: The Foundation in Good Faith and Fair Dealing' (2014) 67 *Current Legal Problems* 297.

[63] Hugh Collins, 'Relational and Associational Justice In Work' (2023) 24 *Theoretical Inquiries in Law* 26.

[64] Hanoch Dagan and Avihay Dorfman, *Relational Justice* (Oxford University Press, 2024).

[65] See also Hanoch Dagan and Avihay Dorfman, 'Just Relationships' (2016) 116 *Columbia Law Review* 1395, 1439–45; Hanoch Dagan and Avihay Dorfman, 'Justice in Private: Beyond the Rawlsian Framework' (2018) 37 *Law and Philosophy* 171, 173, 176.

[66] Dagan and Dorfman, *Relational Justice* (n 64) 8–9.

The problem is that while Dagan and Dorfman appreciate the authority and discretion involved in private law's evolution, they say little about the interactions between relational reasons and structural or allocative reasons, beyond asserting that the latter may override relational justice, provided it is properly engaged and evaluated,[67] and retains its status as private law's distinctive deontic core.[68] This formula raises problems when it comes to values such as autonomy and substantive equality – which, in principle, can entail complex prescriptions, on a social scale, for both public and private agents. Relational justice principles may be sufficient to explain private law, but the further we move towards questions about its evolution – the kind of questions raised by constitutional horizontality – the more systematic and structured our reasoning must be regarding private law's place within the normative universe. This requires not merely leaving room for structural and allocative reasons for regulation but also explaining how they may be reconciled with relational reasons.

A good example of these shortcomings is Dagan and Dorfman's attempt to justify a general tort of discrimination.[69] They highlight its relational justice basis and basic parallels with negligence. However, they ignore many morally relevant factors – for example, distinctions between rights and values or public and private responsibilities – and say little about tort law's role in addressing structural and allocative reasons. This is perhaps not a fatal problem if they intend merely to offer a few reasons, grounded in their version of relational justice, for private law's expansion. But if they aim to offer something that comes closer to an all-things-considered justification about the moral obligations of liberal political collectives concerning private law's evolution, their arguments must be more comprehensive, systematic and ambitious. Importantly, arguments touching private law's evolution must also address its ability to assign responsibilities while deviating from its current moral or conceptual trajectories – a possibility that forces legal reasoning to engage and reconcile structural, allocative and relational reasons for regulation.

5.4. ASSIGNING RESPONSIBILITIES

One of the main problems of weak indirect models is that they reduce private law assignments of responsibilities to the status of policy-oriented exceptions to judicial principles, which merely identify responsibilities. In this picture, common private law helps us conform to reasons that we have apart from the law,[70] largely by responding to relational factors such as consent or causation:

[67] ibid 54, 62.
[68] ibid 4, 22, 32, 170.
[69] ibid 177–99.
[70] On this account of law's authority, see Joseph Raz, 'The Problem of Authority: Revisiting the Service Conception' (2006) 90 *Minnesota Law Review* 1003. See also Lisa Herzog, *Reclaiming the*

for example, by enforcing a contract to which we agreed or imposing liability to pay for a vase that we broke. This leaves relational reasons at the mercy of policy reasons in upstream decisions about the creation, abolition or change of private law regimes, while moving downstream decisions about the details of these regimes away from structural and allocative reasons, unless these reasons are firmly located within the conceptual structure of existing doctrines.

To remedy this situation and better integrate structural, allocative and relational reasons for horizontal rights realisation, we must acknowledge that downstream decisions can also assign responsibilities, thereby both directly realising policy goals and guiding or correcting upstream decisions. The first step in this regard is seeing that responsibility operates in private law not merely as a set of external and factually-sensitive constraints on its evolution or application. Private law forms part of a 'responsibility tapestry',[71] shaped by and shaping other normative systems, such as morality, etiquette, religions, sports, universities and professions. Private law can improve our conformity with reasons from these other systems: for instance, by specifying underdetermined reasons or reconciling conflicting reasons.

Through legal regulation, the political collective can shape not only backwards-looking responsibilities (what can be attributed to us) but also forward-looking responsibilities (what we owe to each other).[72] Such, legally coordinated assignments of responsibility are necessary to resolve moral problems of underdetermination, complexity, conflict or lack of assurance.[73] This is quite clear when it comes to social activities like bankruptcy.[74] This process is also visible in discrimination law. Its responses to social injustice reverberate in and shape moral relationships in complex spheres such as education, housing or employment.[75] It can therefore be said that 'our moral views about discrimination … have been shaped by our legal prohibitions on discrimination',[76] which go beyond merely identifying 'actions that are morally objectionable under some set of pre-institutional moral principles' and instead *ascribe* 'the status of discrimination – and with it, a certain measure of opprobrium – to various forms of action that, if unchecked, would undermine the justness of our basic

System: Moral Responsibility, Divided Labour, and the Role of Organizations in Society (Cambridge University Press, 2013) 23–45.

[71] Peter Cane, *Responsibility in Law and Morality* (Hart Publishing, 2002) 3, 13, 23–25, 181.

[72] See generally Susan Hurley, 'The Public Ecology of Responsibility' in Carl Knight and Zofia Stemplowska (eds), *Responsibility and Distributive Justice* (Oxford University Press, 2011) 187.

[73] Tony Honoré, 'The Dependence of Morality on Law' (1993) 13 *Oxford Journal of Legal Studies* 1; Allen Buchanan, 'Perfecting Imperfect Duties: Collective Action to Create Moral Obligations' (1996) 6 *Business Ethics Quarterly* 27; Henry S Richardson, 'Institutionally Divided Moral Responsibility' (1999) 16 *Social Philosophy and Policy* 218.

[74] Jed Lewinsohn, 'By Convention Alone: Assignable Rights, Dischargeable Debts, and the Distinctiveness of the Commercial Sphere' (2023) 133 *Ethics* 231.

[75] Barbara Herman, *The Moral Habitat* (Oxford University Press, 2021) 167–70, 174–75.

[76] Sophia Moreau, *Faces of Inequality: A Theory of Wrongful Discrimination* (Oxford University Press, 2020) 27.

institutional structures'.[77] Thus, even if justified legal norms are not necessarily moral norms,[78] and possess a distinctively legal normativity, we have good reasons to take legitimate legal norms into account if we want to act morally – which strengthens their force in ways that go beyond their mere validity.

This means that the basic liberal intuition that we can only be held responsible for our actions is inaccurate, at least in a strict sense.[79] We can distinguish in this regard between the voluntaristic core of our agency and its periphery, which can also be shaped by factors beyond our control. For example, by occupying the roles of 'daughter' or 'parent', we expand the scope of our agency, also in ways that respond to our normative environment: for instance, to social expectations or welfare schemes.[80] If private law limits our agency to our choices, it runs the risk of working with and expressing 'a shrivelled public image of our selves'.[81] Our moral powers and duties to push beyond this limited image – to expand our agency by becoming responsible – constitute and contribute to the value of many private relationships, associations and practices. In this sense, when private law assigns responsibilities, it need not be acting solely for policy reasons.[82] It can also reflect the fact that sometimes respect means focusing more on other people's interests than on the limits of our control.[83]

Habitability.[84] A farm manager in South Africa sought to evict a tenant whose occupancy was protected under a legislative scheme, and refused to allow her to make necessary home improvements, at her own expense, despite conceding that her home was unfit for human habitation. The manager and the property owner claimed that recognising the tenant's right to improve the dwelling without the owner's consent raises deep problems, as the legislative scheme also authorises courts to grant compensation for improvements made by an occupier upon their eviction. The owner could then be burdened with what would in effect be a positive duty – to fund the dwelling's improvements.

[77] Patrick S Shin, 'Is There a Unitary Concept of Discrimination?' in Deborah Hellman and Sophia Moreau (eds), *Philosophical Foundations of Discrimination Law* (Oxford University Press, 2013) 163, 181.

[78] On this possibility (that I need not evaluate here), see Steven Schaus, 'A Simple Model of Torts and Moral Wrongs' (2022) 97 *Notre Dame Law Review* 1029.

[79] See also Miller, *National Responsibility and Global Justice* (n 47) 120–124.

[80] On such expansions of agency, see Meir Dan-Cohen, 'Responsibility and the Boundaries of the Self' (1992) 105 *Harvard Law Review* 959; David Enoch, 'Being Responsible, Taking Responsibility, and Penumbral Agency' in Ulrike Heuer and Gerald Lang (eds), *Luck, Value, and Commitment: Themes From the Ethics of Bernard Williams* (Oxford University Press, 2012) 95, 99–100.

[81] Dan-Cohen, 'Responsibility and the Boundaries of the Self' (n 80) 1001–03.

[82] I extend the idea that we have the power to assume responsibilities for relational reasons (see David Enoch, 'Tort Liability and Taking Responsibility' in John Oberdiek (ed), *Philosophical Foundations of the Law of Torts* (Oxford University Press, 2014) 250) to the idea that the state can assign them to us for such reasons.

[83] See Elinor Mason, 'Taking Responsibility' in *Ways to be Blameworthy: Rightness, Wrongness, and Responsibility* (Oxford University Press, 2019) 179, 200.

[84] *Daniels v Scribante and Another* [2017] ZACC 13.

The Constitutional Court's starting point was that the legislative scheme realises the constitutional right of people 'whose tenure of land is legally insecure as a result of past racially discriminatory laws or practices'.[85] It held that, in principle, the horizontal dimensions of constitutional rights can entail positive private duties, considering the nature of the right, its history, its goals, and the threats posed to it by private parties. Such is the case with the right to security of tenure, which may impose positive duties on owners to accommodate tenants.[86]

This constitutionally-grounded private law duty is not merely a duty not to impair the exercise or enjoyment of a right that it is the state's primary duty to realise – like the private law duty in the *Eviction* case, which was mentioned above. In *Habitability*, the duty is, potentially, positive: the owner might not be permitted to prevent the dweller from bringing the dwelling to a habitable condition, and may later be obligated to compensate the dweller for the improvements' costs. We see here a judicial exercise of the authority to assign responsibility – while building on the constitution and background legislation – in response not only to the isolated relationship between the owner and the dweller but also to the unique history and conditions of discrimination and structural injustice in South Africa. The rest of this section explains the nature of this authority and its reliance on structural and allocative considerations.

5.4.1. Role Assumptions

The depth and complexity of responsibility assignments can be further exposed by seeing, with Hart, that responsibility operates in private law not only as a basic capacity, a causal conclusion, or liability, but also as part of roles (or undertakings, tasks, or similar concepts): the conception of responsibility at work here refers to the normative requirements attached to roles – which demand ongoing attention and care in response to the relationships, associations or practices within which they operate.[87] Political collectives regularly shape the processes through which responsibilities, expectations and claims coalesce around roles.[88] This is especially important when it comes to structural moral problems, responses to which must be coordinated – often by legal regulation.[89] As Cass Sunstein notes, 'many norms are intensely role-specific,

[85] The Constitution of South Africa (1996), Art 25(6).
[86] *Daniels* (n 84) paras 39, 49.
[87] HLA Hart, 'Postscript: Responsibility and Retribution' in *Punishment and Responsibility*, 2nd edn (Oxford University Press, 2008) 210, 212–14; Peter Cane, 'Role Responsibility' (2016) 20 *Journal of Ethics* 279.
[88] See Tracy Isaacs, *Moral Responsibility in Collective Contexts* (Oxford University Press, 2011) 132, 149.
[89] See Robin Zheng, 'What is My Role in Changing the System? A New Model of Responsibility for Structural Injustice' (2018) 21 *Ethical Theory and Moral Practice* 869.

and law is often self-consciously concerned with social roles'.[90] This is quite clear when it comes to different forms of private ordering, such as contracts or marriage, which allow private agents to assume, and often shape, roles such as 'landlord', 'seller' or 'wife'. But the legal focus on roles is also important – even if sometimes less pronounced – when it comes to mandatory private law norms.

Protection. A student told a psychologist at the student health service of his intent to kill a woman whom he dated for a while. The psychologist informed campus police, but the university's proceedings ended without informing the woman – who was consequentially murdered by the student. In response to her family's negligence claims, the Supreme Court of California held that mental health professionals have a tort duty to protect third parties from harms by their patients when these patients disclose their harmful intentions to them.[91]

Goldberg and Zipursky explain that mental health professionals – but not religious advisors, teachers or lawyers, for example – are obligated to protect foreseeable third parties from imminent attacks, because of the 'special public health responsibilities' associated with their training and status.[92] Therefore, even without assuming responsibilities to others deliberately through forms of private ordering, duties can be attached to social roles – and not only in response to social or professional conventions (for example, it seems quite justified for discrimination law to prohibit real estate agents from steering potential tenants according to their racial profile, even if this is common practice).

This focus on roles can help state agents reconcile competing considerations in concrete contexts while better guiding private agents by integrating legal norms with other norms that operate in their vicinity, such as professional ethics: it harnesses the normativity of roles in different normative sub-systems and the local knowledge of role-holders to realise public goals in a dynamic manner.[93] As importantly, this focus alleviates some of the concerns that animate the restrictive conception of responsibility. Moral role-responsibilities, such as those to our parents, can be attached to roles that we did not assume and that it is difficult to unburden ourselves of.[94] But the pressures to accommodate voluntaristic concerns are greater when the law determines how normative powers, such as those to contract or marry, may be exercised and even greater when it imposes mandatory duties – for instance, through tort law.[95]

[90] Cass R Sunstein, 'Social Norms and Social Roles' (1996) 96 *Columbia Law Review* 903, 921–23. See also Sari Mazzurco, 'Content Moderation Regulation as Legal Role-Scripting' (2024) 99 *Indiana Law Journal* 1131, 1142–50.

[91] *Tarasoff v Regents of the University of California* 13 Cal 3d 177 (1976).

[92] John CP Goldberg and Benjamin C Zipursky, *The Oxford Introductions to U.S. Law: Torts* (Oxford University Press, 2010) 122–23.

[93] On this form of regulation, see generally Gunther Teubner, 'Substantive and Reflexive Elements in Modern Law' (1983) 17 *Law and Society Review* 239.

[94] See Samuel Scheffler, 'Relationships and Responsibilities' (1997) 26 *Philosophy & Public Affairs* 189.

[95] See Michael O. Hardimon, 'Role Obligations' (1994) 91 *Journal of Philosophy* 333, 352–55.

Thus, discrimination law, for example, alleviates concerns about its demandingness and intrusiveness by imposing mandatory duties only on agents that offer certain services or opportunities to the public, such as employers or sellers. As Tarunabh Khaitan and Sandy Steel note, this design rests not only on structural and allocative reasons that relate to the abilities, resources or privileges of role-holders, but also on reasons of fairness and assurance: private agents can avoid discrimination law duties 'by avoiding entering into one of the legally recognised roles … so long as these roles are clearly identified and relatively limited in number'.[96]

This leaves room for assumptions of responsibility to be tacit and ongoing and for the substantive content of role-responsibilities to change over time,[97] also in response to structural or allocative reasons – as long as there is reasonable foreseeability and legitimate expectations can form:[98] that is, when assigned responsibilities can be effectively and justifiably integrated within rights-and-duties relationships. These processes can be more formalised (for example, through licensing for accountants or lawyers) or more contested (as in debates over whether Uber is the employer of drivers hired through the platform it operates). The crucial point is that they must reconcile concerns about vulnerability and voluntarism within relational normative structures.

Parenthood.[99] A dispute arose about whether a man who cared for his wife's child from a previous relationship (whom he did not adopt) should pay monthly support following a divorce. The Canadian Supreme Court noted that courts must weigh, in such cases, the nature of the relationship, society's values, the interests of the child, and the intentions and representations of the family's members. The Court held that the man should be seen as a step-parent given his representation to the child and the world 'that he assumed full parental responsibility for her' and that he was the only father whom she had known.[100] These relational rather than instrumental normative principles are shaped by the nature of the role and reliance on it by dependent parties.[101]

One of the problems of direct or strong indirect models (and of consequentialism more broadly) is that responsibility assignments rely on goal-oriented reasoning that tends to ignore first-order and second-order relational reasons. Even if we share Robert Goodin's scepticism of the 'conventional philosophical wisdom' about the voluntary nature of responsibilities and duties to

[96] Tarunabh Khaitan and Sandy Steel, 'Wrongs, Group Disadvantage and the Legitimacy of Indirect Discrimination Law' in Hugh Collins and Tarunabh Khaitan (eds), *Foundations of Indirect Discrimination Law* (Hart Publishing, 2018) 197, 217.

[97] On these normative processes, see Hardimon (n 95) 357–62.

[98] For a similar point about undertakings, see Stephen R Perry, 'Protected Interests and Undertakings in the Law of Negligence' (1992) 42 *University of Toronto Law Journal* 247, 285–92.

[99] *Chartier v Chartier* [1999] 1 SCR 242.

[100] ibid 263.

[101] See also Paul B Miller, 'The Morality of Fiduciary Law' (2021) 62 *William & Mary Law Review* 1349.

protect, aid or benefit, and think that more room should be given to need and vulnerability,[102] we must recognise the important role of agency and choice in cases like *Parenthood*. It therefore seems more accurate to say that choice is just not the entire story: it imposes constraints on the assumption of roles and on their possible content, but to determine their attached responsibilities we must also consider broader beneficiary-centered considerations.[103]

5.4.2. Role Delineations

Voluntaristic concerns constrain role-assumptions: we rarely hold that people occupy a role just because it would be socially beneficial if they did. These constraints are weaker, but still operational, when delineating or assigning role-responsibilities. We are mindful of the agent's choices and actions in response to the potential right-holder's interests and needs. The role limits its attached responsibilities: for example, we obligate employers to respect various rights of their employees, but only at the workplace or during work.[104] Private law does not operate against a void in this regard: as soon as a role starts to materialise, social expectations, claims, and therefore responsibilities form around it. This means that assignments must also take into account second-order reasons: for instance, about transition costs or the nature of regulated relationships.

Inheritance. The English Inheritance (Provision for Family and Dependants) Act 1975 creates an exception to the general rule of testamentary freedom: certain portions of estates are reserved for certain family members. The Supreme Court interpreted the exception in a case involving an estranged daughter who had been disinherited by her reclusive mother in favour of animal charities.[105] It was held that need alone is not the measure of reasonable financial provision to family members under the Act, even if the testator's choice is also no longer unrestricted. Weight must also be given to additional factors, including not only testator autonomy but also, for instance, the allocative reason that much of the donations to charities come from wills. These factors must be engaged in the context of the relationship between the testator and the beneficiary. In this case, it was held, a modest award was sufficient, even if it fell short of solving the financial difficulties of the daughter and her family.[106]

[102] Robert E Goodin, *Protecting the Vulnerable* (The University of Chicago Press, 1985) 29–42.

[103] ibid 61.

[104] See, eg, Hugh Collins and Virginia Mantouvalou, 'Human Rights and the Contract of Employment' in Mark Freedland (ed), *The Contract of Employment* (Oxford University Press, 2016) 188, 205–06.

[105] *Ilott v The Blue Cross* [2017] UKSC 17.

[106] See also Brian Sloan, '*Ilot v The Blue Cross* (2017): Testing the Limits of Testamentary Freedom' in Brian Sloan (ed), *Landmark Cases in Succession Law* (Hart Publishing, 2019) 301.

Through a constitutional rights-realisation prism, this case illustrates the need to integrate structural and allocative considerations within the unique normativity of rights-and-duties relationships. To shape roles effectively and justifiably, private law must account for the value of roles and the normative structures within which they operate.[107] Families pose a unique challenge in this regard. But many of the roles dealt with by private law are more amenable to scrutiny and revision. For example, in chapter 3, we talked about the *Drunk Driving* case: about the Canadian Supreme Court's reluctance to impose on house party hosts duties to protect third parties from drunk driving guests.[108] Compared to such hosts, it seems more justified to regularly scrutinise the responsibilities of pub owners with regard to drunk driving from a social perspective – there are weaker second-order reasons to isolate their activity from such scrutiny – and to impose on them heavier burdens. The reason is not only that pub owners are necessarily better placed than house party hosts to mitigate this risk, or that they have a weaker interest in liberty, but also that they occupy a role that involves benefitting from creating this risk and whose normativity and underlying values are less severely harmed by ongoing efforts to mitigate this risk.[109]

Private law responsibility assignments realise not only relational values. For example, by holding contractual parties strictly liable to each other, contract law contributes to their mutual trust, but also to the structural and allocative benefits of markets and practices such as employment.[110] Two tort law classics, *MacPherson* and *Donoghue*,[111] involved such goal-oriented assignments of responsibility. Until these cases, risks of harm by defective products were allocated through contracts: the privity rule allowed consumers to sue only sellers who were contractually obligated to them. These cases tortified manufacturer–consumer relationships by holding manufacturers accountable even to consumers to whom they are not contractually bound: a redistribution of normative burdens in society, which crystallised inchoate moral norms into relational legal norms,[112] and is beneficial both to consumer interests and to the functioning of markets.[113] These seminal cases show that the recognition of private law norms, even in judicial decisions, can operate in a mode

[107] John Gardner, 'Dagan and Dorfman on the Value of Private Law' (2017) 117 *Columbia Law Review* 179, 183–87.

[108] *Childs v Desormeaux* [2006] SCC 18.

[109] See also Moreau, *Faces of Inequality* (n 76) 216, 233–39.

[110] Seana Valentine Shiffrin, 'Enhancing Moral Relationships Through Strict Liability' (2016) 66 *University of Toronto Law Journal* 353.

[111] *MacPherson v Buick Motor Co* (1916) 111 NE 1050; *Donoghue v Stevenson* [1932] AC 562.

[112] John CP Goldberg and Benjamin C Zipursky, 'The Moral of *Macpherson*' (1998) 146 *University of Pennsylvania Law Review* 1733, 1816–17.

[113] See also Cane, *Responsibility in Law and Morality* (n 71) 188.

of active governance and fulfil coordinating roles in response to systematic concerns.[114]

However, it is important that, even when structural and allocative reasons shape role-responsibilities, failures to fulfil these responsibilities can be morally robust relational wrongs, which consist of failures to discharge duties that harm the basic interests of right-holders who reasonably rely on the role-holder.[115] Moral connections exist not only between agents and actions but also between agents and people to whom they are accountable.[116] If private law recognises legitimate norms, integrated within the structure of rights-and-duties relationships, failures to meet them are blameworthy. True, this notion of blame is often distinct from fault, resentment, anger or censure, which tend to foreclose moral dialogue and distance agents from practices of mutual accountability.[117] The blame in failing to discharge legal role-responsibilities can lie in not knowing basic facts about the results of one's conduct (when the situation is clear or can be clarified by consulting others) or not properly responding to these facts. These forms of blame attach to failures to discharge not only roles assumed in special relationships but also roles that form parts of dangerous activities, like driving, medical care or manufacturing. In both cases, a failure to discharge responsibilities, even by omission, is 'but an epicycle on the arc of risk generated by the affirmative conduct' of assuming the role.[118] Thus, for example, while indirect discrimination does not require intent or motive, there is a sense in which we can talk about the negligent failure of role-holders – employers, for instance – to identify or respond to the structural or allocative implications of their actions or policies: implications that discrimination law integrates within the scope of their responsibility.[119] The pervasiveness of roles in private law illuminates its regulatory sides as a normative mechanism that regularly responds to structural and allocative reasons. Weak indirect models largely ignore these regulatory sides, and therefore fail to integrate structural and allocative reasons with relational reasons, often solidified in basic private law principles – except in the circuitous and incremental manner mentioned above. To understand constitutional horizontality, we must explain its use of private law as a regulatory tool in a more principled manner.

[114] But see Aditi Bagchi, 'Law and the Moral Dynamics of Collective Action' (2022) 53 *Seton Hall Law Review* 149, 192–96.

[115] See also Avihay Dorfman, 'Can Tort Law Be Moral' (2010) 23 *Ratio Juris* 205, 213–17.

[116] See Robin Zheng, 'Attributability, Accountability, and Implicit Bias' in Michael Brownstein and Jennifer Saul (eds), *Implicit Bias and Philosophy, Volume 2: Moral Responsibility, Structural Injustice, and Ethics* (Oxford University Press, 2016) 62.

[117] See Robert E Goodin, 'Apportioning Responsibilities' (1987) 6 *Law and Philosophy* 167; Andrea C Westlund, *Answerability Without Blame?* in *Social Dimensions of Moral Responsibility* (n 72) 253.

[118] George P Fletcher, 'The Fault of Not Knowing' (2002) 3 *Theoretical Inquiries in Law* 265, 279–82.

[119] Moreau, *Faces of Inequality* (n 76) 183–208.

5.5. JUSTIFICATORY ASCENT

The jurisprudential possibility of responsibility assignments is vital for understanding constitutional horizontality. First, because advocates of direct models often criticise indirect models for seeing the horizontal dimensions of constitutional rights as addressing only the political morality of state-citizen relations.[120] Under indirect models, the state can be obligated not only to identify but also to concretise or develop relational moral norms. In fact, by seeing the constitutional relationships between private agents as unmediated, direct models ignore or distort the state's important moral coordination roles.

Second, the possibility of assignments sheds a negative light on attempts to isolate private law's ongoing operation from structural and allocative reasons for regulation. While judges can use the tool of identifications quite aggressively and progressively, and non-judicial agents can somehow bridge the gap between relational judicial principles and structural or allocative reasons, weak indirect models envision too rigid a separation between these evolutionary tracks while relying on normatively thin conceptions of private law relationships.

Under weak indirect models, judges are not obligated to engage structural and allocative reasons for the horizontal realisation of constitutional rights or to reconcile them with the relational reasons that dominate private law rights-and-duties relationships. For example, in the *Fertility Treatment* case, mentioned in the previous chapter, in response to a woman's attempt to prevent her former partner from exercising his contractual right to destroy embryos kept at a fertility clinic, the House of Lords focused on the state's interference with the woman's rights, while sidelining the state's duties to address policy concerns related to reproductive rights.[121]

Additionally, under weak indirect models, when non-judicial state agents realise constitutional rights horizontally (and their discretion is broad in this regard), their reasoning tends to be systematic and policy-oriented: for example, ensuring that regulatory schemes offer equal protection to similarly situated agents. When judges interpret such norms compatibly with constitutional rights, their focus is allocative or structural. This creates a gap, familiar in private law theory, between principle and policy, with constitutional rights located quite firmly on the policy side. Thus, while the constitutional distinction between public and private remains less rigid and binary under weak indirect models compared to traditional vertical models, it is still too strong: creating, in practice, two parallel tracks for private law's evolution – one public and progressive, the other private and conservative. There are similarities here to the stunted relations between private law and legislation. Legislative norms, even when

[120] Bhatia (n 57) 60–63; Thomas, *Public Rights, Private Relations* (n 50) 7–8, 14–15; Johan van der Walt, *The Horizontal Effect Revolution and the Question of Sovereignty* (De Gruyter, 2014) 5.

[121] As noted above (ch 4, n 17), such policy concerns were highlighted by the European Court of Human Rights.

recognising rights that private agents exercise with or claim against each other, are often treated as parts of public law:[122] their judicial engagement is limited to policy-oriented interpretation or application and thus they remain foreign objects in private law's relational normative fabric.[123]

These parallel tracks are problematic, first, because responding through private law to the demands of the complex values that underlie constitutional rights requires an integrated and coordinated effort by all state branches. A good example of the outcomes of keeping the tracks too neatly separate is the privacy torts. In the United States, for example, this branch of tort law still gravitates around the four torts identified decades ago in the case law by William Prosser (intrusion, public disclosure, appropriation, and publicity in a false light). Because Prosser restated the case law without grounding it in deeper substantive values, it became difficult for tort law to develop in response to technological and cultural changes, such as social media platforms.[124] The dominance of Prosser's scheme tempts litigants and judges to squeeze their claims into the familiar moulds, and makes it difficult to envision and execute comprehensive legislative reforms that reflect the shifting of normative social boundaries.[125] Somewhat similarly, it was claimed that English law still lacks a pure tort of invasion of privacy because of its incrementalism – as exhibited in the *Campbell* case discussed above, in which the court merely extended the existing tort of breach of confidence.[126] More generally, while private law reforms to protect freedom of expression are often accompanied by a sense of urgency and threat to public debate and to democracy – that is, by normative ascents to a structural perspective – the evolution of privacy-protecting tort rights has been largely incremental and limited.[127] Better collaboration between state agents – with judges not shying away from addressing large-scale reasons for regulation and integrating policy-oriented reforms within the fabric of the common law, thus making relational principles more accessible for non-judicial agents – would be more conducive to effective legal reforms.

The second problem with separating these evolutionary tracks touches not the urgency but the details of private law reform. Weak indirect models rely on a narrow account of private rights-and-duties relationships (often criticised

[122] Shyamkrishna Balganesh, 'Private Law Statutory Interpretation' (2019) 92 *Southern California Law Review* 949.

[123] See also Caleb Nelson, 'The Legitimacy of (Some) Federal Common Law' (2015) 101 *Virginia Law Review* 1.

[124] See Daniel J Solove and Neil M Richards, 'Prosser's Privacy Law: A Mixed Legacy' (2010) 98 *California Law Review* 1887.

[125] On these boundaries, see Robert C Post, 'The Social Foundations of Privacy: Community and Self in the Common Law Tort' (1989) 77(5) *California Law Review* 957.

[126] Thomas DC Bennet, 'Privacy and Incrementalism' in András Koltay and Paul Wragg (eds), *Comparative Privacy and Defamation* (Edward Elgar Publishing, 2020) 24.

[127] Andrew T Kenyon and Megan Richardson, 'Reverberations of *Sullivan*? Considering Defamation and Privacy Law Reform' in Andrew T Kenyon (ed), *Comparative Defamation and Privacy Law* (Cambridge University Press, 2016) 331.

by progressive theorists), which ignores the fact that even in effective and only moderately unjust legal systems, private agents cannot be oblivious to social justice.[128] Such isolation ignores the ties between our agency and our political membership as well as the possible contribution of structural and allocative values to private relationships, associations and practices. For example, in *Habitability*, we saw that landlord–tenant relations were shaped by the past and present of social injustice in South Africa. Thus, even if private actions that harm the interests that underlie constitutional rights are not, in themselves, constitutional rights-violations, they can still be relational moral wrongs – which state agents, when realising constitutional rights, must give adequate weight to, while integrating public and private responsibilities.

To a great extent, this is the point of constitutional horizontality. While it does not subordinate private law to the constitution, it also does not see their relationship as that of considerate neighbours who mind their own business while avoiding loud noises.[129] As a progressive exercise of political authority, constitutional horizontality aims not only to add ad hoc flourishes to private law's traditional focus on life, liberty and property, but to change the ways in which private law evolves – while harnessing its unique regulatory features, such as relational responsibility identifications and assignments. Weak indirect models tend to ignore these ambitious aims by assuming that private law can remain on its current normative trajectories, with which constitutional rights must cross paths to gain weight as justifications for the common law's evolution.

The common law's tendency to evolve incrementally and organically is appealing to conservative thinkers, like Friedrich Hayek, who trust markets more than agents to bring about desirable social distributions and allocations.[130] But the assumption that private law can 'work itself pure'[131] is not only morally dubious, but also conflicts with the very idea of constitutional horizontality. Even if there are good second-order reasons against crude policy reforms, private law's norms and doctrines do not carry more weight in first-order reasoning about rights realisation just because they are currently recognised.[132] Once constitutional rights expand horizontally, such conservatism fails not only in terms of its results, but also in securing a genuine autonomy for private law's relational

[128] See Thomas Nagel, *Equality and Partiality* (Oxford University Press, 1991) 53–54, 59, 86; GA Cohen, 'Introduction' in *Rescuing Justice and Equality* (Harvard University Press, 2008) 1, 10–11; Martha Nussbaum, 'Forward' in Iris Marion Young, *Responsibility for Justice* (Oxford University Press, 2011) ix, xxi–xxii.

[129] Hugh Collins, 'On the (In)compatibility of Human Rights Discourse and Private Law' in Hans-W Micklitz (ed), *Constitutionalization of European Private Law* (Oxford University Press, 2014) 26, 36–37.

[130] FA Hayek, *Law, Legislation, and Liberty: Volume 2 – The Mirage of Social Justice* (Routledge, 1982) 24–25.

[131] Weinrib, *The Idea of Private Law* (n 19) 13.

[132] See also Graham Gee and Grégoire Webber, 'A Conservative Disposition and Constitutional Change' (2019) 39 *Oxford Journal of Legal Studies* 526.

principles – which consists in reconciling them with policy reasons rather than isolating them and subjecting them to ad hoc policy interventions.

5.5.1. Up and Down

To remedy the problems of weak indirect models without reverting to strong indirect models, we must find ways to expose the common law to constitutional scrutiny without ignoring, eroding or distorting private law's unique relational normativity. This idea is not foreign to the common law. For example, Dworkin, one of its leading theorists, claimed that while judges should normally give 'local priority' to norms closer to the cases they resolve, the consideration of more remote and abstract principles – 'justificatory ascent' – is always 'on the cards'.[133] Similarly, Rosco Pound noted that the tension between 'mechanical jurisprudence' and a 'jurisprudence of ends' must be resolved through contextual decisions embedded within a dynamic and systematic normative practice.[134] This transition between modes of legal reasoning can also be tied to the idea of equity, which used to be seen as offering judges greater discretion, but over time became integrated within the law's normal operation.[135]

The challenge is not merely to balance policy goals with concerns about, for instance, legal stability or judicial discretion,[136] but to do so within the unique structure of private rights-and-duties relationships. Consider, for example, the distinction between property law's core and periphery.[137] Because regular reference to the interests that property law serves risks complicating its norms, property law's core, which draws on everyday relational morality, recognises relatively simple and relational ownership rights to control and exclude. However, as we move to property law's periphery – for example, to nuisance, discrimination, overflights or copyright – simple ownership rights must be exposed to more regular goal-oriented limitations.

Nuisance. The neighbours of a cement plant claimed that it produced dirt, smoke and vibrations warranting not merely damages but an injunction – even if this meant closing the plant down. The New York Court of Appeals held that because the harms to the plaintiffs were significantly outweighed by the harms involved in closing the plant down – both the plant owner's investment and

[133] Ronald Dworkin, 'In Praise of Theory' (1997) 29 *Arizona State Law Journal* 353, 356–58. See also Shyamkrishna Balganesh and Gideon Parchomovsky, 'Structure and Value in the Common Law' (2015) 163 *University of Pennsylvania Law Review* 1241.

[134] See Hanoch Dagan, 'Doctrinal Categories, Legal Realism, and the Rule of Law' (2015) 163 *University of Pennsylvania Law Review* 1889, 1891–1908.

[135] See John CP Goldberg and Benjamin C Zipursky, 'From *Riggs v Palmer* to *Shelley v Kraemer*: Judicial Power and the Law–Equity Distinction' in Dennis Klimchuk, Irit Samet and Henry E Smith (eds), *Philosophical Foundations of the Law of Equity* (Oxford University Press, 2020) 291.

[136] On this concern, see Thomas, *Public Rights, Private Relations* (n 50) 33–41; Christina Bambrick, 'Horizontal Rights: A Republican Vein in Liberal Constitutionalism' (2020) 52 *Polity* 401, 415.

[137] Henry E Smith, 'Mind the Gap: The Indirect Relation Between Ends and Means in American Property Law' (2009) 94 *Cornell Law Review* 960.

hundreds of jobs – an injunction was unjustified.[138] The plant's private law right to operate is grounded not only in pre-legal liberty or property rights, which carry less weight in modern regulatory conditions, but also in an allocative relationship, created by legal regulation, in which the plant's employees seem to have the categorically stronger moral claim on the legal system to protect their livelihood, compared to the claims of the neighbours.[139]

The delineation of the core and the periphery – deciding when justificatory ascent is in order – cannot rely on crude policy reasoning. We must engage and reconcile structural, allocative and relational reasons within, for example, the relationships between neigbours. When regulating such relationships, it is not enough to identify structural or allocative wrongs, such as free-riding on beneficial social practices.[140] It is also not enough simply to highlight the myriad of values involved in realisation decisions.[141] We must ensure that legal rights and duties are adequately integrated within private rights-and-duties relationships. For example, that a large company's hiring policy erects barriers for single mothers or for minority members, thereby harming collective efforts to promote equality, is not enough, in itself, to justify the standing and authority of particular right-claimants to call the company to account on their own behalf, reactive attitudes like blame, and remedies.

The contractualist scheme helps here, by explaining why policy reasons not to adopt private law regimes have a certain priority, and why positive policy reasons to adopt such regimes must be integrated with relational reasons to shape the details of rights-and-duties relationships. In the previous chapter, these ideas were discussed to show that strong indirect models envision realisation reasoning as too uniform and consequentialist. Against weak indirect models, I make the converse claim: that even if we take seriously the qualitative distinctions between structural and allocative policy reasons and relational reasons, and the latter's priority in downstream decisions about the details of rights-and-duties relationships, goal-oriented responsibility assignments are not only permitted, but are required and even obligatory.

5.5.2. Inside–Out

The starting point is Scanlon's distinction between the more strictly relational responsibility tied to wrongs and reactions to them and the more loosely

[138] *Boomer v Atlantic Cement Co* 257 NE 2d 870 (NY 1970).

[139] See also Richard W Wright, 'Private Nuisance Law: A Window on Substantive Justice' in Donal Nolan and Andrew Robertson (eds), *Rights and Private Law* (Hart Publishing, 2011) 491, 503–05, 515–23.

[140] See Avia Pasternak, 'The Impact of Corporate Task Responsibilities: A Comparison of Two Models' (2014) 38 *Midwest Studies in Philosophy* 222, 226–30; Stephanie Collins, 'Distributing State's Duties' (2016) 24 *Journal of Political Philosophy* 344, 349.

[141] For such an approach, see David Bilchitz, *Fundamental Rights and the Legal Obligations of Business* (Cambridge University Press, 2021) 220–27.

relational responsibility underlying justifications for obligations: they are justified if we cannot reasonably claim that any agent, including the community in institutional form, owes it to us to help us avoid the normative burden.[142] Thus, reflecting our discussion of role-responsibilities, Scanlon notes that if an agent becomes a milk vendor, it is justifiable to legally penalise them for selling contaminated milk, even if they are not negligent in any way, because they assumed this strict responsibility.[143]

Under contractualism, concern and respect for those affected by our actions require us to reason from a general perspective, regarding the interests of people in their position:[144] we must locate our particular relationships in the societal normative scheme, including the legal system. This is important, for example, in addressing structural injustices, which are created not only through isolated malevolent actions but also through the accumulated effects of countless innocuous actions by many agents towards diffuse groups. Public coordination is essential for holding individual agents responsible for such injustices: social roles can then include moral responsibilities that are forward-looking, politically assigned, and also respond to structural and allocative reasons rather than only to strictly relational reasons.[145] For example, if there are no public institutions that offer free and comprehensive education from a young age, employers might be responsible and obligated to make some accommodations for single parents. Contractualism not only leaves room for but invites the state to impose such duties – to do things that we have no personal responsibility to do, nor would we choose to do, in our private lives.[146]

Because we discharge our role-responsibilities to right-holders as a form of recognition of and respect, the legal frameworks within which state-shaped standards of responsibility operate are relational – as reflected in accountability and remedial private law mechanisms: we must justify ourselves to this person and remedy the specific predicament that we put them in. And because remedies and processes of calling to account are relational, there are strong pressures on primary rights and duties to take relational forms as well.

As noted in the previous chapter, normative integration within such relational frameworks requires reliance on both first-order and second-order reasons. Private law is similar to friendship in this regard: resorting too often

[142] TM Scanlon, 'Forms and Conditions of Responsibility' in Randolph Clarke, Michael McKenna and Angela M Smith (eds), *The Nature of Moral Responsibility: New Essays* (Oxford University Press, 2015) 89, 105–07. See also Emmanuel Voyiakis, *Private Law and the Value of Choice* (Hart Publishing, 2017) 62–65, 105–06.

[143] Thomas Scanlon, *What We Owe to Each Other* (Harvard University Press, 1998) 266.

[144] See Julian Jonker, 'Contractualist Justification and the Direction of a Duty' (2019) 25 *Legal Theory* 200.

[145] Robin Zheng, 'What is My Role in Changing the System? A New Model of Responsibility for Structural Injustice' (2018) 21 *Ethical Theory and Moral Practice* 869.

[146] Thomas Nagel, 'Libertarianism Without Foundations' (1975) 85 *Yale Law Journal* 136, 145–46. For criticism of this idea, see GA Cohen, 'Political Philosophy and Personal Behavior' in *If You're an Egalitarian, How Come You're So Rich?* (Harvard University Press, 2001) 148, 168–74.

or too crudely to instrumentalist calculations in friendship-related decisions, rather than relying on commitments or principles internal to them, makes us worse friends, and under certain thresholds no friends at all – often we should just help a friend without even weighing costs and benefits.[147] The previous chapter was mostly about this idea of exclusion. Here I add that private rights-and-duties relationships, like friendship, are not isolated. Contextualism and relationality must be part of a broader deliberative framework that includes moments of systematic reflection and response. To borrow from Philip Pettit's consequentialist framework, two types of cases can be highlighted as requiring normative ascent: when 'red lights go on' and 'signals of alarm sound', in the sense that the broader wrongful or unjust implications of private actions or activities become apparent (say, if our friend asks us to move a dead body); and, second, we must occasionally reflect on our predispositions, principles, and patterns of behaviour in light of broader goals or commitments.[148]

This deliberative pattern involves the relinquishing of full control, when we just 'go with the (relational) flow'. This allows constitutional horizontality to accommodate relational norms (*contra* strong indirect models). However, we do not offload control completely (*contra* weak indirect models): akin to the cowboy who allows the cattle to roam until they wander too far. This analogy highlights the delicate balance required in legal evolution – recognising the uniqueness of relational reasons while intervening when constitutional rights must be engaged directly. Therefore, reasons that are excluded in certain decisions do not disappear from the normative universe: they continue to pull the strings 'behind the scenes', ready to spring back into action.[149] These parts of constitutional rights will normally operate at a deeper level than relational private law norms, keeping their eyes on the basic structure of society or on allocative institutions and practices, while advocating responses to clear and obvious relational injustices and more incremental recalibrations responding to systemic regulatory problems.[150] Guidance can then be provided not necessarily by isolated norms, but by the body of law taken as a whole – leaving room for specific decisions to operate contextually, provided that they rely in a transparent manner on second-order reasons that locate them in evolutionary legal processes.[151]

[147] John Gardner, *From Personal Life to Private Law* (Oxford University Press, 2018) 30–31, 37–38; Philip Pettit, 'Consequentialism and Moral Psychology' (1994) 2 *International Journal of Philosophical Studies* 1.

[148] Philip Pettit, 'The Inescapability of Consequentialism' in *Luck, Value, and Commitment* (n 80) 45–46. See also Isaacs (n 88) 101–02.

[149] Joseph Raz, *From Normativity to Responsibility* (Oxford University Press, 2011) 176. See also Lawrence G Sager, *Justice in Plainclothes: A Theory of American Constitutional Practice* (Yale University Press, 2004) 86–87, 95–102.

[150] See Brian McElwee, 'The Rights and Wrongs of Consequentialism' (2010) 151 *Philosophical Studies* 393, 407–10.

[151] See Katharina Stevens, 'Setting Precedents Without Making Norms' (2020) 39 *Law and Philosophy* 577.

Importantly, we move towards social justice by relying on the unique normativity and underlying values of private rights-and-duties relationships – yet without limiting ourselves to currently recognised concepts and doctrines. For example, it was claimed that contractual transactions can be exposed to social justice when the duty-bearer has the ability to respond to the other party's disadvantage, and the norms of reciprocity and cooperation in the relevant contractual context can accommodate seeing the parties from a broader societal perspective: for example, as employer and employee.[152] Such relational focus, as we will see in the next chapter, not only allows for better integration of structural and allocative reasons for rights realisation within private relationships, associations and practices, but also – and this is more important for our purposes here – invites and facilitates gradual reform.

For example, even if we find an employer duty to consider the structural and allocative results of all hiring decisions too onerous, we might still find that in some cases they should do so: for instance, if requiring presence in the workplace for long hours harms primary caregivers and is less crucial in some lines of work. Through such cases, we can gradually change the meaning and scope of employer responsibility for equality in employment. This is a form of contextualism, but one that does consider the bigger regulatory picture – a fact that informs second-order reasoning about how to engage particular legal decisions about responsibility assignments. We will see in the next chapter that many novel and policy-infused private law areas (such as employment law, family law, consumer law and discrimination law) and abstract standards (such as good faith or reasonableness) demonstrate this delicate interplay – between different types of first-order reasons for regulation (that must be integrated within rights-and-duties relationships) and between first-order order and second-order reasons for or against reform, which must take into account the unique normativity of regulated relationships, associations or practices.

What weak indirect models miss is the fact that the exclusion of large-scale reasons must form part of a broader scheme, which includes occasional yet principled recourse to structural reasons that touch the delineation of constitutional rights and even more regular recourse to allocative reasons that touch the competing claims of all affected constitutional rights-holders, as part of more extensive and systematic proportionality analysis, evaluating the social implications of private law. Both the horizontal delineation and the realisation of constitutional rights must form part of a practice that serves the protected interests of right-holders better than competing practices.

This exposure to external scrutiny is necessary to ensure that private law's incremental evolution is justified in each case touching constitutional rights – especially given the complex and interconnected nature of the system of rights,

[152] Zhong Xing Tan, 'Where the Action Is: Macro and Micro Justice in Contract Law' (2020) 83 *Modern Law Review* 725.

in which 'a pull on one strand will distribute tensions after a complicated pattern throughout the web as a whole'.[153] Their partial horizontal realisation cannot be justified by blindly relying on formal principles like the separation of powers or the rule of law without actually comparing the impact of legal stability or strict relationality on the interests underlying constitutional rights. Are equality, privacy or dignity better realised under a system in which judges have no constitutional duties to recognise private law norms? My claim is not that the answer is necessarily negative, but that weak indirect models merely assume a positive answer – and this sweeping assumption gives us good reasons to be sceptical about them. As discussed above – and as I will argue in greater detail in the next chapter – private law rights-and-duties relationships can be exposed to ongoing scrutiny, so long as first-order and second-order reasons about their unique relational normativity are taken into account in a principled manner. Many concerns about proportionality analysis and private law (and, indirectly, about the horizontal expansion of constitutional rights) can be alleviated if we see this analysis, in the private law context, as operating within the scheme of priority, exclusion, and reconciliation principles presented above – which balances relationality and contextualism with systematicity and generality.

5.6. THE COMMON LAW

So far, my criticisms of strong and weak indirect horizontality models have primarily focused on substantive reasons: first-order and second-order; structural, allocative and relational. I offered guidelines for their prioritisation and reconciliation in horizontal realisation reasoning. However, I have largely ignored differences between the agents that engage these reasons, which stem from the nature of their authorities, capabilities and interrelationships.

Now, with a better understanding of the substantive features of constitutional horizontality, we can finally examine its institutional side as a practice in which all state branches take part. The judiciary, legislature and executive each contribute in distinctive ways to realising constitutional rights in private law contexts, ensuring that the horizontal application of constitutional principles is not merely a judicial exercise but a collaborative endeavour – whose features further elucidate the shortcomings of weak indirect models.

My general claim in this section is that while constitutional horizontality does not ask the common law to do something it has never done, it calls for a more substantive and comprehensive conception of it – one which includes legislative and administrative activities. The common law should be seen as

[153] Lon L Fuller and Kenneth I Winston, 'The Forms and Limits of Adjudication' (1978) 92 *Harvard Law Review* 353, 395. See also Maris Köpcke, 'Why It Takes Law to Realise Human Rights' in *Legislated Rights: Securing Human Rights through Legislation* (Cambridge University Press, 2018) 55.

a dynamic process of legal evolution that builds on its past, in the sense that responses to normative challenges use tools derived from existing principles and doctrines while moving forward incrementally and contextually.[154] Just as it relies on legal principles to recognise new rights, even in the absence of friendly authorities or the presence of hostile authorities, it now can – and must – rely on constitutional rights. When understood in this light, the judiciary is central to the common law process, but holds no monopoly over it. In fact, the common law works best, transitioning between incrementalism and reform, when each state branch makes a unique contribution to the process of legal evolution.

5.6.1. Adjudication and Litigation

I start with judicial agents because adjudication and litigation are the central deliberative arenas in which constitutional horizontality questions are addressed. Judges can be asked by litigants to bring private law into better conformity with constitutional rights by creating, changing or abolishing private law norms. However, giving this role to judges raises a few institutional concerns, often noted in the literature: notably, retroactivity and the competence of litigants and judges to address complex constitutional questions.

Retroactivity is a general constitutional problem that arises whenever judges are able to change the controlling legal norms. This problem is exacerbated in our context, because the harms of retroactivity are greater when it comes to norms that guide private agents. Both forward-looking and backwards-looking constitutional remedies against the state – say, instructing it to apply a statutory norm differently with regard to a certain class of beneficiaries – raise less severe reliance and fairness concerns. In contrast, constitutional remedies in horizontality cases can change the legal implications of past private actions.

While this problem should not be taken lightly, a flexible remedial approach can allow judges to declare a private law norm unconstitutional, while still applying it to the case before them or even to future cases for a certain period of time.[155] Such flexibility acknowledges that the reliance of private parties on existing legal norms should not be privileged over other interests: generally, the more significant the rights affected, the more severe the harms, and the more effective immediate remedies are likely to be, the less tendency there should be to suspend the results of unconstitutionality. The important point is that there are no good reasons to categorically rule out constitutional horizontality claims without evaluating the results of retroactivity for constitutionally protected

[154] Allan Hutchinson, *Evolution and the Common Law* (Cambridge University Press, 2005) 3–15.

[155] On suspended declarations of invalidity, see Kent Roach, 'Remedies for Laws that Violate Human Rights' in John Bell, Mark Elliott, Jason NE Varuhas and Philip Murray (eds), *Public Law Adjudication in Common Law Systems: Process and Substance* (Hart Publishing, 2016) 269, 277–81. See also de Almeida Ribeiro (n 2) 248–53.

interests on a case-by-case basis – as long as judicial decisions are not arbitrary or opaque, and express the commitments of the legal system, including to the rule of law, better than the previous legal regime.[156]

Another recurring concern that I find less troubling is the authority and competence of judges to resolve political and complex constitutional issues. Again, such concerns – for example, Fuller's famous claim that judges struggle with 'polycentric' problems – apply to traditional vertical cases as well.[157] To the extent that the recognition of loosely relational constitutional rights is justified (and I addressed this issue in chapter 2), it seems difficult to draw distinctions between vertical and horizontal judicial decisions in this regard.

A related problem is the political normative tone and the complexity of constitutional horizontality claims. Again, this problem haunts constitutional law more broadly. Vertical constitutional cases involve the state as an addressee: after a citizen shows that their rights were infringed, the burden shifts to the state to justify the infringement. The state's justification can rely on political and complex reasons: for example, showing that a welfare scheme will likely promote equality or that a criminal law norm will incentivise due care – and that their benefits outweigh their harms in terms of basic interests. While these justifications are addressed at judges, the right-holder can contest them, which means that they may also be required to address normatively and factually complex issues.

Yet the problem in horizontality litigation is worse, because the state is not present as a litigating party, despite the fact that the constitutional rights of the parties obligate the state and not them. In practice, horizontality cases are about conflicts between the state's separate constitutional duties to each litigating party.[158] Even if the state's constitutional duties are shaped, as described above, by relationships between private parties, the basic issue is whether the state fulfilled its constitutional duties. It seems unjustified to allow private parties to make the state's case on this matter. Moreover, concerns also arise that the interests of third parties or the political collective at large will not be adequately represented, and that the information that judges need to address and resolve the case will be lacking. Such concerns underlie more general claims about the introduction of policy reasons in private law litigation.[159]

These are more serious concerns, but they are also not devastating for constitutional horizontality. First, as we saw in many of the cases already discussed,

[156] See Timothy Endicott, 'Adjudication and the Law' (2007) 27 *Oxford Journal of Legal Studies* 311, 317–20.

[157] JWF Allison, 'Fuller's Analysis of Polycentric Disputes and the Limits of Adjudication' (1994) 53 *Cambridge Law Journal* 367.

[158] Collins, 'On the (In)compatibility' (n 129) 49–50.

[159] eg, Rebecca Stone, 'Private Liability Without Wrongdoing' (2023) 73 *University of Toronto Law Journal* 87; Peter Jaffey, 'Policy and Principle and the Character of Private Law' (2020) 11 *Jurisprudence* 387.

and as we will see in the next chapter, many private law decisions are not focused on the immediate relationship of the litigating parties: their law-creating dimensions touch the basic interests of third parties. Second, it is quite common for state agents and civic organisations to contribute to the litigation of high-profile private law and constitutional law cases that have broad implications. Third – and I will revisit this point below – non-judicial agents can respond to and often revise judicial decisions, which rarely recognise concrete and categorical bright line rules. Fourth, routine horizontality litigation will deal with problems that lie closer to the particular and contextual rather than the abstract and systemic end of the spectrum:[160] they will focus on the aspects of constitutional rights implicated in specific relational scenarios – say, workplace surveillance, discrimination by bakeries, or tabloid publications about celebrities.

Second-order reasons justify focusing on concrete problems in litigation, but they leave room for policy reasons and contributions and for inter-branch dialogue. Legal agents cannot ignore these reasons. In this sense, there is no escaping some form of systematicity. This is where weak indirect models falter. As noted above, while they rely on second-order reasons about the authorities of state agents, their reliance is rigid and opaque and they ignore substantive reasons, thereby failing to provide transparent justifications for horizontal realisation decisions, including decisions not to engage in reform, which adequately weigh and reconcile all relevant considerations.

Defamation. Grant, a real-estate developer, sued a newspaper, the Toronto Star, for airing local grievances about a proposed golf course, raising suspicions about political corruption. The reporter tried to verify the allegations, also by approaching Grant, who refused to comment. A jury found the newspaper liable for libel and awarded general, aggravated, and punitive damages. In its appeal to the Supreme Court of Canada, the newspaper claimed that the defences available to journalists under the common law of defamation should be revised to better protect their freedom of expression.[161] The Court agreed, noting that earlier judicial attempts to extend existing defences did not go far enough – including *Hill v Church of Scientology of Toronto* discussed above, which solidified the Canadian weak indirect model.[162] The Court recognised a new defence of responsible communication on matters of public interest.

However, the Court still treated freedom of expression as a mere value, noting that 'the courts will, from time to time, take a fresh look at the common law and re-evaluate its consistency with evolving societal expectations through the lens of Charter values'.[163] This allowed the Court to do little work at the

[160] On this spectrum, see Kent Roach, 'Polycentricity and Queue Jumping in Public Law Remedies: A Two-Track Response' (2016) 66 *University of Toronto Law Journal* 1.
[161] *Grant v Torstar Corp* [2009] 3 SCR 640.
[162] *Hill* (n 8).
[163] *Grant* (n 161) para 46.

second-order level – to frame the decision broadly, as covering online social media and non-journalists as well – rather than focusing on a particular role, its unique normativity, and underlying values. Furthermore, it did not explain why justificatory ascent is justified in this case. Shading into the first-order level of reasoning, the Court did not resort to full-scale proportionality analysis balancing the affected rights – rather, it provided an open list of considerations that express 'the logic of proportionality', such as the public interest, the seriousness of the allegations, the urgency of the matter, and the reliability of the sources.[164] This leaves the substantive decision opaque and unstructured, relying on intuitive balancing. The problem does not necessarily lie with the details of the new principle, but with the ability of its underlying justification to guide its further development in different cases and to prevent mechanical and arbitrary application by judges in similar cases.[165]

This is the kind of case in which proportionality analysis, with its comparison of individual objections touching the social impact of legal regulation – including relational patterns – is important: not only to align private law's evolution with constitutional rights but also to safeguard against ad hoc decision-making. Such reasons were present in the Court's reasoning, but because it is unclear which reasons fall within the scope of the affected constitutional rights and which priority and reconciliation principles led to the realisation result, the new defence is open to unprincipled and policy-oriented deviations – both in future judicial decisions and through legislative and administrative decisions. While flexibility and incrementalism remain crucial in an area such as defamation law, its evolution towards better rights realisation requires a greater degree of stability and structure, and the careful integration of its public goals within the relational normative structures through which it operates.

5.6.2. Collaborative Realisation

The missing aspects of weak indirect models are further exposed when engaging constitutional horizontality as a collaborative regulatory process. The starting point is that judges are uniquely positioned not only regarding law's application, but also regarding its evolution. They regularly engage in normative dialogues with citizens, as part of adversarial processes, about their rights. While court dockets are often shaped by those with the resources to be heard;[166]

[164] ibid paras 98–126.

[165] See Hilary Young, '"Anyone … in any medium"? The Scope of Canada's Responsible Communication Defence' in Andrew T Kenyon (ed), *Comparative Defamation and Privacy Law* (Cambridge University Press, 2016) 17.

[166] See Frederick Schauer and Richard Zeckhauser, 'The Trouble with Cases' in Daniel P Kessler (ed), *Regulation versus Litigation: Perspectives from Economics and Law* (University of Chicago Press, 2010) 45.

and while 'as cases progress up the hierarchy of courts, the primacy of the dispute resolution function gives way to the lawmaking function',[167] judges can transition between these two functions,[168] thereby preserving their ability to act as first-responders in constitutional horizontality cases. Legislative and administrative law-creation processes are often more detached from particular disputes and lack the contextualism and incrementalism that allows judges to break down complex structural and allocative problems into their relational components.[169]

We can therefore say that 'courts are suited to play a mediating role between public and private spheres because they are the most private of our public institutions'.[170] This intermediate position allows judges, as Seana Shiffrin notes, to apply basic relational concepts such as responsibility, reliance or consent to different factual patterns, thereby not only promoting legal coherence but also giving 'voice to a local understanding of our mutual moral relations, one that underpins the governing culture and expectations citizens form about each other'.[171] Judges can not only engage and develop the common law from their unique perspective, but also signal to potential litigators and to non-judicial state agents that certain values are worthy of protection, or that certain normative or factual questions require further exploration. This is especially important when public enforcement is lax,[172] when polarisation erodes the democratic process,[173] or when right-holders find themselves in a political minority position.[174]

Weak indirect models harm this collaboration by granting judges almost unbridled discretion to develop the common law, to highlight matters of constitutional importance, or to integrate inputs from other state branches within private law. Jud Mathews referred to this discretion, under weak indirect models, as 'strategic ambiguity'.[175] It allows judges to keep walking on private law's traditional paths, focusing on relational concepts like consent or causation rather

[167] David Dyzenhaus and Michael Taggart, 'Reasoned Decisions and Legal Theory' in Douglas E Edlin (ed), *Common Law Theory* (Cambridge University Press, 2007) 134, 148.

[168] Owen M Fiss, 'The Forms of Justice' (1979) 93 *Harvard Law Review* 1, 16–28.

[169] See Emily Sherwin, 'The Rules of Obligations' in Andrew Robertson and Tang Hang Wu (eds), *The Goals of Private Law* (Hart Publishing, 2009) 445, 451–56; Douglas A Kysar, 'The Public Life of Private Law: Tort Law as a Risk Regulation Mechanism' (2018) 9 *European Journal of Risk Regulation* 48.

[170] Louis Michael Seidman, 'Public Principle and Private Choice: The Uneasy Case for a Boundary Maintenance Theory of Constitutional Law' (1987) 96 *Yale Law Journal* 1006, 1047.

[171] Seana Valentine Shiffrin, 'Democratic Law and the Erosion of Common Law' in Hannah Ginsborg (ed), *Democratic Law* (Oxford University Press, 2021) 65, 86.

[172] Jamillah Bowman Williams, 'Breaking Down Bias: Legal Mandates vs. Corporate Interests' (2017) 92 *Washington Law Review* 1473, 1502–13.

[173] Myriam E Gilles, 'The Private Attorney General in a Time of Hyper-Polarized Politics' (2023) 65 *Arizona Law Review* 337.

[174] On the contribution of accountability mechanisms to moral progress, see Elizabeth Anderson, 'The Social Epistemology of Morality' in Michael S Brady and Miranda Fricker (eds), *The Epistemic Life of Groups: Essays in the Epistemology of Collectives* (Oxford University Press, 2016) 75.

[175] Mathews (n 4) 186, 191, 195–96.

than on the interests and needs of vulnerable individuals and on structural and allocative reasons for regulation.[176] Yet weak indirect models are too ambiguous. No state agent is under robust duties to develop the common law, which retains much of private law's relational infrastructure.[177] Because weak indirect models are grounded in institutional principles, they leave little room for variation or exceptions in response to pressing substantive considerations. Concerns naturally arise, in this regard, about private common law's questionable track record in responding to the interests and needs of vulnerable individuals – shaped, to a great extent, by the dominance of judicial agents, who operate within strictly relational procedural and remedial structures, and often rely on formalistic reasoning to satisfy democratic and rule of law principles. While constitutional horizontality need not abolish these tendencies, it must push back against them to an extent justified by constitutional rights. Hanging the common law's evolution on the content of private law's current principles and doctrines, as weak indirect models do, is morally and constitutionally arbitrary.[178]

A significant issue here is judicial legitimacy. In modern liberal legal systems, judicial autonomy cannot be merely assumed or grounded in legal conventions that sit uneasily with the justificatory and regulatory aspects of constitutional rights (a point also made against traditional verticality). Judges are not neutral arbiters but state agents who also make law in the name of the political collective. Thus, their common law decisions cannot be fully immune to constitutional scrutiny. This leads to a second and more results-oriented point: the effective and justified horizontal realisation of constitutional rights depends on regulatory communication among the state's branches. As we drift towards more systemic reasoning about private relationships, associations and practices from structural or allocative perspectives, adjudication must be complemented by legislative and administrative activities – which often rely on judicial or 'lawyerly' translation to engage relational values and principles. What weak indirect models often disregard – and what strong indirect models press too strongly – is that private law, including its common law foundations, must be integrated within the regulatory system and therefore subjected to similar (yet not identical) scrutiny in light of public goals.

Private law must embrace – not merely tolerate – legislative and administrative policy-oriented interventions, which are integral to its evolution towards better rights realisation: both directly, by creating or changing private law norms, and indirectly through ongoing dialogue with judges. Legislators have the democratic authority and legitimacy to resolve controversial or complex

176 See Vladislava Stoyanova, 'Common Law Tort of Negligence as a Tool for Deconstructing Positive Obligations under the European Convention on Human Rights' (2020) 24 *International Journal of Human Rights* 632, 645–48.

177 See Katharina Pistor, *The Code of Capital: How the Law Creates Wealth and Inequality* (Princeton University Press, 2019) 167–69, 210–12.

178 See Larry Alexander, 'The Public/Private Distinction and Constitutional Limits on Private Power' (1993) 10 *Constitutional Commentary* 361, 362–67.

moral conflicts,[179] while expressing collective commitments to basic values.[180] This is evident in many constraints on markets – for example, in employment law, consumer law or discrimination law. Thus, for example, in many legal systems, the daily practice of promoting equality focuses on the application and development of norms located in equality and civil rights laws.

Administrative agencies and tribunals, in turn, offer expertise and a certain remoteness from the political process that often best places them to bring constitutional rights to bear on issues like insurance contracts, online privacy or workplace safety.[181] The institution of law commissions is interesting in this regard: the government, and through it the legislature and judiciary, receive advice from bodies comprised of judges, practitioners, academics, civic organisations and other interested parties, with regard to possible legal reforms.[182] It is more political than adjudication as commissions openly engage structural and allocative reasons; but it is less political than legislation as commissions tend to make incremental prescriptions that often build on judicial principles – even when these prescriptions mature into legislation, like the Unfair Contract Terms Act 1977 or the Contracts (Rights of Third Parties) Act 1999.

When facing novel challenges – say, stem cell research, euthanasia or artificial intelligence – constitutional horizontality must therefore balance stability, integrity, and existing judicial principles, with openness to diverse normative inputs. Legislation and adjudication, alongside contributions from law commissions or other hybrid bodies, are all necessary in this regard – and therefore there is little sense in seeing them as mutually exclusive or antagonistic. We must move from accounts of rights as judicially-enforced constraints on non-judicial state activities, to accounts of rights as regulatory ideals whose realisation is a collaborative effort,[183] which relies on unwritten second-order constitutional principles.[184] This leaves room, for example, for judges to reform the law based on recommendations of law commissions that parliament did not act on (as was the case with ownership after cohabitation), and for parliament to amend the law in response to judicial reform (as was the case with joint and several liability in tort).[185] For this process to be effective and justified, judges must not only leave room for other agents' input, but also change the tone of

[179] Virgilio Afonso Da Silva, 'Comparing the Incommensurable: Constitutional Principles, Balancing and Rational Decision' (2011) 31 *Oxford Journal of Legal Studies* 273, 299–301.

[180] Seana Valentine Shiffrin, 'Democratic Law' in *Democratic Law* (n 171) 17.

[181] Mathews (n 4) 194.

[182] See generally Matthew Dyson, James Lee and Shona Wilson Stark (eds), *Fifty Years of the Law Commission: The Dynamics of Law Reform* (Hart Publishing, 2016).

[183] Grégoire Webber and Paul Yowell, 'Introduction: Securing Human Rights Through Legislation' in *Legislated Rights* (n 153) 1.

[184] Aileen Kavanagh, *The Collaborative Constitution* (Cambridge University Press, 2024).

[185] Barbara McDonald, 'Law Reform in Private Law' in *Fifty Years of the Law Commission* (n 182) 297, 300.

their reasoning: a change already evident, for example, in judicial decisions in South Africa, which often, as we saw in the *Habitability* case, locate private law norms in their historical, sociological, political and moral background.[186]

We can see this by comparing the Canadian *Grant* case (*Defamation*) with the parallel development of English law. The starting point is the *Reynolds* case where, in response to the former Irish prime minister's claims that a newspaper article about his resignation (alleging he misled parliament) amounted to defamation, the House of Lords offered a non-exhaustive list of 10 factors to determine whether media statements on matters of public concern meet standards of reasonable journalism (such as the source of the information, its verification, the tone of the article, and its account of the victim's side).[187] The defence was an extension of existing doctrine (qualified privilege), and only in later cases, in response to concerns about how the open-ended nature of the defence and its underlying justifications left room for courts to apply it as rigid hurdles, was it accepted that *Reynolds* forms a novel doctrine.[188]

Dissatisfaction with this situation was one of the motivations for the lengthy parliamentary deliberations culminating in the Defamation Act 2013.[189] After *Reynolds* was engaged from many legal and moral perspectives, it was decided to explicitly replace it with a defence of statements made on matters of public interest, whose publishing the defendant reasonably believed was in the public interest.[190] While portrayed as continuous with *Reynolds*,[191] and while the language of responsibility can be reintroduced by holding that a belief is reasonable only if certain steps were taken to verify it, the Act shifts the focus to the duty-bearer's belief-forming processes – in an attempt to realise the policy goal of imposing simpler and narrower duties on contributors to public debates.[192] This process is an example of collaborative rights realisation, but notice that there is a discontinuity between the shift of focus, which is grounded in policy reasons, and the common law principle of relational responsibility that *Reynolds* failed to state in a clear manner, offering instead a list of general principles and values. More principled judicial reasoning, which better integrates structural, allocative and relational factors, would have served as a better normative foundation for political debates about legal reform.

[186] Edward Béchard-Torres, 'Social Rights and Transformative Private Law' (2023) 60 *Osgoode Hall Law Journal* 375, 400–16.

[187] *Reynolds v Times Newspapers* [2001] 2 AC 127.

[188] *Jameel v Wall Street Journal* [2007] 1 AC 359; *Flood v Times Newspapers* [2012] UKSC 11.

[189] For replies to some of the criticisms, see Gavin Phillipson, 'The "Global Pariah", the Defamation Bill and the Human Rights Act' (2012) 63 *Northern Ireland Legal Quarterly* 149.

[190] s 4.

[191] Ministry of Justice, *Defamation Act 2013 Explanatory Notes* (2013) § 29.

[192] See Alastair Mullis and Andrew Scott, 'Tilting at Windmills: The Defamation Act 2013' (2014) 77 *Modern Law Review* 84, 90.

Inheritance. In 1902, a couple executed a joint will, bequeathing several properties to their children – holding that they can only be passed on to male descendants until the fourth generation. In 2015, one of their grandchildren died with no male children, leaving his shares in an inherited farm to his daughters. The Constitutional Court of South Africa had to decide whether the discriminatory clause was valid.[193] It held that while freedom of testation is grounded in the constitutional rights to dignity, property and privacy, the common law rule of largely unfettered discretion cannot be maintained.[194] To conform with 'the spirit, purport and objects of the Bill of Rights', the principle of the unenforceability of clauses contrary to public policy must be developed,[195] and a bright line rule must be adopted: 'it can never accord with public policy for a testator, even in the private sphere, to discriminate against lineal descendants unknown to her or him purely on the ground of gender'.[196]

While adopting such rules will not necessarily be justified in complex cases like *Defamation*, the adoption of more concrete and clear norms grounded in a coherent system of principles is an ideal that constitutional horizontality must aim to meet.[197] For example, in *Inheritance*, structural reasons trumped the relational reasons that support freedom of testation in respect of discriminatory choices; and the replacement of *Reynolds* relies on structural reasons about public debate. In such cases, private law's evolution towards better rights realisation through categorisation and simplification requires policy reasons to be gradually integrated within private rights-and-duties relationships. If in *Inheritance* a bright line rule seems justified, cases like *Defamation* must rely more heavily, and therefore more transparently, on systems of priority and reconciliation principles that leave room for second-order reasons and on the common law's ability to evolve incrementally – while relying on contributions from different actors, reflecting their normative perspectives.[198] This sheds light on the importance of the common law, construed broadly, for constitutional horizontality – but also on the importance of an overarching normative structure, which weak indirect models tend to neglect or obscure.

[193] *King v De Jager* [2021] ZACC 4.
[194] ibid paras 64, 70.
[195] ibid paras 49–50.
[196] ibid para 84.
[197] See Jochen von Bernstorff, 'Proportionality Without Balancing' in Liora Lazarus, Christopher McCrudden and Nigel Bowles (eds), *Reasoning Rights: Comparative Judicial Engagement* (Hart Publishing, 2014) 63.
[198] See also Jane Wright, *Tort Law and Human Rights*, 2nd edn (Hart Publishing, 2017) 27–34.

5.7. CONCLUSION

Building on the previous chapter's critique of strong indirect models and the distinctions between structural, allocative and relational reasons, this chapter criticised weak indirect models by introducing the idea of responsibility assignments and portraying horizontal rights realisation as an ongoing collaborative practice. It describes the common law broadly, as an attempt by all state branches to transition between particularity and generality while relying on second-order reasons to gradually push private law towards better conformity with constitutional rights. The core idea of indirect models, in a way, is to operate through an enriched version of the common law. This picture, as the next chapter will show, is not entirely disconnected from legal practices: private law is not oblivious to public goals, and many of its norms are created or changed by legislative or administrative agents – even if it remains slow to respond to structural and allocative reasons for regulation, and if the involvement of non-judicial state agents remains sporadic and unprincipled.

Having said that, the basic features of the rights-realisation picture painted in this chapter are not foreign to modern legal systems – which means that they already have the tools to realise constitutional rights effectively and justifiably in private social spheres. This chapter exposed and elucidated these basic features not with the goal of making the conflicts and tensions disappear – after all, they are signs of a healthy legal system, which operates in conditions of moral pluralism – but to place the process of reconciling the competing considerations on more solid ground. The next chapter will further unpack the realisation scheme described in this chapter, while highlighting its ability to operate in the more pluralistic normative conditions of modern private law.

6

Modern Private Law

6.1. A MIDLIFE CRISIS

THE PREVIOUS CHAPTERS touched on the horizontal delineation and realisation of constitutional rights. They explained why such rights obligate primarily state agents but also address private activities and actions; and why their requirements from private law should not subordinate it to constitutional goals nor isolate it from effective constitutional scrutiny. We ended up with a rough sketch of constitutional horizontality as a collaborative effort of all state branches to realise constitutional rights in private relationships, associations and practices – a process that transitions between upstream decisions about the adoption of private law regimes, where structural and allocative reasons take priority, and downstream decisions about the details of private law rights-and-duties relationships, where relational reasons take priority.

So far, the nature and limits of private law have been regularly considered, because, to be effective and justified, constitutional horizontality cannot ignore the normative structure and underlying values of private rights-and-duties relationships. However, while discussing many examples of private law responses to basic interests and policy goals (*Fertility Treatment*, *Parenthood*, *Habitability*, *Eviction*, *Inheritance*, *Nuisance*, *Drunk Driving*, *Discrimination*, *Surveillance*, *Defamation, Privacy*, and others), we largely stayed at its borders. We focused on the outside–inside interface – the translation of constitutional rights into private law rights – without going too deeply into private law itself.

This chapter takes this further step by exploring additional procedural, institutional and substantive features of private law. It therefore removes some of the scaffolding used to engage the horizontal dimensions of constitutional rights: certain assumptions and abstractions about the operation and evolution of private law's normative core, which generally push back against the beneficiary-centredness and teleological orientation of general constitutional rights. This chapter shifts the focus from the horizontal dimensions of constitutional rights – the kind of pressures that they apply to private law – to private law's ability to respond to these pressures, which has so far been presented, because of its inherent relationality, as uniformly strong.

This shift of focus serves two main purposes. First, it sheds further light, upstream, on the horizontal dimensions of constitutional rights, filling the framework presented earlier with additional content. For example, we can distinguish between private law domains in terms of their ties to the restrictive conception of personal responsibility – and thus the strictness of their relationality and resistance to constitutional scrutiny. Constitutional horizontality reasoning must account for such distinctions. Second, this shift complements the constitutional perspective by taking a look, downstream, at the framework's possible integration within and implications for private law. By taking a closer look at private law, on the ground, we can gain further insight into the ways in which it can better accommodate constitutional rights in the future.

This chapter relies on a general distinction between the loosening of private law's relationality by agent-centered reasons and by beneficiary-centered reasons. While building on this distinction, this chapter will touch upon another overarching issue that was kept latent in the previous chapters: the rights and duties of corporations. The more instrumentalist and structured corporate activities are – and distinctions must be made in this regard between, for instance, multinational for-profit corporations and churches or small coffee shops – the more intense and ongoing constitutional scrutiny can be, because of how the agency and well-being of affected individuals are implicated.

We will also see the door opened for more intense and ongoing constitutional scrutiny in cases involving unincorporated individuals. In some such cases, choices are more remote from moral agency: for instance, when agreeing to certain online contracts or engaging in risky activities while being insured. In other cases, choice and agency are tied more strongly to private law norms, but the interests and needs of people who rely on the agent's role-responsibility – say, as a parent, a seller or an employer – justify stronger forms of constitutional horizontality. While domains like family law, consumer law, labour law and discrimination law are sometimes referred to as peripheral (or, to borrow John Gardner's words, 'private-law-lite'),[1] they are central for the practice of constitutional horizontality – as avenues through which constitutional rights regularly shape private relationships, associations and practices.

After understanding how and when private law can tolerate stronger forms of constitutional horizontality, we can further highlight the ways in which the strictly relational bubble – that traditional private law theories often highlight – has already burst. Private law contains not only surgical responsibility identifications through concrete norms but also abstract standards, such as good faith or reasonableness, through which responsibilities can be assigned on a more ongoing basis to private agents. Even looser relationality typifies cases in which insurers carry the burdens of liability and where administrative agencies monitor and respond to the actions and activities of duty-bearers – for example, overseeing workplace safety policies.

[1] John Gardner, 'Dagan and Dorfman on the Value of Private Law' (2017) 117 *Columbia Law Review* 179, 199.

Private law's expanding margins raise many theoretical and practical questions. What is clear is that they cannot be treated as mere exceptions (or worse, aberrations) in an attempt to present private law as uniformly strictly relational. However, this chapter will claim that seeing private law as more diverse in terms of its relationality need not bring about its disintegration as a coherent normative system. My goal is not to offer a definition of private law that has concrete doctrinal implications or to describe its timeless essence. Rather, it is to show that constitutional horizontality can not only accommodate private law's unique regulatory role – shaping the normative DNA of private relationships, associations and practices, by recognising morally robust rights and duties – but also protect this role from erosion or distortion.

Recognising private law's inherent relationality does not necessitate reducing it to a homogeneous and abstract construct. As we will see, its relationality performs morally important roles even in its more policy-infused margins – and, in this sense, can be said to tie it together as a coherent cluster of legal domains. Importantly, the realisation of constitutional rights in all these domains must rely on the priority and reconciliation principles presented in chapter 4, and on the incremental and collaborative common law process presented in chapter 5. This framework is important not only because it contributes to the effectiveness and justification of the horizontal realisation of constitutional rights, but also because it strengthens private law's autonomy – which consists in integration within rather than in isolation from the regulatory system.

To a great extent, this is the starting point of a political theory of private law – a topic I touched upon in the first chapter. The nature and limits of private law as an exercise of state authority and power must take into account not only the complex social, economic, political and cultural conditions to which private law must respond, but also the nature of the standards that it must meet as a form of regulation – chief among them, the horizontal dimensions of constitutional rights. This chapter therefore concludes by stressing that constitutional horizontality not only constrains private law but also grants it moral legitimacy as a unique political exercise of authority.

6.2. CORPORATIONS

Corporations are prevalent in modern societies. The creation and provision of many goods and services – from food, through sports, to religion – are tied to corporate activities. In the constitutional horizontality context, corporations are both a threat and a promise. On the one hand, concerns arise that the horizontal expansion of constitutional rights will serve corporations more than it does individuals, as corporations often have better means of vindicating their rights. Thus, constitutional horizontality can tilt the balance of power even more toward the already stronger party in many private law relationships.

On the other hand, because corporations already possess significant power over essential goods and services (like electricity or water), constitutional rights can guarantee basic procedural or substantive moral standards.

In this section, I address these issues without going too deeply into philosophical questions about whether the corporation is an agent or a mere aggregation of agents.[2] Legal systems have long recognised the agency of corporations. They can, for example, sign contracts, hold property, and discharge (or violate) duties of care. While they are comprised of individual agents – owners, shareholders, managers, employees, and so on – and often conceived as a 'nexus of contracts',[3] it still makes sense to say, for example, that 'McDonald's sold this burger' or that 'Meta operates this online platform'.[4] Much of corporate law is dedicated to the consolidation of corporations as agents who can claim rights and bear duties.[5]

But corporations are not real persons, in the sense that their well-being and agency have no intrinsic but merely derivative moral importance.[6] This invites distinctions between corporations. Some corporations are associations of individuals in a robust sense. They are not impersonal like public for-profit corporations, and are tied more closely to the well-being and agency of their members: for instance, cooperatives, clubs, sports teams, universities, churches, labour unions, political parties, and other forms of private ordering that organise around a corporate person for different practical purposes.

While I need not rule out the possibility that public for-profit corporations can be associational in this sense, it is clear that some such corporations – for example, Exxon Mobil, McDonald's, Walmart, Apple, Meta, Amazon, Visa and Tesla – operate in ways that distance them from the agency and well-being of any stable group of individuals. Not only are many of their shareholders passive and see them as financial investments, but their stocks are often owned by institutional investors – like pension, mutual or hedge funds.[7] In practice, they are frequently operated by small groups of managers located at the top of hierarchical structures.

[2] See Richard Schragger and Micah Schwartzman, 'Some Realism about Corporate Rights' in Micah Schwartzman, Chad Flanders and Zoë Robinson (eds), *The Rise of Corporate Religious Liberty* (Oxford University Press, 2016) 345.

[3] See John Armour, Henry Hansmann, Reinier Kraakman and Mariana Pargendler, 'What is Corporate Law?' in *The Anatomy of Corporate Law: A Comparative and Functional Approach*, 3rd edn (Oxford University Press, 2017) 1, 5.

[4] See Meir Dan-Cohen, *Rights, Persons, and Organizations: A Legal Theory for Bureaucratic Society* (University of California Press, 1986) 13–40.

[5] Elizabeth Pollman, 'Constitutionalizing Corporate Law' (2016) 69 *Vanderbilt Law Review* 639.

[6] Philip Pettit, 'Two Fallacies About Corporations' in Subramanian Rangan (ed), *Performance and Progress: Essays on Capitalism, Business, and Society* (Oxford University Press, 2015) 379.

[7] See David Ciepley, 'Beyond Public and Private: Toward a Political Theory of the Corporation' (2013) 107 *American Political Science Review* 139, 148; James D Nelson, 'The Freedom of Business Association' (2015) 115 *Columbia Law Review* 461, 496–99.

When thinking about whether corporations can hold constitutional rights and about the intensity of the constitutional scrutiny of their activities, we should keep this entire spectrum in mind. My claims in this section are that we can see corporations as holders of constitutional rights with horizontal dimensions in some cases, and that the nature of their agency gives state agents more leeway to burden them with demanding private law duties.

6.2.1. Corporations as Right-holders

While in many cases corporations are recognised as constitutional right-holders (for instance, to property or freedom of expression),[8] such recognition often meets resistance – especially when constitutional rights are conceived as stronger and more categorical. Thus, in the United States, deep concerns and heated debates arose following the Supreme Court's decisions to recognise corporate rights to freedom of political speech[9] and to the free exercise of religion.[10] The second case, *Hobby Lobby*, is noteworthy, because despite not dealing directly with constitutional rights but with their realisation through the Religious Freedom Restoration Act (1993), it does address what is a typical constitutional horizontality question: whether a private business corporation, with thousands of employees, should pay for their health insurance coverage of contraceptives, if their use contradicts the religious beliefs of the family members who own the corporation. The Supreme Court exempted the corporation from this duty, holding that less restrictive means exist to promote the policy goal of insurance coverage – in effect, using a version of proportionality analysis to reconcile the conflicting interests and rights.

Such decisions naturally create a temptation to deny that corporations should be recognised as constitutional right-holders. But this is too sweeping a solution. The concerns raised by cases like *Hobby Lobby* could also be addressed at the realisation stage. As explained earlier, at the delineation stage we rely mostly on structural reasons, about the ongoing operation of constitutional rights as part of the basic structure of society. We must therefore ask, at this level of generality, which normative connections exist between corporate activities and individual agency and well-being.[11] Two paths can be identified in this regard.[12]

[8] eg, Anat Scolnicov, 'Human Rights as Derivative Rights: The European Convention on Human Rights and the Rights of Corporations' in Tsvi Kahana and Anat Scolnicov (eds), *Boundaries of State, Boundaries of Rights: Human Rights, Private Actors, and Positive Obligations* (Cambridge University Press, 2016) 194.

[9] *Citizens United v Federal Election Commission* 558 US 310 (2010).

[10] *Burwell v Hobby Lobby* 573 US 682 (2014).

[11] Margaret M Blair and Elizabeth Pollman, 'The Derivative Nature of Corporate Constitutional Rights' (2015) 56 *William & Mary Law Review* 1673.

[12] See Dan-Cohen, *Rights, Persons, and Organizations* (n 4) 55–57.

The internal path focuses on how corporate activities serve relatively stable and identifiable groups of individuals. In *Hobby Lobby*, for example, it was the family members who owned the corporation. However, this group could also consist of managers and employees, and even customers: they could be dedicated to, say, not selling certain products or to closing on holy days.[13] Such associational connections tend to be stronger when referring to non-profits, but categorical distinctions need not be drawn here.[14] In principle, all corporations could come to be intricately bound with the autonomy and identity of a distinct group of individuals.

The second, external, path focuses on the impact of corporate activities over larger and more diffuse groups of individuals: for example, the right to freedom of commercial speech could be tied to the interests of consumers in making informed decisions.[15] If corporate rights are tied to their broader societal impact, values like autonomy or identity will fail to justify, for example, a form of corporate speech that harms public debate.[16] The external path is, therefore, not necessarily weaker when corporate activities are heavily influenced by economic incentives.[17] In general, the recognition of rights through this path raises complex questions, which require evaluating the impact of corporate activities as parts of the basic structure of society.

6.2.2. Corporations as Duty-Bearers

The imposition of demanding duties on corporations raises fewer concerns compared to their imposition on individuals – especially on large business corporations operated by a managerial group whose main goal is making profits: these entities can perform complex duties; their accountability is more weakly tied to moral integrity; and their relationships with other legal agents are largely of derivative value. This seems to open the door for direct horizontality, especially when corporations engage in traditionally public activities, such as incarceration or electricity provision.[18] In such cases, corporations have a public state-like

[13] Alan J Meese and Nathan B Oman, '*Hobby Lobby*, Corporate Law, and the Theory of the Firm: Why For-Profit Corporations are RFRA Persons' (2014) 127 *Harvard Law Review Forum* 273.

[14] Waheed Hussain, 'Corporations, Profit Maximization and the Personal Sphere' (2012) 28 *Economics and Philosophy* 311.

[15] *Virginia State Pharmacy Board v Virginia Citizens Consumer Council* 425 US 748 (1976).

[16] See Meir Dan-Cohen, 'Freedoms of Collective Speech: A Theory of Protected Communications by Organizations, Communities, and the State' (1991) 79 *California Law Review* 1229, 1248–54.

[17] See also Seana Valentine Shiffrin, 'A Thinker-Based Approach to Freedom of Speech' in *Speech Matters: On Lying, Morality, and the Law* (Princeton University Press, 2014) 79, 98–102.

[18] See Eric W Orts, *Business Persons: A Legal Theory of the Firm* (Oxford University Press, 2013) 109–31; Nien-hê Hsieh, 'Corporate Moral Agency, Positive Duties, and Purpose' in Eric W Orts and N Craig Smith (eds), *The Moral Responsibility of Firms* (Oxford University Press, 2017) 188.

status (often masked by their portrayal as a form of private ordering),[19] even if – unlike the state – they can unburden themselves of responsibilities and duties by withdrawing from social spheres and activities.[20]

Having said that, at least in well-functioning legal systems (on which we focus), there is still the problem of authority: duties to realise general constitutional rights involve an ongoing exercise of discretion. This is a main reason for the strong resistance to the privatisation of foundational public activities, such as incarceration.[21] Similar concerns arise about imposing on corporations constitutional duties that require, for instance, the reconciliation of the freedom of speech, dignity and privacy of the users of social media platforms. This reconciliation must be performed by agents accountable to the public not only through litigation, where corporations have inherent advantages, but also through more robust institutional mechanisms.

However, the smaller scale of the problems of complexity, intrusion, crowding out and scrutiny means that indirect horizontality can take stronger forms: it can rely more heavily on consequentialist reasons and shape private law duties as more complex standards. Corporations are operated by and interact with individuals, and therefore the ways in which they observe relational norms – say, of promise-keeping – have implications for the status of such norms in society.[22] However, limiting our reasoning about, say, the regulation of corporate agreements about mergers or the extraction of natural resources to strictly relational moral principles of promise-keeping, overextends the jurisdiction of relational morality into structural and allocative domains (unless structural or allocative reasons invite this extension).[23] This tendency to overextend relational morality is pervasive and reduces our ability to alleviate problems like environmental pollution, employee exploitation, corruption of the democratic process, and the sale of dangerous products, such as guns.

We saw this in the *Eviction* case, in which the Supreme Court of the United Kingdom deferred to the existing statutory balance between the rights to property and home by refusing to subject a lending company's eviction claim to substantive fairness tests.[24] The Court was rightly concerned about direct horizontality and about evaluating the proportionality of all eviction claims. However, we can distinguish between small-scale individual landlords and large companies that specialise in home loans, on whom the imposition of clear and

[19] Ciepley (n 7); Grant M Hayden and Matthew T Bodie, 'The Uncorporation and the Unravelling of "Nexus of Contracts" Theory' (2011) 109 *Michigan Law Review* 1127, 1127–30.

[20] See David Jason Karp, *Responsibility for Human Rights: Transnational Corporations in Imperfect States* (Cambridge University Press, 2014) 89–151.

[21] See generally Avihay Dorfman and Alon Harel (eds), *The Cambridge Handbook of Privatization* (Cambridge University Press, 2001).

[22] Seana Valentine Shiffrin, 'The Divergence of Contract and Promise' (2007) 120 *Harvard Law Review* 708, 746–49.

[23] See Joseph Heath, *Morality, Competition, and the Firm* (Oxford University Press, 2014) 12–19.

[24] *McDonald v McDonald* [2016] UKSC 28.

general duties that require responses (even if procedural) to threats to constitutionally protected interests, can be justified more easily.

There are often good reasons for state agents to apply full-scale proportionality analysis more strongly to the regulation of corporate activities. In doing so, state agents should consider how heavier burdens fit within rights-and-duties relationships, while taking the nature of corporate activities into account: for instance, the imposition of substantive constraints on eviction claims by individuals must be firmly grounded in relational notions like fairness or consent, whereas such constraints on corporations can be more loosely relational and focus on the risks created by business ventures and their social roles in credit or housing markets, to which complex responsibilities can more easily be assigned. In this sense, as Nagel noted, all corporations – even universities or political parties – 'come under a kind of public morality'.[25]

Social Security. A private company's contract with the state for the administration of a social security grant program was cancelled after it started administering it due to problems with the bidding process. The Constitutional Court of South Africa had to decide which duties the company should have until a contract could be agreed with another company.[26] It was held that because the company assumed obligations to exercise a public power that realises the constitutional right to access to social security, private autonomy considerations gain much less weight, and therefore the company was obligated to continue to administer the program.

Thomas claims, about a structurally similar case, that a company providing electricity is only under procedural duties like granting a fair hearing to non-paying customers before terminating their service, but under no duties to provide the good because it creates or substantially contributes to it.[27] Under the approach presented here, the relational normativity of roles such as electricity provider or social security program administrator exceeds the agent's actions towards particular right-holders, thus making more room for structural and allocative concerns to justify assignments of affirmative responsibilities and duties. Because corporate activities are often tied more weakly to individual interests and corporate capabilities are often greater, their activities in sensitive social spheres (such as electricity provision, social security or social media) are tied to expanded moral expectations and accountability to a larger public, which can underlie society-facing remedial obligations (such as ensuring that the electric grid or public debate do not overload).

Market Share. The justifications for deviating from strict relationality in private law relationships with corporations are evident in a case involving

[25] Thomas Nagel, 'Ruthlessness in Public Life' in Stuart Hampshire (ed), *Public and Private Morality* (Cambridge University Press, 1978) 75, 82.

[26] *AllPay Consolidated Investment Holdings (Pty) Ltd v Chief Executive Officer of the South African Social Security Agency* [2014] ZACC 12.

[27] Jean Thomas, *Public Rights, Private Relations* (Oxford University Press, 2015) 231.

the sale of a drug that caused cancer to the daughters of women who took it during pregnancy. The problem for a certain claimant was that she did not know which company's version of the drug her mother used. The Supreme Court of California held that each company that produced the drug during the relevant time-frame was liable according to its market share, unless it could prove that it could not have possibly caused the woman's harm (which is quite difficult).[28] Importantly, there is no strict correlation here between rights and duties. The companies failed to take due care, thereby negligently creating risks of physical harm. These wrongful activities justified secondary duties to compensate, bits and pieces of which were put together to assemble the claimant's right to full compensation. In a sense, by assuming the role of a pharmaceutical company, these agents assumed duties as part of the industry. Similar claims could arise about gun or tobacco manufacturers, even if stretching responsibilities and duties like this is much more difficult when it comes to individual agents. As noted above, this opens the door for more progressive and robust forms of constitutional horizontality.

6.3. AGENCY AND CHOICE

Implicit in the discussion above is the idea that when individuals relinquish a degree of choice and control over their affairs (for instance, by entrusting the directors and managers of a corporation with their financial interests), the ties to the restrictive conception of responsibility are weakened, and therefore regulatory reasoning can be less strictly relational: there is more room in rights-and-duties relationships for structural and allocative reasons.

This section develops this idea, while removing additional scaffolding used to simplify the argument. So far, we have treated the individual as an agent who takes charge of their life through well-informed and diligent decisions. Such assumptions are necessary because private law must be general enough to guide behaviour. But only up to a point. Sometimes, this section claims, our agency falls short of two abstract figures that lurk behind private law theory and practice: the autonomous Kantian agent and the rational economic chooser. Biases, predispositions and deliberate choices often undermine our control over our normative situation. The fact that this does not stop private law from empowering us or imposing duties on us has drawn criticisms in private law theory. But to the extent that private law continues to do these things, there is less resistance to stronger forms of constitutional horizontality.

The normative implications of our limited agency are generally less significant at the stage of constitutional rights delineation, because this stage relies

[28] *Sindell v Abbott Laboratories* 26 Cal 3d 588 (1980). A somewhat similar solution was adopted by the House of Lords regarding negligent exposure to asbestos under several employers in *Fairchild v Glenhaven Funeral Services Ltd* [2003] 1 AC 32.

on basic assumptions about the individual to allow rights to operate as general ideals. However, at the stage of constitutional rights realisation, limited agency has important implications, which private law must respond to in order to avoid a coarse and anachronistic clinging to an idealised image of the private agent.[29]

6.3.1. Contractual Consent

The erosion of agency is felt across private law. But it is most pronounced in contract law, given its emphasis on the choice of contractual parties to assume mutual legal duties.[30] Such emphasis often accompanies a focus on the relational morality of promising or exercising normative powers,[31] which distinguishes contract law's normativity from tort law's mandatory and duty-imposing normativity: contract law empowers us to assume duties deliberately rather than incidentally.[32] In this sense, autonomy and choice serve as the moral foundations of contract law.[33]

Even if we assume that contract law is, in most cases, strongly connected to autonomy and choice and that contract law should therefore generally rely on the relational morality of promises or agreements,[34] these connections weaken in some contractual contexts. Take, for example, contracts that operate on a rolling basis and include future terms, that list some terms separately, or that we enter merely by opening a box or clicking 'I agree' on a website.[35] Even if it is morally justified to recognise such contracts as valid while reducing our consent to obligate ourselves to hypothetical assent (and there are some doubts here),[36] this falls short of robust consent. Concerns can therefore arise about the alienation of rights (for example, not to be discriminated against by employers) under the guise of exercising a normative power.[37]

[29] See generally Steve Hedley, 'Corrective Justice – An Idea Whose Time Has Gone?' in Maksymilian Del Mar and Michael Lobban (eds), *Law in Theory and History* (Hart Publishing, 2016) 305, 319–25.

[30] Nancy S Kim, 'Relative Consent and Contract Law' (2017) 18 *Nevada Law Journal* 165.

[31] Charles Fried, *Contract as Promise: A Theory of Contractual Obligation* (Harvard University Press, 1981).

[32] Curtis Bridgeman and John CP Goldberg, 'Do Promises Distinguish Contract from Tort?' (2012) 45 *Suffolk University Law Review* 873.

[33] See Hanoch Dagan and Michael Heller, *The Choice Theory of Contracts* (Cambridge University Press, 2017).

[34] See also Dori Kimel, *From Promise to Contract: Towards a Liberal Theory of Contract* (Hart Publishing, 2003); Prince Saprai, *Contract Law Without Foundations: Toward a Republican Theory of Contract Law* (Oxford University Press, 2019) 22–35.

[35] See Nancy S Kim, *Wrap Contracts* (Oxford University Press, 2013); Margaret Jane Radin, *Boilerplate: The Fine Print, Vanishing Rights, and the Rule of Law* (Princeton University Press, 2013).

[36] Radin (n 35) 19–32.

[37] ibid.

However, there are good policy reasons to recognise and enforce some such contracts, as they facilitate many beneficial and justified social activities (such as online commerce), provided they do not harm the basic interests of the parties involved – either by being imposed on them or by violating inalienable rights. It is therefore justified to hold us responsible, to some degree, for agreeing to enter such contracts, given our knowledge of their general contours in many social spheres – and doing so can help solidify our responsibility for our choices, even ones made casually. To the extent that enforcing such contracts is justified, one might argue that policy reasons not explicitly included in the contracts should not be imposed on the parties.

However, if a contract relies on less than full consent, at least by one of the parties – say, the party clicking 'I agree' – there are fewer reasons based in agency and choice or in the relational morality of agreements to exclude constitutional (or, more broadly, policy) reasons: with implications both for their validity and for substantive interventions in their content. Once we recognise that agency comes in degrees, we can also recognise that we need not dignify all contracts with the strict relationality that accompanies more robust forms of consent. Thus, the fact that the recognition of certain interactions as valid contracts is heavily shaped by policy reasons means that such reasons can also more easily justify deviations from the details to which the parties allegedly agreed: for example, it could be justified to read substantive fairness or good faith standards into certain contracts or to hold their drafters to increased transparency requirements. In some cases, this will justify duties that amplify agency and choice: for example, on sellers to ensure adequate consumer consent, even by taking active and protective measures.

Undue Influence. A parallel can be drawn here to a case decided by the House of Lords, concerning the claims of wives whose family homes were mortgaged to banks to secure their husbands' loans. After the loans went unpaid, the banks sought possession of the properties to sell them. The wives argued that they had been pressured or misled into signing and sought to cancel the guarantees. The court held that when a bank knows that a guarantee might involve pressure – such as in loans benefiting only one spouse – it must ensure the guarantor receives independent legal advice and understands the risks for the contract to be valid.[38]

This case is important because while focusing on relationships with banks, it engages choice and consent substantively, thereby viewing them as shaped by external factors such as the relationship between guarantors and their spouses. This sensitivity could be extended further – not only to factors that shape the ability to agree to transactions (for example, ensuring that minorities are communicated with in their language and cultural context) but also to concerns

[38] *Royal Bank of Scotland plc v Etridge (No 2)* [2002] 2 AC 773.

that fit less neatly in the strictly relational picture of isolated relationships between contractual parties. If some types of contracts involve less detailed choice and consent, there is less resistance to the introduction of structural and allocative reasons into them. For example, if consumers rarely read the details of online transactions, there is less resistance to including pro-consumer norms: for example, a minimal cancelation period or substantive fairness standards. This can be done not only through defaults that contractual parties can deviate from, but also through mandatory norms. This is where the erosion of consent ties into our discussion, in the next section, of heightened duties that respond to vulnerability and need. But before that we must address a slightly different context in which agency is not fully present.

6.3.2. Tort Liability

Tort law imposes general duties which tend to be negative and categorical or fault-based, as well as more demanding and affirmative duties when agents assume special roles. Like contract law, tort law aims to preserve a reasonable congruence between our choices and our duties and liabilities to others. However, given its mandatory nature, tort law is less sensitive to choice and control. It is often criticised, for example, for adopting objective or strict standards that some agents struggle to meet, for imposing liabilities for brief moments of inattention, for disproportions between liability and culpability, and for disparities between agents who act similarly.[39] The distance between personal responsibility and tort liability is even greater when considering that tortfeasors often do not participate in legal proceedings or compensate victims: their insurers regularly do so.[40] Many tort disputes do not even reach litigation: they end in settlements, the details of which are often remotely tied to particular tortious interactions or tort norms, and are shaped, instead, by instrumental and profit-oriented corporate policies.[41]

The heavy involvement of liability insurance is not merely an external market factor. To a great extent, it has shaped and continues to shape tort law's development – for example, by allowing liability to expand without financially

[39] See Larry Alexander and Kimberly Kessler Ferzan, 'Confused Culpability, Contrived Causation, and the Collapse of Tort Theory' in John Oberdiek (ed), *Philosophical Foundations of the Law of Torts* (Oxford University Press, 2014) 406.

[40] Richard Lewis and Annette Morris, 'Tort Law Culture: Image and Reality' (2012) 39 *Journal of Law and Society* 562; Rob Merkin, 'Tort, Insurance and Ideology: Further Thoughts' (2012) 75 *Modern Law Review* 301; Kennth S Abraham and Catherine M Sharkey, 'The Glaring Gap in Tort Theory' (2024) 133 *Yale Law Journal* 2165.

[41] Richard Lewis, 'Humanity in Tort: Does Personality Affect Personal Injury Litigation?' (2018) 71 *Current Legal Problems* 245.

devastating tortfeasors.[42] While often ignored by traditional tort theory,[43] there is an opening here for stronger forms of constitutional horizontality, which could alleviate some concerns about tort law's responses to vulnerability and responsibility – even if we see tort law's ongoing operation as inherently relational. Liability insurance could be seen as an ex-ante way of taking responsibility: of ensuring that we can remedy the harms we cause.[44] It might then be claimed that not purchasing insurance when engaging in dangerous activities is a form of negligence. This idea has important implications. It allows allocative reasons – including ones grounded in constitutional rights – to justify imposing mandatory duties of insurance on participants in activities like driving.[45] These could also be public law duties, which are not owed to any agent in particular, but which nonetheless shape tort law rights-and-duties relationships: if engagement in certain activities is or should be conditioned on purchasing insurance, standards of care may be increased and causation requirements may be relaxed.[46]

A concern could arise that the force and value of tort norms would diminish if the shadows they cast in terms of accountability grow too dim: if private agents can buy tort law immunity, why should they pay attention to how their actions affect others?[47] Basic interests might be reduced to the ability to bargain for favourable settlements with insurance companies – which is worrying both because many bargains will be unfair and because tort law rights against harms and deprivations are not mere price tags. It is morally wrong to falsely imprison, batter, defame, cause nuisance or drive recklessly, even if insurance covers the costs of harms. One option – and policy reasons are central in this regard – is for contract law to come to tort law's aid by not recognising certain insurance contracts. The commodification of some tort rights – for example, against defamation or sexual harassment – could violate constitutional rights: for example, to dignity or bodily integrity. Thus, constitutional rights can justify prohibiting liability insurance in certain cases.

[42] Richard Lewis, 'Insurers and Personal Injury Litigation: Acknowledging the Elephant in the Living Room' (2005) 1/05 *Journal of Personal Injury Law* 1; Tom Baker, 'Liability Insurance as Tort Regulation: Six Ways that Liability Insurance Shapes Tort Law in Action' (2005) 12 *Connecticut Insurance Law Journal* 1; Rob Merkin and Jenny Steele, *Insurance and the Law of Obligations* (Oxford University Press, 2013) chs 8–9; Kenneth S Abraham, 'Tort Luck and Liability Insurance' (2017) 70 *Rutgers University Law Review* 1.

[43] Christopher J Robinette, 'Two Roads Diverge for Civil Recourse Theory' (2013) 88 *Indiana Law Journal* 543, 564–66; Hanoch Sheinman, 'Tort Law and Distributive Justice' in *Philosophical Foundations of the Law of Torts* (n 39) 354, 381–83.

[44] Tony Honoré, 'The Morality of Tort Law: Questions and Answers' in *Responsibility and Fault* (Hart Publishing, 1999) 67, 74–75; Arthur Ripstein, 'Some Recent Obituaries of Tort Law' (1998) 48 *University of Toronto Law Journal* 561, 566.

[45] See, eg, Rob Merkin and Sheila Dziobon, 'Tort Law and Compulsory Insurance' in TT Arvind and Jenny Steele (eds), *Tort Law and the Legislature* (Hart Publishing, 2012) 303.

[46] Merkin (n 40).

[47] *See* John CP Goldberg, 'Ten Half-Truths About Tort Law' (2008) 42 *Valparaiso University Law Review* 1221, 1264–70; John CP Goldberg and Benjamin C Zipursky, 'Civil Recourse Defended: A Reply to Posner, Calabresi, Rustad, Chamallas, and Robinette' (2013) 88 *Indiana Law Journal* 569, 607–08.

The aforementioned scenarios of mandatory or prohibited insurance raise complex questions, but are more straightforward than the third scenario, in which insurance is permissible. The challenge here arises from the assumption that tort duties can be more extensive because the tortfeasor is insured or has chosen not to purchase insurance. Agency operates in this scenario, but it is coloured in allocative shades: we focus on the choice to engage in insurable risky activities and assume that the costs of harms can be dispersed among many agents through insurance, thereby allowing greater consideration for the interests and needs of tort victims – such as by lowering the bar for tort claims in terms of fault or causation.[48] These ideas help explain why drivers are exposed to liability for 'moments of carelessness',[49] and why employers face vicarious liability for employee actions.[50] Thus, the very possibility of insurance opens the door for constitutional reasons to shape not only choices about whether insurance should be mandatory or prohibited, but also its nuanced implications for rights-and-duties relationships where it is merely permitted: it allows giving greater weight to vulnerabilities and needs – the topic to which we now turn.

6.4. VULNERABILITY AND NEED

Also common in private law's expanding margins are cases in which relationality is loosened and the door is opened to policy reasons, not because agent-centered reasons about choice and control are weaker, but because beneficiary-centered reasons about vulnerability and need are stronger. There are many private law domains in which assumptions of roles are accompanied by special duties to people who rely on role-holders – crucially, even if the role-holder did not create the vulnerabilities or needs to which they must respond. These beneficiary-centered impositions of duties are important because they push back, even more strongly than the agent-centered ones, against the free-market paradigm that dominates traditional conceptions of private law – thereby justifying more cooperative and compassionate legal schemes.[51]

It could be said that vulnerabilities and needs justify mandatory tort law layers over forms of private ordering. The Supreme Court of the United Kingdom noted, in this vein, that state agents have more leeway to balance

[48] Christopher J Robinette, 'Harmonizing Wrongs and Compensation' (2021) 80 *Maryland Law Review* 343.

[49] Jeremy Waldron, 'Moments of Carelessness and Massive Loss' in David G Owen (ed), *Philosophical Foundations of Tort Law* (Clarendon Press, 1995) 387.

[50] Andrew Robertson, 'Justifying Liabilities and Duties' in Simone Degeling, Michael Crawford and Nicholas Tiverios (eds), *Justifying Private Rights* (Hart Publishing, 2021) 201, 209–10.

[51] See Hanoch Dagan, *Property* (Oxford University Press, 2011) 42–45. See also Michael J Sandel, 'Market Reasoning as Moral Reasoning: Why Economists Should Re-engage with Political Philosophy' (2013) 27 *Journal of Economic Perspectives* 121.

rights and interests through tort law compared to contract law.[52] Yet it must be emphasised that vitiating factors in contract law need not be seen only as remedying defects in consent or choice during contract formation: they can also be understood as ensuring due care; minimising the creation, exacerbation or exploitation of vulnerabilities; preventing severe unfairness; and promoting public policies or goals. Thus, contractual duties to interfere with the administration of justice, restrain trade, commit a crime, or further immoral purposes, to give a few examples, are often unenforceable even if duly agreed.[53]

On the other hand, private law does not ignore agency when imposing mandatory protections on forms of private ordering. Rather, it focuses on roles in special relationships within which a vulnerable party reasonably and foreseeably relies on the agent's adequate care. While general mandatory duties tend to be negative and focus on physical harms, more demanding and affirmative duties – say, to protect from third parties or not to cause non-physical harms – are imposed only within special relationships, often alongside contractual norms (as is the case, for example, with some of the duties of landlords, employers and lawyers). For example, the *Protection* case, discussed in the previous chapter, recognised the duties of mental health experts to protect third parties from their patients;[54] banks must take due care not to cause pure economic harms negligently to people who reasonably and foreseeably rely on their diligence;[55] and universities must protect intoxicated students from foreseeable risks of physical harm,[56] and even take reasonable measures to protect students from foreseeable suicide attempts.[57] We can see in such cases judicial exercises of authority that assign demanding role-responsibilities. This element of authority – and its grounding in relational role-responsibilities – grow more visible as we circle out towards more novel and markedly policy-oriented areas of private law, to which I refer as its expanding margins. I will briefly mention four examples: family law, consumer law, labour law and discrimination law. My goal in touching on these areas is to further elucidate the ways in which private law responds to vulnerability and need in ways that are hospitable to indirect and even relatively strong indirect forms of horizontality.

[52] *McDonald v McDonald* (n 24) para 46. On judicial restraint and the resulting limited influence of constitutional rights in the contractual context, see also François du Bois, 'The Impact of Human Rights on English Contract Law' in Luca Siliquini-Cinelli and Andrew Hutchison (eds), *The Constitutional Dimension of Contract Law: A Comparative Perspective* (Springer, 2017) 1.

[53] Mindy Chen-Wishart, 'The Nature of Vitiating Factors in Contract Law' in Gregory Klass, George Letsas and Prince Saprai (eds), *Philosophical Foundations of Contract Law* (Oxford University Press, 2014) 294.

[54] See ch 5, n 91.

[55] Peter Benson, 'The Problem with Pure Economic Loss' (2009) 60 *South Carolina Law Review* 823, 861–65.

[56] Nathan F McGuire, 'When Does a University Have a Duty to Protect Students from Campus Harms? The Fall of the Bystander Era and the Rise of a Special-Relationship Theory of Duty' (2022) 55 *Suffolk University Law Review* 405, 406–22.

[57] Betsy J Grey, 'Preventing Student Suicide: Nguyen v. Massachusetts Institute of Technology' (2023) 16 *Journal of Tort Law* 107.

6.4.1. Policy-Oriented Domains

Family Law. Much of the legal infrastructure of the family could be thought of in terms of contract and property, as a form of private ordering. Some attempts to shape the family in light of policy goals rely on this relational basis: for example, grounding the justification of property sharing regimes among married or cohabiting partners in implicit intentions to protect the financially weaker party upon the relationship's breakdown.[58] But such explanations often fall short, because choice exists at such a high level of abstraction that it does not really address many financial and legal eventualities. Then, choice is merely one factor alongside others – such as protecting vulnerable family members or fairly rewarding care work.[59] Thus, roles like 'partner' or 'parent' are voluntarily assumed, but many of their attached responsibilities and duties are legally imposed. As Lucinda Ferguson notes, focusing on personal responsibilities in such cases distracts us from collective responsibilities – partly assigned to private agents – to alleviate social injustices, like inequality, which are manifested and exacerbated in family relations.[60] Therefore, we can talk, for instance, about property law's 'familialisation', when it is pulled away from principles of private ordering towards mandatory and beneficiary-centered principles.[61] There are strong criticisms of this nuanced form of privatisation;[62] and it is clear that the law cannot ensure that family members show concern and care to each other.[63] But the point remains that the law can integrate structural and allocative concerns within normatively robust legal rights-and-duties relationships by facilitating processes through which expectations, claims and responsibilities form around family roles and the normativity of dependence and care.[64]

Consumer Law. Atop traditional contract law doctrines like fraud, duress or misrepresentation lies a layer of norms that diverges quite strongly from a private ordering approach, towards a mandatory approach.[65] It regulates

[58] John Eekelaar, *Family Law and Personal Life*, 2nd edn (Oxford University Press, 2017) 52.

[59] Robert Leckey, 'Cohabitants, Choice, and the Public Interest' in Elizabeth Brake and Lucinda Ferguson (eds), *Philosophical Foundations of Children's and Family Law* (Oxford University Press, 2018) 115, 128–29.

[60] Lucinda Ferguson, 'Family, Social Inequalities, and the Persuasive Force of Interpersonal Obligation' (2008) 22 *International Journal of Law, Policy, and the Family* 61, 82–84.

[61] Andrew Hayward, '"Family Property" and the Process of "Familialisation" of Property Law' (2012) 24 *Child and Family Law Quarterly* 284.

[62] Anne L Alstott, 'Private Tragedies? Family Law as Social Insurance' (2010) 4 *Harvard Law and Policy Review* 3.

[63] See generally Jo Bridgeman, Heather Keating and Craig Lind (eds), *Regulating Family Responsibilities* (Ashgate, 2011).

[64] On this normativity's openness to regulation, see Martha Minow and Mary Lyndon Shanley, 'Relational Rights and Responsibilities: Revisioning the Family in Liberal Political Theory and Law' (1996) 11 *Hypatia* 4.

[65] Roger Brownsword, 'Regulating Transactions: Good Faith and Fair Dealing' in Geraint Howells and Reiner Schulze (eds), *Modernising and Harmonising Consumer Contract Law* (Sellier Publishers, 2009) 87, 100.

the manner in which information is presented to consumers, the conditions in which transactions can be made, and occasionally their substantive conditions. The justifications of many such norms are not merely agent-centered but are also shaped by the risks created by commercial enterprises.[66] For example, Shiffrin explains duties against deceptive advertising (even when the deception is unintentional and results from not entirely reasonable consumer inferences) as expansions of the seller's moral responsibility beyond their control.[67] Thus, there is no pre-legal relational moral wrong here. Rather, sellers are treated, due to their 'greater control and access to modes of production', as 'decentralized agents of the public cooperative project' of allocating goods in society.[68] The last several decades have shown that this additional layer of protective private law norms can be gradually translated into basic moral features of private rights-and-duties relationships between consumers and sellers in mass markets.[69]

Labour Law. In the past century or so, responding to claims about the commodification of labour and its central roles in our identity and social life,[70] legal systems deviated from traditional *laissez-faire* ideas by imposing mandatory duties on employers. For example, the British Workmen's Compensation Act 1897 obligated employers in some lines of work (such as railways, factories or mines) to compensate employees for injuries caused by accidents arising out of and in the course of employment (unless there was severe contributory negligence). Gradually, additional duties were imposed regarding working conditions and how labour relations may start and end. It is inaccurate to locate these norms in public law,[71] as they are exercised and claimed by private agents in employment relations with private employers. However, they move from a private ordering model, in which contract is the exclusive source of duties,[72] towards a mandatory model, aiming not only to allow employees to look after their own interests by equalising their bargaining power, but also to ensure that

[66] Iris Benöhr, *EU Consumer Law and Human Rights* (Oxford University Press, 2013) 81.

[67] Seana Valentine Shiffrin, 'Deceptive Advertising and Taking Responsibility for Others' in Anne Barnhill, Mark Budolfson and Tyler Doggett (eds), *The Oxford Handbook of Food Ethics* (Oxford University Press, 2018) 471.

[68] ibid 489–91.

[69] Gregory Klass, 'False Advertising Law' in Andrew S Gold, John CP Goldberg, Daniel B Kelly, Emily Sherwin and Henry E Smith (eds), *The Oxford Handbook of the New Private Law* (Oxford University Press, 2020) 391, 396–400.

[70] See Hugh Collins, *Regulating Contracts* (Oxford University Press, 1999) 17.

[71] Cynthia Estlund, 'The Fall and Rise of the Private Law of Work' in Hanoch Dagan and Benjamin C Zipursky (eds), *Research Handbook on Private Law Theory* (Edward Elgar Publishing, 2020) 412. See also ACL Davies, 'Labour Law as Public Law' in Alan Bogg, Cathryn Costello, ACL Davies and Jeremias Prassl (eds), *The Autonomy of Labour Law* (Hart Publishing, 2015) 231.

[72] See John Gardner, 'The Contractualisation of Labour Law' in Hugh Collins, Gillian Lester and Virginia Mantouvalou (eds), *Philosophical Foundations of Labour Law* (Oxford University Press, 2018) 33.

their basic interests are well protected.[73] This model relies on a rich organisational conception of employer authority, holding employers responsible to alleviate risks created by their enterprise: both internally, with regard to harm by co-workers, and externally – say, with regard to employee harms to or by third parties.[74] Thus, we see, again, how the unique normativity of a social activity – here, employment – makes it easier to shape private law norms in light of structural and allocative reasons, touching vulnerability and need.

Discrimination Law. This area of law wears its policy goals on its sleeve. It aims to ensure that individuals do not suffer adverse treatment because of protected traits such as race, gender or age, in social spheres such as housing, commerce and employment (and thus it overlaps to some extent with the previous two domains). It is a distinctively political and progressive attempt to go beyond private law's traditional responses to inequality while operating within the normative structure of rights-and-duties relationships: role-holders are not simply enlisted as public agents, and right-holders are not empowered as private attorneys general who claim rights on the public's behalf.[75] Discrimination law's relational focus is reflected, for example, in the fact that less onerous duties are imposed in personal or intimate settings, regardless of the implications in terms of social equality;[76] and in the insistence on preserving substantive tort law requirements like causation or reasonableness.[77] Discrimination law is also, in this sense, an extension of tort law's special duties branch: imposing complex and demanding duties – for example, to prevent workplace harassment, to accommodate disabled workers, or to make sufficient efforts to hire members of underrepresented groups – on role-holders on which vulnerable parties foreseeably and reasonably rely.

6.4.2. Safety Valves

The private law domains discussed above deviate from strict relationality in response to vulnerabilities and needs by imposing mandatory duties on agents that occupy structurally or allocatively important roles. However, responses to vulnerability and need can be more general and indirect. I will present two additional ways in which private law's relationality is loosened – and thus in which constitutional rights can apply stronger pressures on it.

[73] Hugh Collins and Virginia Mantouvalou, 'Human Rights and the Contract of Employment' in Mark Freedland (ed), *The Contract of Employment* (Oxford University Press, 2016) 188.

[74] See, eg, *Burlington Industries, Inc v Ellerth*, 524 US 742 (1998); *Faragher v City of Boca Raton*, 524 US 775 (1998); *Bazley v Curry* [1999] 2 SCR 534; *Jacobi v Griffiths* [1999] 2 SCR 570.

[75] But see Benjamin Eidelson, *Discrimination and Disrespect* (Oxford University Press, 2015) 68.

[76] See Hugh Collins, 'Discrimination and the Private Sphere' in Kasper Lippert-Rasmussen (ed), *The Routledge Handbook of the Ethics of Discrimination* (Routledge, 2017) 360.

[77] See Tom Kohavi, 'Discrimination Law as Private Law' (forthcoming) *Albany Law Review*.

Abstract Standards. Standards like reasonableness or good faith are sprinkled throughout private law, allowing moral concerns to shape its application to particular cases.[78] They are often tied to indirect horizontality, because their interpretation – for instance, determining what amounts to an illegal and unenforceable contract – can incorporate the reconciliation of rights and competing reasons for regulation, while deviating from strictly relational reasoning.[79]

These standards need not be construed as obligating private agents to engage in large-scale and complex forms of reasoning, like proportionality analysis. I argued extensively in the previous chapters why such duties raise deep moral concerns. It is therefore more accurate to see proportionality and balancing as background principles, shaping the general features of norms like illegality,[80] good faith,[81] or fairness.[82] As I claimed above, in the context of rights-and-duties relationships, structural and allocative reasons must be diluted and integrated with relational reasons to be properly realised. The concept of good faith, for example, has inherently relational normative content that cannot be stretched to include duties to hire members of minority groups because they are underrepresented in certain professions – but it can include duties to ensure that members of such groups have the ability and resources to meaningfully participate in negotiations of contractual terms. The difference is not grounded in some large-scale policy calculation, but in the relational nature and limits of the concept of good faith and the manner of its operation in private rights-and-duties relationships.

While the application of abstract standards need not amount to direct or strong indirect horizontality, it is important to see that upstream choices to include or not to include them in different areas of law are subject to robust proportionality analysis. Without these standards, many areas of law would be too rigid – able to respond to certain vulnerabilities and needs only through judicial contortionism or sporadic non-judicial interventions. For example, Andrew Burrows notes that despite his strong preference for concrete legal rules, he recognises the justification of judicial discretion and flexibility when applying the illegality defence in contract law, and therefore supports the United Kingdom Supreme Court's decision to construe it as involving open-ended

[78] See Aditi Bagchi, 'Contract as Procedural Justice' (2016) 7 *Jurisprudence* 47, 79; Felipe Jimenez, 'A Formalist Theory of Contract Law Adjudication' (2020) *Utah Law Review* 1121, 1145.

[79] See Aharon Barak, 'Constitutional Human Rights and Private Law' in Daniel Friedmann and Daphne Barak-Erez (eds), *Human Rights in Private Law* (Hart Publishing, 2001) 13.

[80] Sarah Green and Alan Bogg (eds), *Illegality after* Patel v Mirza (Hart Publishing, 2018).

[81] Hugh Collins, 'Implied Terms: The Foundation in Good Faith and Fair Dealing' (2014) 67 *Current Legal Problems* 297. See also Zhong Xing Tan, 'The Proportionality Puzzle in Contract Law: A Challenge for Private Law Theory?' (2020) 33 *Canadian Journal of Law and Jurisprudence* 215.

[82] Collins and Mantouvalou (n 73) 203–06; Pnina Alon-Shenkar and Guy Davidov, 'Applying the Principle of Proportionality in Employment and Labour Law Contexts' (2013) 59 *McGill Law Journal* 375.

balancing (following the recommendations of the Law Commission).[83] While some standards are difficult to implement (for example, hate speech codes vaguely condemning stigmatising or demeaning speech in universities),[84] and thus we should aim to translate them, incrementally and contextually, to more concrete rules, some flexibility is necessary. This flexibility is one of the benefits of standards, and it enables constitutional rights to indirectly push private law towards better responses to constitutionally protected interests.

Institutional Structures. Another feature of private law that has been largely ignored so far is the involvement of public third parties in private rights-and-duties relationships. We have previously talked about private insurance companies. But there are also public insurance schemes and agencies that regulate specific social activities. It could therefore be said that private law actually operates against a dense background of 'overtly systemic and consequentialist' public institutions, which regularly bring policy reasons to bear on its operation and evolution.[85] Even family relations, for example, are now increasingly subject to state supervision and potential intervention.[86]

Take, for instance, labour law. In its *laissez-faire* past, employers and employees had almost complete leeway to define their contractual relations. Today, however, it is not only that states impose many constraints on contracts of employment but that administrative agencies regulate issues like workplace health and safety and intervene in workplace disputes (involving labour unions or not),[87] often, as noted above, against the background of publicly administered insurance schemes for work-related injuries, funded by employers.[88]

Take consumer law as another example. Beyond licensing and prior approval requirements – for example, for professions like physicians or products like pharmaceuticals – we see legal norms allowing interest groups, consumers' associations and state agencies to contest contractual terms or business practices on substantive grounds, like fairness.[89] Beyond that, in some legal systems, the use of class actions (similar in certain functions to labour unions) is quite common: we see lawyers and litigants act – with the state's approval, and often joined by state agents – as private attorneys general, calling private agents (often,

[83] Andrew Burrows, 'A New Dawn for the Law of Illegality' in *Illegality after* Patel v Mirza (n 80) 23.

[84] Erwin Chemerinsky, 'The Challenge of Free Speech on Campus' (2018) 61 *Howard Law Journal* 585.

[85] TT Arvind and Joanna Gray, 'The Limits of Technocracy: Private Law's Future in the Regulatory State' in Kit Barker, Karen Fairweather and Ross Grantham (eds), *Private Law in the 21st Century* (Hart Publishing, 2017) 237, 237.

[86] eg, Andrew Bainham, 'Private and Public Children Law' (2013) 25 *Child and Family Law Quarterly* 138.

[87] See Hanoch Dagan and Roy Kreitner, 'The Other Half of Regulatory Theory' (2020) 52 *Connecticut Law Review* 607.

[88] See C Arthur Williams Jr, *An International Comparison of Workers' Compensation* (Springer, 1991).

[89] See Peter Cartwright, *Consumer Protection and the Criminal Law: Law, Theory, and Policy in the UK* (Cambridge University Press, 2001) 11, 41–44.

for-profit corporations) to account for violating the rights of diffuse groups of private parties.[90]

Our final stop in this section is one of the most active sites of evolution and disagreement with regard to policy's place in private law: the tort duty not to harm others negligently. It is generally accepted that policy reasons can, for example, shape or negate the recognition of such duties even if an agent creates a foreseeable risk of physical harm.[91] When it comes to non-physical harms – say, economic or emotional – or to duties to protect or aid, we saw that policy reasons are intermingled with relational reasons: they shape, for example, the duties of banks or therapists. Importantly in our current context, public law norms – for example, regulatory standards about water pollution – can also negate or shape the scope and content of duties of care in negligence.[92] Thus, it is not only that constitutional rights themselves can influence rights-and-duties relationships (according to the priority and reconciliation rules discussed above), but also that regulatory agencies can translate constitutional rights into more concrete public standards, which then apply more direct pressure on tort law's operation and evolution.

Thus, we can see public pathways into private law not only in its novel and policy-infused margins – in domains whose declared purpose is to respond to deficiencies in traditional private law regimes – but also in its normative core; and within this core, not only when general standards are used, but also when public institutions more directly shape private rights-and-duties relationships. While these regulatory paths are not unconstrained – efforts must still be made to stay within the perimeter established by the normativity of private rights-and-duties relationships – the possibility of responsibility-assignments leaves much room for constitutional rights realisation. In this sense, constitutional horizontality is not entirely foreign to private law. This raises a concern that has not been directly addressed thus far: not of top-down constitutional imperialism, but of bottom-up private law disintegration.

6.5. DISINTEGRATION

The sections above painted a picture of private law that is quite different from the one presented in previous chapters – where private law's relationality was highlighted and presented as pushing back against both direct and

[90] See generally Michael L Rustad, 'Torts as Public Wrongs' (2011) 38 *Pepperdine Law Review* 433.

[91] *Cooper v Hobart* [2001] 3 SCR 537; Restatement (Third) of Torts: Liability for Physical and Emotional Harm (American Law Institute, 2012) §7(b); *Robinson v Chief Constable of Yorkshire Police* [2018] AC 736.

[92] See Maria Lee, 'Safety, Regulation and Tort: Fault in Context' (2011) 74(4) *Modern Law Review* 755.

indirect forms of constitutional horizontality. This chapter has shown that private law's relationality often loosens in response to corporate involvement, partial agency and choice, and special vulnerabilities and needs. This looser relationality is accompanied by abstract standards and institutional supervision through which structural and allocative reasons for regulation flow more freely into private law rights-and-duties relationships. This dynamic invites stronger forms of horizontality, which rely on policy-oriented responsibility assignments – not only in upstream decisions about private law regimes but also in downstream decisions closer to private law's ongoing operation.

This raises questions about the argument so far and about private law as a unified system and concept with practical significance. While it is encouraging that policy reasons are not foreign to private law, doubts arise about this book's underlying theme: that constitutional horizontality is inherently in tension with private law's relational structure. One could agree with the assertion that relational structures of standing, responsibility, accountability, reactive attitudes, and remedies are central to private law, while adding that their resistance to structural and allocative reasons for regulation may not be as strong as previously suggested. The sections above demonstrate, the thought could continue, that there is no neat separation between public law and private law; and that the private law label lacks the stability, coherence and integrity to do any meaningful work in legal reasoning. Private law is a cluster of norms weakly held together to the extent required by policy calculations – to which constitutional horizontality merely adds additional considerations.

6.5.1. Pulling Threads

It seems that any attempt to depict private law as homogenously and strictly relational is doomed to fail – and that reasoning about its application and evolution must regularly address structural and allocative considerations. However, once these normative threads are pulled, we start to feel the earth shaking beneath private law's feet. For example, if private corporations that assume public roles can be tasked with demanding goal-oriented duties, such as promoting equality; if the distinctions between such corporations and smaller corporations and associations or even individual role-holders are merely quantitative rather than qualitative; and if proportionality analysis shapes and infiltrates all these duties – what is left of private law, as the domain of distinctively private rights-and-duties relationships? Its distinction from public law seems to be a matter of degree and policy choices between regulatory techniques.

Even if constitutional rights can be claimed only against the state, the osmosis process through which they constitutionalise private law could therefore erode distinctions external and internal to private law that solidify it as a normative system and legal category. Take, for example, distinctions between tort law and criminal law. Wrongdoers in both legal domains might be seen as committing public wrongs that merely happen to affect certain victims more directly than others. Even if the accountability and liability structures in the domains are different, tort law right-holders can be granted the standing to hold duty-bearers accountable based on abstract standards on the public's behalf, while operating in tandem with administrative regulatory bodies.[93]

The borders between private law domains could also be destabilised by pressures to adopt mandatory norms or more general and standardised norms in social spheres currently regulated by forms of private ordering. For example, ensuring that the constitutional rights of family members are adequately protected[94] could induce a simultaneous process of grounding family-related agreements (for instance, about separation, adoption or surrogacy) more firmly in general contract law (with the aim of ensuring adequate consent),[95] while also limiting them with more rigid mandatory constraints (that, for instance, protect children). Family law could then be seen as a public risk-allocation tool that responds to certain disruptions to affective life.[96]

It could also be claimed that policy-based limits on forms of private ordering, recognised by allegedly peripheral private law domains, should be seen as public law norms – now also grounded in constitutional rights. This means that the application and development of norms in these domains should be free from the shackles of relational private law principles: for example, that discrimination law duties should not be restricted to assumed roles or by causation requirements.[97] From here it is a short distance to seeing abstract standards in traditional domains such as tort, contract and property as sites of strong constitutional horizontality; and the background regulatory activities of administrative bodies or statutory private law norms as policy-oriented interventions in the common law. The justification of such norms will then be measured by how effectively they realise policy goals or constitutional rights. Thus, constitutional horizontality can push the entire body of private law towards the public and political, while tearing at the weak seams that hold it together as a legal category.

[93] *See* Keneth W Simons, 'The Crime/Tort Distinction: Legal Doctrine and Normative Perspectives' (2007) 17 *Widener Law Journal* 719, 720–21.

[94] Shazia Choudhry and Helen Fenwick, 'Taking the Rights of Parents and Children Seriously: Confronting the Welfare Principle under the Human Rights Act' (2005) 25 *Oxford Journal of Legal Studies* 453.

[95] Brian H Bix, 'Private Ordering in Family Law' in *Philosophical Foundations of Children's and Family Law* (n 59) 257, 263–72.

[96] Anne L Alstott, 'Private Tragedies? Family Law as Social Insurance' (2010) 4 *Harvard Law & Policy Review* 3.

[97] See Kohavi (n 77) Part II.A.

6.5.2. Resistance

Private law's pluralistic tendencies raise taxonomical concerns: its nature and borders as a legal category seem to grow obscure to the point of reducing our ability to reason about its operation and evolution. Legal categories, even without direct doctrinal implications, are important both for the law's application by public and private agents (in their own affairs) and for its effective and justified development. Coherence and integrity are rightly celebrated as legal virtues, tied to the common law and the rule of law. Constitutional horizontality could then act as the cuckoo in the private law nest, pushing it away from the features that give it force and value as a system of regulatory tools.[98]

These concerns induce many private law theorists to adopt an attitude Nigel Simmonds referred to as 'resistance': they hope to preserve the traditional picture of private law by treating most of its expanding margins and their ties to collective or policy considerations as exceptions (or even aberrations).[99] They argue that abstracting away from private law's broader political, social, cultural and economic background and treating its normative core as homogeneous and unified in its resistance to policy reasoning are necessary for private law's survival.[100] The recurring concern is that adopting foundational forms of pluralism – accepting that private law actively pursues structural and allocative goals – will reduce its coherence and integrity and exacerbate problems of incommensurability, which will induce forms of deliberation, reasoning and decision-making that are less clear, fair and predictable.[101]

To address these concerns, we must first note that any closed list of substantive principles or values will struggle to explain or guide all areas of private law.[102] This is no surprise, considering the incremental and contextual manner in which it evolves and regulates different relationships, associations and practices.[103] We must be careful not to presuppose 'some sort of timeless essence of private wrongs',[104] located in a pre-modern world of discrete and isolated interactions.[105] There is a difference between preserving private law's coherence as a normative category and seeing it as rigid and static.

[98] See also William Lucy, *Philosophy of Private Law* (Oxford University Press, 2007) 368–70, 383–87.

[99] NE Simmonds, 'Private Law, The Market, and the State' in *The Decline of Juridical Reason: Doctrine and Theory in the Legal Order* (Manchester University Press, 1984) 120.

[100] See, eg, Ernest Weinrib, 'Deterrence and Corrective Justice' (2002) 50 *UCLA Law Review* 621, 638; Arthur Ripstein, *Equality, Responsibility, and the Law* (Cambridge University Press, 1999) 11.

[101] See, eg, Goldberg, 'Ten Half-Truths' (n 47) 1248–55; Goldberg and Zipursky, 'Civil Recourse Defended' (n 47) 592–93; Robert Stevens, *Torts and Rights* (Oxford University Press, 2007) 325.

[102] See Izhak Englard, 'The Idea of Complementarity as a Philosophical Basis for Pluralism in Tort Law' in *Philosophical Foundations of Tort Law* (n 49) 183, 184–85.

[103] See Christopher J Robinette, 'Can There be a Unified Theory of Torts? A Pluralist Suggestion from History and Doctrine' (2005) 43 *Brandeis Law Journal* 369.

[104] Michael L Rustad, 'Torts as Public Wrongs' (2011) 38 *Pepperdine Law Review* 433, 495.

[105] Gregory C Keating, 'Is Tort Law "Private"?' in Paul B Miller and John Oberdiek (eds), *Civil Wrongs and Justice in Private Law* (Oxford University Press, 2020) 351, 367.

The regulatory diversity described in the previous sections, and the pressures applied to private law to respond to social justice and constitutional rights, leave little room for rigid divisions of labour that portray private law as focusing on the strict relationality of isolated interactions, while ignoring structural and allocative reasons. Such attempts to impose order on private law fail in terms of both fit and justification: private law is applied and developed in complex institutional environments while responding to policy reasons; and this complexity relies on solid moral foundations, because isolating private law from reasons for regulation on a larger scale erodes its very legitimacy and authority.[106] Some tensions and inconsistencies within the domain of private law and in its concept are therefore unavoidable.[107] The challenge of disintegration, therefore, cannot be sidelined: it must be addressed head on.

6.6. REINTEGRATION

The blurring of private law's borders and distinctness seems like an almost inevitable outcome of constitutional horizontality. However, for constitutional horizontality to be an effective and justified legal process, it must preserve private law's internal coherence and integrity and its external distinctions (yet not isolation) from public law. My claim in this section is that constitutional horizontality can not only tolerate private law's uniqueness as a legal category, but actually solidify it by recognising its constitutional importance as a form of regulation. This idea has been running through the previous chapters, but it must be placed on more solid ground to respond to the pluralistic picture presented in this chapter. Doing so is important not only to alleviate the concerns of private law theorists and practitioners, whose contribution is vital to the success of constitutional horizontality, but also from the constitutional perspective: seeing private law as applied constitutional law or as public law in disguise will often lead to regulatory failures.

While private law's value, like all areas of law, is derived from its ability to improve people's lives, and thus relies on values similar to those realised by other legal domains, it need not be fully contingent: private law cannot simply be replaced by other regulatory tools if they outperform it (whatever that means). Private law realises values in a normatively unique way: as parts of private rights-and-duties relationships. While corporate involvement, objective or abstract standards, and complex institutional supervision can stretch this normative

[106] See Steve Hedley, 'The Shock of the Old: Interpretivism in Obligations' in Charles EF Rickett and Ross Grantham (eds), *Structure and Justification in Private Law* (Hart Publishing, 2008) 205, 208–10; Hanoch Dagan and Avihay Dorfman, 'Against Private Law Escapism: Comment on Arthur Ripstein, Private Wrongs' (2017) 14 *Jerusalem Review of Legal Studies* 37.

[107] Stephen R Perry, 'Professor Weinrib's Formalism: The Not-so-empty Sepulchre' (1993) 16 *Harvard Journal of Law & Public Policy* 597, 609–12, 617–19; Christopher J Robinette, 'Torts Rationales, Pluralism, and Isaiah Berlin' (2007) 14 *George Mason Law Review* 329.

structure, it remains – with its relational constitutive components – the foundation upon which more complex regulatory activities build.

The convergence towards indirect and nuanced forms of constitutional horizontality is underpinned by the recognition that private law must be exposed to constitutional scrutiny, but that this exposure must be incremental and carefully transition between contextualism and reform to make the best constitutional use of private law's relationality. The crucial point in our context is that distinctions between public and private – agents, legal domains, and social spheres – are essential aspects of constitutional horizontality: legal agents must rely on them when reasoning about the application or evolution of legal norms towards better conformity with constitutional requirements, because of the ties between these norms and deeper moral principles.[108]

This does not commit us to specific public–private distinctions or private law regimes. The reconciliation of policy reasons, moral principles and rule of law values such as practicality, stability and coherence is complex and contextual. However, when introducing constitutional right-based reasons into decisions about, say, tort law's replacement by criminal law, administrative oversight, or insurance; about tortifying contract law or contractualising family law; or about relaxing substantive duties or causation requirements – we must ensure that private law's coherence and integrity as a regulatory tool are preserved. Against the centrifugal disintegration forces, this requires us to adhere even more carefully to the principles underlying horizontal delineation and realisation presented above – touching the distinctions between and the reconciliation of structural, allocative and relational reasons for regulation.

6.6.1. Centripetal Forces

The starting point in thinking about private law's constitutional role is that it regulates the actions and activities of agents not obligated by constitutional rights (excluding special rights, such as against torture or slavery). Constitutional rights are realised through private law, which regulates by reconising rights and duties that private agents exercise with or claim and enforce against each other. This means that relational normative phenomena like standing, responsibility, accountability, reactive attitudes, and remedies are constitutive parts of private law relationships. This remains true even if these relationships form parts of associations or practices, if corporations are involved, if the state operates in the background as a regulator or insurer, or if legal norms grow abstract and policy-infused. If anything, because private law's ties to relational morality do

[108] See Saprai (n 34) 48–63; Dan Priel, 'Two Forms of Formalism' in Andrew Robertson and James Goudkamp (eds), *Form and Substance in the Law of Obligations* (Hart Publishing, 2019) 165, 172–75, 185–86.

not vanish but merely become more nuanced, we must, to guarantee private law's force and value, pay even closer attention to how the constitutive parts of private rights-and-duties relationships constrain and shape the influence of large-scale policy reasons.

Thus, even if the relationality of private law is often looser, we have good moral reasons to think about constitutional horizontality while keeping the relational normativity of rights-and-duties relationships as our central case and point of reference. The priority and reconciliation framework presented above – structural and allocative reasons take priority in choices of regulatory regimes, and relational reasons take priority in decisions about the details of private law regimes – still holds, even in more peripheral private law areas.

This is true even when corporations are involved, because they are central parts of our normative ecology, operate through individual actions, and regularly interact with individuals. The relational morality of rights and duties is a crucial counterweight against the profit-oriented rationality of many corporations. Similarly, this relational morality is necessary to avoid enlisting duty-bearers as public agents, even when their agency and choice are weaker, or when they assume structurally or allocatively important social roles. We saw that even in policy-oriented areas of private law, such as discrimination law, privacy law or defamation law, relational reasons have a strong pull – and for good moral reasons. If anything, against strong policy pressures, and when legal norms grow abstract or are developed by public bodies, it is even more important to consider how the unique normativity of rights and duties is reflected in private law concepts that should shape the realisation of constitutional rights. In this sense, constitutional horizontality requires private law to function as a regulatory ideal that can shape it on an ongoing basis.

6.6.2. Private Law as an Ideal

I claimed that there are strong reasons to see constitutional rights as general ideals that guide political and legal activities, and that private law's privateness and relationality depend on effective and justified public law institutions. Here I add that the ability of constitutional rights to operate as general ideals – in a sense, their publicness – depends on private law's ability to function as a morally robust ideal in legal reasoning and as a distinctively private category in the general architecture of the legal system. A liberal constitutional order cannot operate without a distinctively relational ideal of private law – even if it takes a looser and more complex form in practice, after it is reconciled with competing values and ideals. The regulatory ideal of private law must operate as an Archimedean point in political and legal deliberations, so as to allow constitutional rights to focus on distinctively public values and forms of reasoning.

Interpretive private law theories can contribute to constitutional horizontality by illuminating the nature and limits of this regulatory ideal: they are uniquely positioned, equipped and motivated to highlight the distinctiveness of private law rights-and-duties relationships and their constitutive components – for example, reasonableness, consent, causation or responsibility. Of course, such theories must be careful not to assume that conceptual or doctrinal claims can resolve prescriptive questions of legal evolution. For this purpose, we must pay more attention to broader normative factors. However, the practice of constitutional horizontality would lack relational nuance without the unique contribution of traditional private law theories.

Private law's regulatory roles are quite complex, of course. It has, for example, not only action-guiding but also expressive and educational dimensions. As modern societies grow marketised and technologically-mediated, private law's role in communicating to members of the political collective what they owe to each other grows in importance.[109] Private law cultivates, facilitates and solidifies practices of mutual recognition, respect and accountability. It must therefore not only avoid harming relational morality but also develop it, thereby contributing to the morality and constitutionality of private relationships, associations and practices – whether they involve individual agents or sophisticated corporate agents.[110] Private law is important because even against the erosion of the individualistic notion of restrictive responsibility (reflected in many of the examples provided in this chapter), it is still premature to declare the triumph of collectivistic or consequentialist notions, which remain distant from how individuals conduct their daily lives and call each other to account.[111]

In practical terms, constitutional horizontality must still distinguish between types of roles within different private relationships, associations and practices. We must determine in what ways different constitutional rights can and should shape different actions or activities: for example, the implications of equality for charities, privacy for employers, or dignity for journalists. We must not only consider the place and weight of structural or allocative reasons in rights-and-duties relationships in the abstract, but also rely on relational private law principles when doing so. Private law, I have argued, serves as a centuries-old repository of principles addressing what we owe to each other. Even critical moral theorists, such as Bernard Williams, have recommended taking private law seriously from a philosophical perspective:[112] both its concepts and doctrines and, more generally its ways of engaging the policy questions falling within its normative jurisdiction.

[109] See, eg, Dan Priel, 'A Public Role for the Intentional Torts' (2011) 22 *King's Law Journal* 183.

[110] See also Seana Shiffrin, 'Compelled Association, Morality, and Market Dynamics' (2007) 41 *Loyola of Los Angeles Law Review* 317.

[111] Samuel Scheffler, 'Individual Responsibility in a Global Age' in *Boundaries and Allegiances: Problems of Justice and Responsibility in Liberal Thought* (Oxford University Press, 2002) 32, 41–44.

[112] Bernard Williams, 'Afterword: What Has Philosophy to Learn from Tort Law?' in *Philosophical Foundations of Tort Law* (n 49) 487.

This means that in private law's margins as well we must be careful to avoid imposing roles on private agents. We must also preserve a correlation between their responsibilities and their legal duties. Even if we can be more instrumental regarding some corporate agents or abstract standards, we must see instrumentalism as the exception to avoid over-extending it. Crucially, reasoning from relationality to policy ensures a better balance between the two, which is more sensitive to the roles of agency, choice, vulnerability and need in private rights-and-duties relationships, than reasoning the other way around – from policy to relationality. Even policy-infused domains like discrimination law or employment law cannot be reduced to crude policy-promotion, which ignores the priority of relational reasoning in downstream decisions about the details of rights-and-duties relationships – and this almost goes without saying with regard to reasoning about abstract standards like good faith or reasonableness.

The cure to the fact that relational principles 'exert a tenacious hold on the legal mind, and are often applied in adjudicative contexts in which they are anachronistic or have little or no place'[113] is therefore not to discard relationality or to see it as instrumentally grounded in policy reasons. We must reject zero-sum accounts of the relations between public and private, constitutional rights and private law, or policy and relationality. Private law's pluralism demonstrates the careful interplay between them – and its ability to absorb constitutional reasons. Private law is still importantly private as a regulatory ideal, focused on private rights-and-duties relationships. Losing sight of this ideal means losing sight of private law itself. And losing sight of private law, I stress, is losing sight of constitutional horizontality. Because it is pulled towards indirect and intermediate forms, it relies on private law not only in a shallow sense, of imposing constitutional standards on existing private law norms, but also in a deep sense of adopting forms of reasoning that are shaped and informed by the nature and limits of private law as a regulatory tool – a tool that is indispensable for constitutional horizontality to be effective and justified.

This means that it could be constitutionally justified not to take regulatory private law paths not only for reasons external to private law (for example, when the difficulties of locating and calling wrongdoers to account threaten constitutionally protected interests),[114] but also for reasons internal to it. For example, replacing tort law with insurance schemes can be not only fairer to victims (who might receive quicker and more reliable compensation) and to tortfeasors (who might pay premiums better reflecting the risks they created),[115] but also relieve

[113] Cass R Sunstein, 'The Limits of Compensatory Justice' in John W Chapman (ed), *Compensatory Justice: Nomos XXXIII* (New York University Press, 1991) 281, 285.

[114] *KU v Finland*, App no 2872/02 (ECtHR, 2 March 2009), paras 43, 47 (a case in which a wrongdoer operated online anonymously).

[115] Alexander B Lemann, 'Coercive Insurance and the Soul of Tort Law' (2016) 105 *Georgetown Law Journal* 55.

pressures on tort law to find ways to impose liability by stretching relational concepts like foreseeability or causation – against its own principles.[116] It might even be justified to see private agents as responsible only for part of the harms they cause, thereby securing a better fit between liability and responsibility.[117] Thus, structural and allocative reasons could justify not putting too much pressure on tort law, thereby indirectly strengthening its relationality.[118]

Similarly, structural and allocative reasons could justify not dignifying certain agreements with contract law's coverage – not only when they threaten policy goals but also when they harm moral values associated with agency, responsibility and consent: for instance, when agreements rely on manipulation, biases or power disparities.[119] In such cases as well, relational reasons can shape and join forces with structural and allocative reasons and push towards less binary regulatory paths: for example, the drafting party could be burdened with duties to assist the other party; particular terms or contract-types could be categorically forbidden, allowed, or require regulatory pre-approval; and stronger forms of consent can be required when it comes to terms affecting constitutionally protected interests.[120]

Thus, while constitutional horizontality destabilises some private law structures, it must still rely on their underlying principles to reason about their potential replacement or change – and when doing so it can actually push them towards better adherence to these principles. Crucially, many choices of regulatory regimes will be strongly pulled towards private law, because public regulation will be less effective and justified: for example, because of the expressive value of granting private rights;[121] because top-down regulation can send people on the defensive – or, if sanctions are seen as prices, even increase the prohibited conduct;[122] or because of concerns about lax public regulation and enforcement, especially when it comes to political minorities.[123] Private law has the ability to ground norm-conformity in respect to particular others as moral agents. Morally robust private rights and duties can be more effective and justified by tying duties to the claims of particular individuals, who will be wronged if the duty-bearer fails to discharge their duties. The history of discrimination law, for example, echoes this idea: we saw that when perceived as political and distributive, it meets difficulties in garnering support from legal

[116] Rob Merkin and Jenny Steele, *Insurance and the Law of Obligations* (Oxford University Press, 2013) 207.

[117] See Alex Kaiserman, 'Partial Liability' (2017) 23 *Legal Theory* 1.

[118] See also Steve Hedley, 'The Unacknowledged Revolution in Liability for Negligence' in Sarah Worthington, Andrew Robertson and Graham Virgo (eds), *Revolution and Evolution in Private Law* (Hart Publishing, 2018) 99, 108–09.

[119] Radin, *Boilerplate* (n 35) 30, 33–51, 154–85.

[120] ibid 217–42; Kim (n 35) 174–210.

[121] See, eg, Findlay Shark, 'Tort Law, Expression, and Duplicative Wrongs' in *Civil Wrongs and Justice in Private Law* (n 105) 441.

[122] Uri Gneezy and Aldo Rustichini, 'A Fine is a Price' (2000) 29 *Journal of Legal Studies* 1.

[123] Chapter 5, nn 172–174.

actors. Top-down regulation can therefore be less effective than forms of regulation that leave more room for duty-bearer discretion and facilitate their ongoing dialogue with different right-holders – often through different local mechanisms that utilise the local knowledge of different private actors.[124]

This implies that there could be constitutional reasons not only to take private law paths, but also to ensure their effectiveness by tying them to morally-grounded relational principles. To take another example, we already touched the fact that private law disputes are only occasionally resolved in court: whether because court proceedings are briefer and shallower or because of the prevalence of out-of-court settlements.[125] This trend is exacerbated by contractual duties to arbitrate.[126] Adjudication and litigation were privatised, allegedly in the name of autonomy and efficiency; and often without scrutiny of the implications for the rights of litigants or third parties or the state's ability to sustain social or constitutional justice. This trend is supported, in a way, by accounts of private law that see its point not as ensuring that justice is done, but as providing an avenue for private parties to exercise their rights.[127] Constitutional horizontality pushes back by calling for a comprehensive comparison of the impact of different rights-claiming and enforcement schemes on the realisation of constitutional rights – which could require treating some private law rights as mandatory, while preserving their unique relational normativity.[128]

Thus, to conclude this section, private law must remain a coherent regulatory ideal not only because its relationality shapes and constrains the ways in which structural and allocative reasons can be integrated within private rights-and-duties relationships. This ideal also has important roles to play in upstream choices of regulatory regimes: whether pushing regulation away from private law, pulling regulation towards private law, or calling for mixed regimes. The justified and effective realisation of constitutional rights at such regulatory junctures must draw on relational reasons, which are often reflected in and developed by private law principles. We therefore have good reasons to draw on the framework of priority, exclusion and reconciliation principles presented above – which expresses the qualitative uniqueness of relational reasons for regulation – even if we accept private law's deep pluralism and the collective obligation to subject it to comprehensive and ongoing constitutional scrutiny.

[124] Frank Dobbin and Alexandra Kalev, 'Are Diversity Programs Merely Ceremonial? Evidence-Free Institutionalization' in Royston Greenwood, Christine Oliver, Thomas B Lawrence and Renate E Meyer (eds), *The Sage Handbook of Organizational Institutionalism* (Sage Publishing, 2017) 808.

[125] Nora Freeman Engstrom, 'The Diminished Trial' (2018) 86 *Fordham Law Review* 2131.

[126] Judith Resnik, 'Diffusing Disputes: The Public in the Private of Arbitration, the Private in Courts, and the Erasure of Rights' (2015) 124 *Yale Law Journal* 2804.

[127] John CP Goldberg and Benjamin C Zipursky, *Recognizing Wrongs* (Harvard University Press, 2020) 277–88.

[128] Susan James, 'Rights as Enforceable Claims' (2003) 103 *Proceedings of the Aristotelian Society* 133.

6.7. CONCLUSION

This chapter has shown that there are many public inroads into private law through which constitutional reasons for regulation can flow more freely: corporate involvement, partial agency and choice, the reliance of vulnerable individuals on role-holders, abstract standards, and background regulatory regimes. These paths are central both in the practice of private law and from the constitutional horizontality perspective, which engages private law as a set of regulatory tools. However, I claimed that there are still good reasons to see relationality as the moral heart of private law: it must still shape upstream decisions about whether to adopt private law regimes and has priority in downstream decisions about the details of rights-and-duties relationships. If anything, the centrifugal forces that influence private law as a cluster of regulatory domains with distinct purposes call for greater care in exposing and explaining its relationality. As questions about how to use private law effectively, justifiably and constitutionally grow more complex, it becomes more important to ground our reasoning in robust normative foundations, which draw not only on moral principles but also on private law's history of successes and failures. This also means that we must not ignore the inherent tensions between constitutional rights and private law: even when they blur in practice, understanding when and how they materialise and how we can further facilitate the dialogue between these domains requires going down to their foundations – where they often keep pulling our reasoning in different directions. The challenge of constitutional horizontality, in this sense, cannot and should not be resolved – it forms part of our collective, slow, and often frustrating progress towards social justice.

7

Conclusion

THE NATURE AND limits of constitutional horizontality were explored in this book, with each chapter building on the previous ones. The first chapter situated the challenge of constitutional horizontality in its historical context, as part of the post-war ascendence of the ambitious regulatory state. The chapter framed the challenge as rights-based, because it is rights that drive the constitution most forcefully into private spheres while simultaneously pushing against such expansion, reflecting the more traditional moral paradigm of the restrained state. The second and third chapters elaborated on these colliding normative forces. On the one hand, many constitutional rights (such as to liberty, equality, dignity or privacy) are general, beneficiary-centered, and loosely relational. Contrary to traditional vertical models, these rights address not only public but also private actions and activities. On the other hand, contrary to direct horizontality models, such constitutional rights normally obligate only public but not private agents, because imposing demanding constitutional duties on private agents raises problems of complexity, intrusion, crowding out, scrutiny and authority.

The deficiencies of traditional verticality and direct horizontality led us to indirect horizontality. Such models see general constitutional rights as addressing both public and private activities and actions, but as obligating only state agents. The focus of constitutional horizontality is then on the realisation of constitutional rights by state agents through private law. The fourth chapter argued that the normativity of private rights-and-duties relationships – comprised of interdependent and morally robust notions such as claims, standing, accountability, responsibility, blame and remedies – pushes back not only against direct horizontality but also against strong indirect horizontality, which construes realisation reasoning as optimising rights and values, in a consequentialist manner. Such models fail to respond to the inherently conflicting normative forces underlying constitutional rights and private law. For private law to be effective and justified, its relational features must be engaged on their own terms and in their normative habitats. For horizontal realisation reasoning to respond to the implications of moral pluralism, it must therefore draw qualitative distinctions between types of reasons for regulation and reconcile them in a principled manner. I claimed that distributive reasons about the basic structure of society and allocative reasons about institutions and practices have priority in upstream decisions about the adoption of regulatory regimes, yet must be integrated with relational reasons to gain weight in downstream decisions about the details of private law rights-and-duties relationships.

The fifth chapter added that, contrary to weak indirect models, downstream decisions about private rights-and-duties relationships cannot be isolated too strongly from structural and allocative reasons – even if relational reasons have a certain priority in them. It was argued that private law not only identifies responsibilities in response to relational factors but also assigns responsibilities in response to large-scale considerations – including so-called policy reasons. The second-order reasons that justify protecting rights-and-duties relationships from regular political influence are not absolute: they leave room for justificatory ascents – taking into account the sensitivity of private relationships, associations and practices to such exposure. The dependence of constitutional horizontality on goal-oriented responsibility assignments sheds light on its collaborative nature as a regulatory practice: not only do all state branches play important roles in this practice, but there must also be a meaningful dialogue between them: this requires judges to often use a regulatory normative key when deciding cases, and non-judicial state agents to remain aware of the doctrinal foundations and implications of their decisions.

Armed with this account of constitutional horizontality as a regulatory practice, the previous chapter went back to private law. It found that while it resists direct and unprincipled forms of horizontality, many of its areas can tolerate principled indirect forms, even relatively strong ones, which bring constitutional rights to bear on private law's operation and evolution: corporate activities, limited agency and choice, and increased vulnerability and need, invite policy reasons not only into allegedly peripheral domains such as family law, labour law, consumer law and discrimination law, but also to private law's traditional core – for instance, through the delineation of standards like reasonableness or good faith or the background involvement of regulatory agencies. While there are concerns that such public inroads, coupled with constitutional horizontality, will erode private law's distinctness and value as a normative system, it was argued that these concerns can be mitigated by recognising that distinctions between public and private agents, legal domains, and social spheres are essential aspects of constitutional horizontality. Horizontality practices must therefore rely on a robust conception of private law as a regulatory ideal, and they must acknowledge the importance of relational reasons (shaped by basic concepts that private common law refines) and their priority in decisions about rights-and-duties relationships.

Following this crude summary, there are a few loose ends that must be tied and clarifications that must be made. First, it is worth reiterating that my goal was not to solve concrete policy problems or to make definitive claims about how constitutional rights should be realised in different private settings. My goal was to set the stage for such concrete claims, which often either target legal doctrine without addressing its broader constitutional dimensions or move too quickly from social justice or constitutional rights to specific regulatory solutions, without recognising the challenges of horizontal realisation. It bears noting that constitutional horizontality is not only relatively novel, but also suffers from its location on the borders of constitutional law and private law. Theorists and practitioners addressing either of these domains rarely take serious account of the nature and limits of the other. This results, as I claimed, in constitutional and human rights lawyers gravitating towards direct or strong indirect horizontality, and private lawyers being drawn to traditional verticality or weak indirect horizontality. This book has endeavoured to place, side by side, central principles from both domains – with basic principles from legal, political and moral theory serving as normative bridges.

My goal, in this regard, was more ambitious than a mere *modus vivendi*: constitutional horizontality can facilitate a coherent and principled dialogue. However, I did not aim to create a synthesis or a grand theory of constitutional horizontality. I grouped the basic principles I advocated under contractualist moral principles and the common law method, but there is no single theme tying them together – except, perhaps, the theme of moral pluralism. Thus, I leave room for further exploration both regarding concrete policy issues and regarding the general principles and ideals that define and shape constitutional horizontality in specific legal systems.

Of course, there is a risk of allowing incrementalism to devolve into conservative rigidity. I highlighted this concern with regard to private law (and justifiably so, given its historical track record), but constitutional law could also isolate the private from the public by construing general rights (for instance, to freedom of religion or expression) as rigid constraints against state intervention in private spheres.[1] Against such conservatism, we can press not only the teleological and merely loosely relational aspects of modern constitutional rights, but also the conception of private law as a set of regulatory tools that assign responsibilities and shape roles within rights-and-duties relationships while regularly responding to structural and allocative reasons.

This connects us to another concern: criticisms of the language of rights, which claim that because of its individualism, it tends to distort individual and collective reasoning about social justice and about what we owe to each other.[2] I tried to show that the language of rights can also accommodate loose and not only strict relationality, and thus make room for collective values and for considerations that exceed the direct relations between isolated right-holders and duty-bearers. While no framing is perfectly neutral,[3] the language of rights is helpful because of its progressive force and its ability to build bridges

[1] See Elizabeth Sepper, 'Free Exercise Lochnerism' (2015) 115 *Columbia Law Review* 1453, 1498–1507.

[2] See Mary Ann Glendon, *Rights Talk: The Impoverishment of Political Discourse* (The Free Press, 1991).

[3] See Cass R Sunstein, 'Moral Heuristics' (2005) 28 *Behavioral and Brain Sciences* 531.

between constitutional law and private law. As Hannah Arendt noted, there is a sense in which if everybody is responsible – if we all take responsibility indiscriminately – no one really is.[4] The language of rights is helpful for constitutional horizontality because it highlights its ability to integrate collective and beneficiary-centered responsibilities within relational structures of mutual recognition, respect and accountability.

Constitutional horizontality's ability to complement public regulation and social norms is crucial in this regard. Take the example of efforts to curb corporate activities benefitting from addictive goods. Robert Rabin observed that because it was difficult to call tobacco companies to account through private law litigation, the decline in tobacco use in the past decades was achieved mostly by public health campaigns, public space restrictions, and taxation.[5] This demonstrates normative progress, but it remains limited, leaving open other paths to benefits from addictive goods such as pain killers, social media, firearms or gambling. The relationality and depth of private law reasoning are beneficial in responding to such concerns: it can not only enhance coherence and systematicity across different regulatory domains by bridging legal norms and their political and moral foundations, but also integrate the products of legal reasoning more firmly in the societal normative fabric by reshaping the relational DNA of private relationships, associations and practices.

Part of the point of constitutional horizontality is therefore to uncover the ways in which collective responsibilities can shape private relationships, associations and practices – whether as an omnipresent leviathan or as a more elusive Cheshire cat.[6] In both forms, the constitution exerts constant pressure on private law. Take, for example, the debates about replacing tort law with alternative insurance schemes. These debates have largely subsided in the past decades, but a robust practice of constitutional horizontality urges us to keep them going. We cannot continue thinking about private law as a purely private domain, free to stick to its old ways. Instead, we are compelled to address questions about its broader constitutional justification.

This pressure exists not only because private law creates the normative foundations of capitalistic markets.[7] This point can be extended to the very foundations of liberal democracy. As modern ideals like truth, science, expertise, democracy and rights come under pressure from political forces pulling regulation back to the *laissez-faire* days, private law's constitutional roles expand. The regulation of freedom of speech or data mining on online social

[4] Hannah Arendt, 'Personal Responsibility Under Dictatorship' in *Responsibility and Judgement* (Jerome Kohn ed, Schocken Books, 2003) 28.

[5] Robert L Rabin, 'Tobacco Control Strategies: Past Efficacy and Future Promise' (2008) 41 *Loyola of Los Angeles Law Review* 1721.

[6] I borrow this imagery from Mirjan R Damaška, *The Faces of Justice and State Authority: A Comparative Approach to the Legal Process* (Yale University Press, 1986) 72.

[7] Katharina Pistor, *The Code of Capital: How the Law Creates Wealth and Inequality* (Princeton University Press, 2019) 222.

media platforms, for example, is clearly not only about what private agents owe to each other. The policies and rules under which such platforms operate shape not only electoral outcomes but also deep and entrenched predispositions, beliefs, values and attitudes regarding the democratic process. This point extends further to concerns about wealth accumulation, access to education, housing patterns and employer authority. Regulating such forms of political power solely through market-oriented and strictly relational normative frameworks risks undermining the foundations of liberal democracy. The reliance of constitutional horizontality on both top-down and bottom-up collaborative inputs and its capacity to integrate constitutional concerns into private domains helps reinforce the principles essential to sustaining a thriving democracy. Because it draws its force from deep moral foundations and relies on common law responses to our collective commitments, it can push back against populist shifts in electoral politics. Constitutional horizontality is therefore not only a bridge between public ideals and private rights but also a stabilising force that can preserve the moral integrity of political communities.

It is customary to conclude a discussion about a theoretical topic by saying that much work remains to be done. This conclusion is no exception. As noted above, while already several decades old and despite receiving ample scholarly attention, constitutional horizontality is still in its adolescence in terms of its entrenchment in legal practices and the sophistication of its underlying principles. However, if we take one thing from this book, it is that constitutional horizontality, with all its inner tensions, cannot be ignored by theorists and practitioners occupied with constitutional law and private law. Indeed, constitutional horizontality is not merely an academic puzzle or a conceptual curiosity. Whether we aim to understand legal practices or to bring them into better conformity with social justice, we must understand constitutional horizontality – and its implications for complex regulatory challenges. This book has sought to equip readers with the tools to navigate the complexities of this foundational process and to build solid bridges between collective commitments to safeguard basic interests in all social spheres, and what we owe to each other within private relationships, associations and practices.

Index

www.ingramcontent.com/pod-product-compliance
Ingram Content Group UK Ltd.
Pitfield, Milton Keynes, MK11 3LW, UK
UKHW021905150926
475560UK00004B/343